The Spectre of the Other in Jungian Psychoanalysis

This volume explores Jung's theories in relation to the concept of Other and in conjunction with the lived experience of it, while examining current events and cultural phenomena through the lens of Jungian and post-Jungian psychology, sociology, literature, film and philosophy.

The contributors examine global expressions of these various viewpoints, disciplines and life experiences and how cultural, political and sociological complexes evoke challenges as well as invitations to the idea of the Other from intersecting and convergent perspectives.

The Spectre of the Other in Jungian Psychoanalysis is timely and important reading for Jungian and post-Jungian analysts, therapists, academics, students and creatives.

Marybeth Carter is a Jungian analyst in private practice in Southern California and a member of the C. G. Jung Institute of Los Angeles. She serves on the board of directors of the International Association for Jungian Studies.

Stephen Anthony Farah is the co-founder and head of learning at The Centre for Applied Jungian Studies based in Cape Town, South Africa. He serves as co-chair of the International Association for Jungian Studies.

'*The Spectre of the Other in Jungian Psychoanalysis* could not be timelier nor more important. This superb collection of new research dissects Jung's eurocentrism, diagnoses his racism and repositions his psychoanalysis as uniquely poised to bring transdisciplinary illumination to the Other in a twenty-first century of multiple crises. Drawing on indigenous, artistic, historical and psychological perspectives, *The Spectre of the Other* is an international volume extending clinical research into the collective. It thereby reinvigorates Jungian studies by enlarging the scope of the field. No serious scholar of psychology and othering can afford to miss it'.

Susan Rowland, *author of* Jungian Arts-based
Research and the Nuclear Enchantment of
New Mexico *(2021)*

'This bold volume gives flesh and blood specificity to the notion of the Other, a term which can easily feel like an all-purpose nostrum when applied indiscriminately. The insightful contributors to this finely differentiated book enable us to explore the Other as it appears in the creative arts, sociology, psychology and even the ultimate Other, the anus'.

Thomas Singer, *editor of the award-winning* Cultural
Complexes and the Soul of America

'Open this marvellous book to any page, and you will discover another facet of that protean notion of the Other that you likely have not considered before. These chapters evoke the cultural complexes emergent from contributors from seven countries encompassing intrapsychic, sociocultural, historical and archetypal dimensions. The essential paradox of the Other, in eternal syzygy with the Self, is revealed as both the *sine qua non* of consciousness and unconscious shadow laden with destructive potential – and as that third which unites these seeming opposites. Illuminating, erudite and crucially relevant to our times, this book is a rich feast for mind, heart and soul'.

Frances Hatfield, *senior training analyst at the*
C. G. Jung Institutes of San Francisco and Santa Fe,
poetry editor of Jung Journal: Culture and Psyche,
and author of Rudiments of Flight

'This ground-breaking collection of essays – expertly curated by Marybeth Carter and Stephen Farah – captures the archetypal valence of the pressing struggles and conflicts faced by humanity in the 21st century. No stone is left unturned, as the authors fearlessly tackle wide-ranging topics, detailing how alterity is constellated and expressed by the psyche. The key question readers are forced to ask is: what do we do when we are conscious of how processes of othering materialise? In this regard, *The Spectre of the Other in Jungian Psychoanalysis: Political, Psychological and Sociological Perspectives* practises what it preaches; it marks a paradigmatic shift in Jungian and post-Jungian studies. While the book explores topics and presents methods that are second nature to the field, it also unapologetically confronts, in equal measure, the very issues that have been ignored and banished to the fringes. By making that which is unconscious, conscious, the book's ethos is completely aligned with the topic with which it so skilfully engages. Stated another way, this collection will stand the test of time, not only because of its vision and intersectional spirit, but also because it captures where our field has been and points to where it is going – indeed, where it needs to go'.

Kevin Lu, PhD, *Head of Department, Department of*
Psychosocial and Psychoanalytic Studies,
University of Essex

'This important and innovative collection of chapters inspired by the IAJS international conference held in Cape Town covers a wide range of in-depth perspectives that creatively examine the ever-prescient phenomenology of the Other through three parts: the Transpersonal Other; the Socio-Political Lives of Otherness and the Mythopoetic Other as explored through Film, Art and Literature. Each chapter, written by talented and experienced Jungian analysts, psychotherapists and academics, explores fresh perspectives on the theme of otherness, particularly during times of global crises where blame and scapegoating the Other becomes increasingly visible and open to complex, interdisciplinary and international scrutiny'.

Dr. Phil. Elizabeth Brodersen, *accredited training*
analyst, supervisor and member of the research
commission of the C.G. Jung Institute,
Küsnacht, Zürich

The Spectre of the Other in Jungian Psychoanalysis

Political, Psychological and Sociological Perspectives

Edited by Marybeth Carter
and Stephen Anthony Farah

Routledge
Taylor & Francis Group

LONDON AND NEW YORK

Designed cover image: Ekely | © Getty Images

First published 2023
by Routledge
4 Park Square, Milton Park, Abingdon, Oxon OX14 4RN

and by Routledge
605 Third Avenue, New York, NY 10158

Routledge is an imprint of the Taylor & Francis Group, an informa business

British Library Cataloguing-in-Publication Data
A catalogue record for this book is available from the British Library

Library of Congress Cataloging-in-Publication Data
Names: Carter, Marybeth, editor. | Farah, Stephen Anthony, editor.
Title: The spectre of the other in Jungian psychoanalysis: political,
psychological, and sociological perspectives / edited by
Marybeth Carter and Stephen Anthony Farah.
Description: Abingdon, Oxon; New York, NY: Routledge, [2023]
| Includes bibliographical references and index.
Identifiers: LCCN 2022032256 | ISBN 9781032121871 (hardback) |
ISBN 9781032121864 (paperback) | ISBN 9781003223481 (ebook)
Subjects: LCSH: Jungian psychology. |
Other (Philosophy)—Psychological aspects.
Classification: LCC BF173.J85 S576 2023 |
DDC 150.19/54—dc23/eng/20220914
LC record available at https://lccn.loc.gov/2022032256

ISBN: 978-1-032-12187-1 (hbk)
ISBN: 978-1-032-12186-4 (pbk)
ISBN: 978-1-003-22348-1 (ebk)

DOI: 10.4324/9781003223481

Typeset in Times New Roman
by codeMantra

Contents

Contributors

Gustavo Beck, PhD, is a clinical psychologist with a private practice in Mexico City as well as a translator of books and essays on psychology and the humanities. He received his PhD in Mythological Studies from Pacifica Graduate Institute in Santa Barbara, California, and is currently a senior candidate in the analytic training program at the C.G. Jung Institute of Chicago. His interests revolve essentially around post-Jungian thought and archetypal theory, particularly regarding its impact on contemporary social, cultural, environmental and political issues.

John Beebe is a Jungian analyst and author of *Integrity in Depth* (1992) and *Energies and Patterns in Psychological Type* (2016). He is the co-author, with Virginia Apperson, of *The Presence of the Feminine in Film* (2008). He has written more than 30 film reviews as well as many articles and chapters in which films are used to demonstrate depth psychological processes.

Fanny Brewster, PhD, MFA, is a Jungian analyst and professor at Pacifica Graduate Institute. She is a writer of nonfiction, including *African Americans and Jungian Psychology: Leaving the Shadows* (2017), *Archetypal Grief: Slavery's Legacy of Intergenerational Child Loss* (2018) and *The Racial Complex: A Jungian Perspective on Culture and Race* (2019). Her poems have been published in *Psychological Perspectives* where she was the featured poet. Dr. Brewster is an international lecturer and workshop presenter on Jungian-related topics that address culture, diversity and creativity. She is a faculty member at the New York C.G. Jung Foundation and the Philadelphia Association of Jungian Analysts.

Roger Brooke, PhD, ABPP, is a professor of psychology at Duquesne University and a psychoanalytically and Jungian-oriented psychotherapist in private practice. He is best known for his book *Jung and Phenomenology* (1991/2015) and other writings on the interface between the Jungian, psychoanalytic and phenomenological traditions. His formative professional years were in the 1980s in South Africa. In 2018 he was recipient of the

Pennsylvania Psychological Association's Public Service Award for his work with veterans.

Marybeth Carter, PhD, is a psychologist and Jungian analyst with a degree in religious studies with honours from Indiana University and a doctorate in clinical psychology from Pacifica Graduate Institute where she is now an adjunct faculty. She is also an executive member of the International Association for Jungian Studies (IAJS). Marybeth has a special interest in the creative arts, transcendent states and the process of individuation. Marybeth's previously published work includes 'Crystalizing the Universe in Geometrical Figures: Diagrammatic Abstraction in the Creative Works of Hilma af Klint and C. G. Jung' and 'Painting Transcendence: A Jungian Lens on the Work of Hilma af Klint', both published in *Jung Journal: Culture & Psyche*. She also had an extensive career in non-profit leadership and has published in the victim and trauma services field.

Stephen Anthony Farah, MA, is the co-founder and head of learning at The Centre for Applied Jungian Studies in South Africa and an executive member and current co-chair of the International Association for Jungian Studies (IAJS). Stephen holds an honours degree in analytical philosophy from the University of the Witwatersrand and a master's degree in Jungian and Post-Jungian Studies from the University of Essex. His areas of interest include psychoanalysis, film, consciousness, individuation and psychoeducation. A chapter, 'True Detective and Jung's Four Steps of Transformation', was published in *The Routledge International Handbook of Film Studies* (2018).

Johann Graaff is a retired sociologist from the University of Cape Town. He trained as a Jungian analyst at the C.G. Jung Institute in Zürich and now has an analytic practice. His ongoing project is to construct a viable Jungian Sociology around topics like the culture of narcissism, nationalism, authoritarianism, conspiracy theories and modern consumerism.

Denise Grobbelaar is a clinical psychologist and Jungian analyst in private practice in Cape Town, South Africa. Denise is passionate about dreams, shamanism and mythology. She has tracked her own dreams for 30 years and has participated in numerous Dream Appreciation groups since 2013. She has a profound sense of reverence for Nature.

Amanda Hon, MA, is a member of the Association of Jungian Analysts, London, and has a master's in Jungian and Post-Jungian Studies from the University of Essex. Originally, she trained with the Centre for Transpersonal Psychology, London, of which she continues to be a member. Formerly a director/trustee of FreshStart Psychotherapy, a charity providing low-cost psychotherapy to members of the Greater London community, she now works in private practice with individuals and couples and is a supervisor of psychotherapists. Her chapter 'Rethinking Virginity: A Post-Jungian Reframing' was published in Gottfried Heuer's *Sexual Revolutions, Psychoanalysis, History and the Father* (2010).

Barbara Helen Miller, PhD, has a private practice and works in co-operation with the Research Group Circumpolar Cultures. She has a PhD in anthropology and a diploma in analytical psychology from the C.G. Jung Institute, Zürich. Many of her publications attempt to bring analytical psychology and anthropology into fruitful dialogue. In 2021 these efforts resulted in the publication of 'Visions at Work: When an Untold Story Becomes a Ghost', co-authored with Sigvald Persen, in *Healing Power, Living Traditions, Global Interactions*, and 'I Ching and Analytical Psychology: Case Study on I Ching Reading and Dream Analysis' in *Jung Journal: Culture & Psyche* (Spring 2021).

Karen H. Naifeh, PhD, is an analyst member of the C.G. Jung Institute of San Francisco, where she teaches in the internship and analytic training programmes and is co-chair of the ad hoc Committee on Diversity and Inclusivity. Her analytic practice with adults is in Burlingame and San Francisco, California. Her areas of special interest are trauma, the shadow and cultural diversity.

Konoyu Nakamura, PhD, is a Professor Emeritus at Otemon Gakuin University in Osaka, Japan. She contributed chapters to several English books, and she translated *Jung: A Feminist* Revision by Susan Rowland (2021) into Japanese. She also published *Jungian Psychology in the East and West* (2021). She was a member of the executive committee of the International Association for Jungian Studies and was a co-chair of the 2019 IAJS Regional Conference at Otemon Gakuin University.

Renos K. Papadopoulos, PhD, is a professor in the Department of Psychosocial and Psychoanalytic Studies and the director of the Centre for Trauma, Asylum and Refugees and of the post-graduate programmes in Refugee Care at the University of Essex. He is an honorary clinical psychologist and systemic family psychotherapist at the Tavistock Clinic as well as a Jungian psychoanalyst. As a consultant to numerous organisations, he works with survivors of political violence and disasters in many countries. His writings have appeared in 16 languages.

Andrew Samuels is one of the founders of the field of Jungian and Post-Jungian Studies. He works internationally as a political and organisational consultant and is in practice as a Jungian analyst and therapist in London. He was one of the two founders of Psychotherapists and Counsellors for Social Responsibility and is a former chair of the UK Council for Psychotherapy. He is a professor of analytical psychology at the University of Essex and a training analyst of the society of analytical psychology.

His many books have been translated into 21 languages and range from *Jung and the Post-Jungians* (1985) to *A New Therapy for Politics?* (2015) and *Analysis and Activism: Social and Political Contributions of Jungian Psychology* (edited with Emilija Kiehl and Mark Saban, 2016).

Stephani Stephens, PhD, is a Jungian-oriented psychotherapist and a lecturer in counselling at the University of Canberra. She has a PhD from the University of Kent, Canterbury, UK, in Jungian psychology. She is the author of *C.G. Jung and the Dead: Visions, Active Imagination and the Unconscious Terrain* (2019).

Douglas Thomas, PhD, LCSW, has a psychotherapy practice in Pasadena, California, and teaches at Pacifica Graduate Institute in Carpinteria, California. He holds a master's degree from the USC School of Social Work and a PhD from Pacifica Graduate Institute. Areas of specialisation include work with Queer clients, alternative sexualities and dream tending. He has published and co-authored articles for the *Journal of Jungian Scholarly Studies* and will soon have a book published by Routledge entitled, *The Deep Psychology of Kink and BDSM: Jungian and Archetypal Perspectives on the Soul's Dark Necessities.*

Acknowledgements

Thank you to our contributors for your chapters and staying involved through the many iterations of this manuscript. We also acknowledge the conference presenters whose papers were published in the special conference issue of the *International Journal of Jungian Studies*, vol. 10, no. 3, as well as those papers we could not include due to the focus and length of this volume.

We give special thanks to editor Alexis O'Brien, with Routledge Mental Health, Taylor & Francis Group, who gave the green light to produce this volume and who has steadfastly accompanied us throughout the publishing process. Appreciation is extended to editor Susannah Frearson, also with Taylor & Francis, who expressed an initial interest in this book and to the Routledge production team for their assistance with proof editing, indexing and general support.

We truly appreciate the work of copyeditor LeeAnn Pickrell, who brought extensive professional experience to the copyediting and manuscript preparation of this collection. Her guidance and suggestions made it possible to complete this volume. And we give special thanks to Elizabeth "Liz" Brodersen, PhD, Jungian analyst, for her support with the conference, the co-editors' efforts and this volume.

We gratefully acknowledge the Global White Lion Permission Trust for their permission to publish the images in Chapter 5.

We acknowledge Brill Publications for permission to reprint 'Jung's Fantasies of Africa' by Roger Brooke, which appeared in the *International Journal of Jungian Studies*, 11(2) 140–59, https://doi.org/10.1163/19409060-01101003

We are also grateful to Jeffrey Moulton Benevedes, PhD, Jungian analyst and editor of *Jung Journal: Culture & Psyche*, and to the San Francisco C.G. Jung Institute, for permission to include three articles published in *Jung Journal: Culture & Psyche.*

Denise Grobbelaar, 'The white lion as symbol of the archetype of the Self and the cannibalisation of the Self in canned hunting', *Jung Journal: Culture & Psyche*, 2020 © C.G. Jung Institute of San Francisco. Reprinted by permission of Taylor & Francis Ltd, http://www.tandfonline.com on behalf of C. G. Jung Institute of San Francisco.

Karen H. Naifeh, 'Encountering the Other: the white shadow', *Jung Journal: Culture & Psyche*, 2019 © C.G. Jung Institute of San Francisco. Reprinted by permission of Taylor & Francis Ltd, http://www.tandfonline.com on behalf of C. G. Jung Institute of San Francisco.

Marybeth Carter, 'Satan's mouth or font of magic: what is it about the anus?', *Jung Journal: Culture & Psyche*, 2022 © C.G. Jung Institute of San Francisco. Reprinted by permission of Taylor & Francis Ltd, http://www.tandfonline.com on behalf of C. G. Jung Institute of San Francisco.

Other permissions include the following:

Ben Highmore, *The Everyday Life Reader.* © 2002 Ben Highmore for selection and editorial matter; individual chapters © the contributors. Reproduced by permission of the Licensor through PLSClear.

Ian McCallum, 'Wilderness', *Wild Gifts.* © 1998. By permission of the author.

Fanny Brewster, "We Have Just Survived," appears by permission of the author.

Excerpts from *The Book of Sand and Shakespeare's Memory* by Jorge Luis Borges, translated by Andrew Hurley, copyright © 1998 by Maria Kodama; translation copyright © 1998 by Penguin Group (USA) Inc. Used by permission of Penguin Books, an imprint of Penguin Publishing Group, a division of Penguin Random House LLC. All rights reserved.

All references from Jung's *Collected Works* listed in this collection are translated by R.F.C. Hull and edited by H. Read, M. Fordham, G. Adler and W. McGuire and published in the UK by Routledge, London, and in America by Princeton University Press, Bollingen Series XX, 1953–1992. These references are listed to paragraph number. Page numbers are cited for Jung's *Memories, Dreams, Reflections.*

In all cases where client material has been used, the confidentiality and anonymity of client identity has been protected.

Editors' Preface

Marybeth Carter and Stephen Anthony Farah

The Spectre of the Other in Jungian Psychoanalysis: Political, Psychological and Sociological Perspectives started as a conversation among colleagues at the International Association for Jungian Studies (IAJS) conference in Cape Town, South Africa, in 2017. That we decided to meet and explore the topic of otherness in the modern birthplace of the struggle for equality now seems like a prescient warning. Little did we know that a few years after the conference we would be living in a 21st-century global pandemic. What surfaced as a novel virus, an *infectious Other*, caused massive illness, death and suffering throughout the world. This public health crisis was superimposed on other crises, some historical and some new, that have highlighted the personification of the Other in our current social gestalt. Politically, sociologically, spiritually, ecologically and psychologically, encounters with the Other are manifest in the rise of identity politics and keenly heard in the current social discourse concerning refugees and immigration, LGBTQ individuals and gun violence. Othering has been seen in the rise of pandemic-related violence towards Asian Americans. We also see it in Brexit and the restructuring of the European Union; the MeToo anti-sexual assault movement; and the Black Lives Matter movement, all of which have highlighted the massive scale of the issue. As we go to press with this book, there are several wars occurring in countries around the globe. History will reveal how othering emerged in the polarisation of communities and opinions, in the fragmentation of 'truth' into partisan camps over the issues of scientific data and vaccination protocols and the shunning of COVID-infected as well as unvaccinated individuals. These visceral experiences of otherness could hardly have been imagined when we began these discussions in 2017.

Jung stated, 'Where there is no "other", or it does not yet exist, all possibility of consciousness ceases' (Jung, 1968, CW9ii, para. 301). Paradoxically, othering is as natural to the development of consciousness as any other psychological process. Without a doubt, there is a significant price paid for projecting the shadow onto others as well as living within the shadow of otherness. All too often, the experience of otherness, experienced by those who are forced to carry it, fuels negativity and violence. Yet, the encounter

with otherness, especially when experienced in the emergence of consciousness, is a fundamentally positive possibility as well as a goal of individuation. Renos K. Papadopoulos was the first post-Jungian scholar to introduce
the concept of the Other, which he developed through his reading of Lacan.
In his Foreword to this volume, Papadopoulos presents the concept of the
Other as an experience of wholeness and as a lived experience of the projected shadow. Papadopoulos's contribution provides a framing of the notion of the Other – the subject of this compilation.

In a harbinger of what is to come, 'Sinking Like a Stone: Activism, Analysis and the Role of the Academy', by Andrew Samuels, both calls our
attention to encounters with the Other and challenges us to examine our
relationship with this shadow experience. Samuels shares his experience as
a Brit who was jailed in South Africa during the apartheid era. That experience greatly informed him about problems of class and race. Samuels
uses this experience as the basis to critique the clinical discipline of Jungian
analysis, which he claims has historically provided therapeutic services to a
limited few. He also challenges researchers to consider the actual contribution their research makes to the greater good.

International contributors were selected from the gathering in Cape Town
to contribute to this volume to further develop the concept of the conceptual, interpersonal, artistical, social and intra-psychic Other. The dialectic
between Jung's theories in relation to the lived experience of the Other is the
object of their contemplation. Each of the selections, in their unique way, is
connected through points of intersection as well as points of convergence,
inviting the reader to examine the question of the Other. In this way, these
chapters respond to the urgency that Papadopoulos and Samuels expose by
confronting contemporary culture with the need to better understand and
respond to the nature of the Other – the shadow and illumination.

Part I: The transpersonal Other: dreams, ancestors and the psyche

Part I, 'The transpersonal Other: dreams, ancestors and the psyche', explores the many ways that the experience of the Other manifests through
the psychogenic realm. In Chapter 1, 'Jung's fantasies of Africa and the individuation process, and Africa's healing of analytical psychology', Roger
Brooke posits that Jung's dreams about Africa reveal the whiteness and
colonialist assumptions typical of the 20th-century educated European.
Brooke reviews Jung's visits to Africa and New Mexico and discusses his
dreams related to these visits. He shows how, even decades later, Jung failed
to use his own theory of dreaming with regard to these dreams. According to Brooke, this was an unfortunate consequence for the development
of Jung's thinking and, consequently, of his theory about the individuation
process. Jung's oppositional thinking in terms of white and Black remained

as a concrete transference fantasy as well as a colonialist attitude towards his inner world. Brooke suggests that the Nguni term *ubuntu* can be used to reimagine individuation in more explicitly ethical and socially embedded ways and posits that if Jung's dreams of Africa had managed to 'heal' him, Jungian psychology would look somewhat like it does today: post-colonial.

In Chapter 2, 'The spectre and its movement: the dynamic of intra- and transgenerational influence', Stephani Stephens examines the meaning of the word 'spectre' as a wonderfully complex word. 'Spectre' is derived from the Latin root words specere and spectare, meaning to watch. The author asks, 'What is so compelling about the association of these words is the question that arises as to who exactly is doing the watching. Does the derivation speak to one's ability to perceive an apparition, or rather, is it that a presence is watching them?' Stephens proposes that a spectre establishes an inherent engagement as the Other, which proceeds to work often unknowingly and yet sometimes in conjunction with the psyche. Stephens then explores the idea of intra- and transgenerational influences, beginning with 'the voices of the "Unanswered, Unresolved, and Unredeemed"' of generations inhabiting the psyche of offspring. She explores how a spectre leaves footprints, spaces or perhaps a mark, as Jung calls it, and then influences and interferes with the destiny of succeeding generations, which the author maintains, raises the crucial question of whether transgenerational influence constitutes haunting.

Marybeth Carter, in Chapter 3, 'Satan's mouth or font of magic: what is it about the anus?', explores the symbolic and archetypal aspects of the anus and the alimentary canal including their psychological and psychosocial significance as a site of psychic coniunctio. Carter considers the standard default of Freudian anal regression and Jungian alchemical 'shit into gold' interpretations in terms of both their illumination and obfuscation of these symbols as well as their expression of a heterosexist repressive ideologue. She explores alternate archetypal and symbolic meanings of the anal-coniunctio, reflecting on the incidence of patient dreams and fantasy material around anal penetration and its possible psychic significance. The chapter concludes that the disavowal of the anal-coniunctio is an instance of othering that precludes potentially fertile considerations.

Douglas Thomas explores BDSM in Chapter 4, 'My kinky shadow: the poetics of the sadomasochistic Other'. He describes the historical stance of a mental health profession that has pathologised a range of sexual behaviours, activities and relationships that are now commonly known as BDSM (bondage and discipline, domination and submission, sadism and masochism) or, more commonly, kink. Thomas suggests that cultural attitudes and clinical opinions are changing regarding these practices such that a Jungian perspective can offer new and valuable clinical insights regarding the archetypal meaning of BDSM and the relationship dynamics that develop in this context. He concludes that, in particular, Jung's concept of the syzygy provides a framework to understand the value BDSM finds in the creation of a conscious Other. He advocates that this creative meaning-making aspect of BDSM and kink constitutes a form of poetics, offering new possibilities for integrating countercultural aspects of the psyche.

In Chapter 5, 'The white lion as symbol of the archetype of the Self and the cannibalisation of the Self in canned hunting', Denise Grobbelaar examines the Jungian concept of the archetype of the Self, equating the role of the white lion as an 'ordering principle' in nature with the Self as the regulating centre in the human psyche. The lions' deep-rooted symbolic and mythological significance is considered, with specific emphasis on the importance of white animals in spiritual traditions. Her hypothesis is contextualised in an ecological perspective, which demands a fundamental interconnectedness – as is implicit in the South African concept of Ubuntu. The numinosity of the sacred hunt is juxtaposed with the great myth of 'The Infernal Hunt' in which the accursed hunter perpetually chases transitory worldly objects driven by an insatiable urge. The author further explores the concept of Wetiko – a cannibalistic spirit driven by insatiable greed and selfish excessive consumption without regard for others, thereby cannibalising the life-force. Grobbelaar arrives at the significant conclusion that 'canned hunting', a grotesque caricature of the sacred hunt in which lions are killed for trophies in organised fenced-in circumstances, is a cannibalising of the Self and a desecration of nature.

Part II: Sociopolitical lives of otherness: pain and possibility

In Part II of the book, 'Sociopolitical lives of otherness: pain and possibility', the stark reality of humanity's actions is examined in relation to the societal expressions that create the Other, suggesting possibilities for different approaches that can make for a better present and future. Fanny Brewster writes in Chapter 6, 'In remembrance and celebration of Other', that when the people of the African Diaspora arrived on American soil, they brought with them the essence of a rich African heritage. Separated by time and the painful remembrance of what became of those who once travelled across the waters, Brewster advocates that people of the African Diaspora are always in search of their African otherness – not the socially constructed imposed Other, but the one to which they belong in remembrance and reverence. She describes how African Americans and others of the African Diaspora re-created their African lives in many ways: through music, architecture, literature, medicine and healing, spirituality and much more. Their pain and trauma helped forge, for those who survived, a cause to remember and celebrate their existence, not to be ashamed. Brewster calls for descendants of the diaspora to resist the post-colonial pressure to only be seen as the constructed, mythological Other.

In Chapter 7, 'Encountering the Other: the white shadow', Karen H. Naifeh suggests that despite Jung's encounter with the spirit of the depths that he describes in *The Red Book* and his reverence for other cultures, he remained, in some ways, very much a man held by the spirit of the times in which he lived. Eurocentrism, even unconscious patronising racism, is evident in Jung's writings. The author asks the reader, 'How, due to the impact of the spirit of the time on *us*, do we unconsciously express attitudes, writings and actions that are offensive to the Other?' There are embedded forms of racism and thereby oppression that members of the dominant group learn not to see, to keep in the shadows. Naifeh explores, through a reflective and personal consideration, the 'white shadow' in the form of unconscious racial micro-aggressive beliefs and actions, white privilege and white fragility. She asks, 'What forces keep unconscious racial bias alive and active in our societies?' This paper utilises the writings of Jung and post-Jungians, such as Samuel Kimbles, Thomas Singer and Fanny Brewster, as well as examples from philosophy, relational psychoanalysis, film and literature that depict culture's shadow. She also explores the relationship of culture's shadow to Jung's 'geology' of the personality as diagrammed in one of his 1925 lectures. The author steers these explorations towards new ways of understanding the creation and maintenance of the sense of the Other in the psyche, thereby furthering the work of bringing culture's shadow into consciousness.

Chapter 8, 'Sitting on an impossible bench: reflections on the bridge between social and analytical justice', by Gustavo Beck provides a psychological exploration of the relationship between economic inequality and the psychotherapeutic relationship. By using the author's experience of his own analysis, he examines the impact and implication that social injustice can have on the psychotherapeutic process, proposing that psychotherapy may participate in such injustice. Beck's objective is to examine otherness under the light, or the shadow, cast by the gap created between people through economic inequality.

In Chapter 9, 'Jung's Others: society, nationalism and crowds', Johann Graaff writes that in 1936 and again in 1946, Jung set out his views on society, nationalism and crowds. The author advocates that when put alongside more recent sociological or social-psychological writing, Jung's views are one-sided and, at times, cynical. For example, Jung was quite dismissive of social institutions, traditions and culture and advocated that one must work only with individuals to create change in society and other groups. German Nazism, in particular, and European nationalism, in general, were, for Jung, products of an alienated modernity by peoples who were easily 'possessed' by particular archetypes. Crowds, said Jung, within the context of this bleak modernity, had a strong tendency to morph into mindless mobs, and they easily fell into 'mass psychosis'. The author proposes that such an emphasis in Jung's writings has set a negative example for later Jungians writing about sociology. Graaff aims to supplement Jung's writings with more recent sociological approaches to writing about the relationship of individuals and groups to conceptualise a viable 'Jungian sociology'.

Chapter 10, 'Picturing the Sámi and *participation mystique*', written by Barbara Helen Miller, highlights that throughout Europe, folklore in the 19th century contributed to the establishment of and support for the idea of national culture. At the time, theories in folklore studies employed the concept of cultural borrowings and evolution, a paradigm that had played out in Europe for some 200 years and then, as described by Franz Boas (1858–1942) in modern anthropology, was effectively abandoned. Miller explains how Boas developed a theory of culture that was pluralist and anti-racial but came under attack by those who conflated race and nation. The author then asks whether there are 'comparable adjustments of theory in analytical psychology'. Miller sketches the effects of viewing the Sámi with an ethnocentric lens using Lévy-Bruhl's concept of *participation mystique* while, at the same, suggesting an adjustment to the application of Jung's theory. Miller makes the argument that this adjustment allows for the practice of participation: the sharing of one's own stories and myths, which facilitates the sense of cohesion in one's own group. She concludes that the practice of participation forms cohesion among people and among the various motivational systems operative in an individual.

Part III: The mythopoetic Other through film, art and literature

Part III, 'The mythopoetic Other through film, art and literature', explores the experience and depiction of the Other using the creative arts. In Chapter 11, 'On being an Other', John Beebe describes going to movies with his mother at the age of six. One of the films they saw, Otto Preminger's 1944 film *Laura,* contributed to his own early initiation into otherness. Beebe sees 'the character Laura as an "anima woman" who exists for, and is controlled by, the projections of others until she begins to find herself when she learns that she has mistakenly been believed to be the victim of a murder'. A portrait of Laura shows her more as a fantasy than a real woman, revealing her disconnection to her own spirit, or animus. Beebe helps the reader identify the parts of Laura's personality using his eight-function, eight-archetype model of psychological type.

Chapter 12, 'The Freak: in search of Jung's second personality', by Stephen Anthony Farah, advocates the position that psychoanalysis, with the introduction of the unconscious, posits an intrapsychic internal Other. He explores *the Freak* as this internal Other, an archetypal structure and its location in the Jungian model of the psyche. He posits the Freak as a telos of the individuation process and as the subject's authentic identity. He examines the Freak in myth, film and psyche, in particular exploring the character

'Chauncy Gardiner' as a cinematic depiction of the second personality, or 'Freak', in the film *Being There*. Farah formulates an analysis of how this sacred relationship with the Other might be conceived of and negotiated.

Next, in Chapter 13, Konoyu Nakamura brings us *'ONE PIECE*: diversity and borderlessness'. Here she writes an archetypal and thematic exploration of Japanese *anime*, a genre that became popular in the 1990s, with a focus on *ONE PIECE*, by Eiichiro Oda, a series that includes comics, films and television programmes. The protagonist is a 17-year-old named *Luffy* who with his friends, called 'the team of straw', searches for a legendary treasure, the titular *ONE PIECE*. Nakamura explores the idea of 'the team of straw' as an individual. She then discusses the 'variety and differences' that these characters represent not only in terms of the differentiation of an individual but also in relation to the diversity represented by the cultural and national borderlessness that societies face today.

This book concludes with Chapter 14, 'What is it about *The Singing Ringing Tree?*' by Amanda Hon. She applies Jungian concepts on not only the content but also the reception of the East German film *The Singing Ringing Tree*, which was broadcast on British children's television in the 1960s and 1970s. The author contextualises the analysis in relation to post-WWII and 1960s British culture by linking consideration of fairy tales, social critique, social science and media studies with underpinnings of Jungian and post-Jungian concepts. In this way, Hon illustrates how the film is a lens on cultural analysis.

Reference

Jung, C.W. (1968). *The collected works of C.G. Jung: Vol. 9ii. Aion.* (H. Read, M. Fordham, G. Adler & W. McGuire, Eds.). (R. F. C. Hull, Trans.). Princeton University Press.

Foreword
Jung and the Other in historical and theoretical perspectives

Renos K. Papadopoulos

The basic assumption of the present volume is that the examination of aspects of the Jungian opus from the perspective of the Other is not only a fruitful undertaking for academic research but also deepens one's understanding of Jung's theories and extends their applicability. However, before anything is considered in relation to the Other, it is essential that certain fundamental clarifications are made.

At the outset, it should not be forgotten that the very word or term *Other* does not refer to any specific entity or process or phenomenon, unless it is explicitly indicated. On its own, it does not have the basic clarity that terms such as the *unconscious* or *projection* or *victimisation*, for example, convey. Although there are endless debates about the particular interpretation of what, precisely, these three examples may be referring to, at least, the reader knows what they are denoting in some basic way. This tentative intelligibility does not exist at all when one speaks about the Other because the Other is directly contingent on a 'this', and how one understands this 'this'. It is for this reason that I called the Other a '"counter-index" word' (Papadopoulos, 1980, 1984, 1992). Whereas words such as *here, tomorrow, I, he, you, same, foreign, current* and so on, are termed *indexicals* or *index words*, the *Other*, in a sense, counters the index word by referring to something other than what the given index word indicates.

The study of indexicals and indexicality is of great importance not only in linguistics but also, on a much wider scale, in disciplines such as anthropology, philosophy, semiotics and sociology. Without going into unwarranted details, it suffices to clarify that index words (or indexicals) refer to words that have no meaning on their own outside the context within which they are used. For example, unless we are aware of their specific referring context, words such as *here, tomorrow, current* and *same* do not provide any clear meaning. These words become intelligible only if linked directly with their context. For example, the 'here' and 'now' for me, writing this now in my home in London, is very different from what 'here' and 'now' mean to you, while reading this in your own space, now.

The danger with ordinary words that become terms is that the user tends, often erroneously, to assume that the reader has a clear understanding of their connotation, and the Other is a particular case in point: on its own and without an unambiguous referring context, the Other is a meaningless term or even word. To start with, is the *other* used as a simple adjective, to indicate another entity; or is the *Other* used as a noun, identifying an object or a person as being 'other' to what was already referred to; or is it used as a verb to suggest an act of distancing oneself from an 'other' person or group of people?

Above all, in relation to Jung, it should not be forgotten that in German, there are two words for Other, *Andere* and *Fremde*, and in the English translations of Jung's works both tend to be translated as 'Other'. Whereas *Andere* is more equivalent to the English colloquial *other*, as different, another and so on, *Fremde* covers more marked connotations such as strange, alien, foreign and unfamiliar. These subtle differences are not always conveyed when Jungian writings are translated into English.

The basic point of departure is to appreciate that Jung did not use the Other in one specific way, and, in short, he did not have any theory of the Other (Papadopoulos, 1980). In fact, using the Other in the context of Jung started only in the 1970s, when I first introduced the term in relation to Jung (Papadopoulos, 1974), culminating with my PhD thesis in 1980, entitled *The Dialectic of the Other in the Psychology of C.G. Jung: A Metatheoretical Investigation*. Then, it took several years before anyone else started using the Other in the context of Jungian psychology.

My interest in the Other was ignited by my reading of the theories of Jacques Lacan. I was intrigued and inspired by the richness of Lacan's understanding of the Other, and immediately I connected it with Jungian ideas (Papadopoulos, 1978), both at theoretical and clinical levels (1979). My reading of the Lacanian ideas of language as the realm of the Other, that is, as a form of what I called 'collective structures of meaning' (Papadopoulos, 1980, 2021), sparked off strong overtones with my reading of the Jungian theorising about the collective reservoir of meaning 'stored' in the archetypal realm of the collective unconscious. With excitement, I recognised the potential of using the concept of the Other (which Lacan introduced to provide a deeper understanding of Freudian theories) in fruitfully applying it to enrich our understanding of the Jungian opus, and this is what I undertook to investigate for my PhD research.

In order to locate my examination of the Other in its relevant historical and philosophical traditions, in my PhD research, first, I developed a theory of the Other in Heraclitus and in Plato and then articulated a comparable theory in Hegel. Using those foundational formulations, I constructed a metatheoretical framework within which I examined the Jungian opus. This framework was based on my central claim that Jung was driven by a predominant quest, which I termed 'the problematic of the other', that is, a fundamental preoccupation to grasp how one's personality (a) is formed in close interaction with 'other' realms and (b) is composed of various 'inner others', which are in constant dynamic interaction among themselves and with the other parts of the personality (Papadopoulos, 1980).

Accordingly, in my thesis, I identified Jung's early childhood imaginary games with the fire, carved manikin and pebble (Jung, 1961) as his first attempts at connecting with the boundaries of his personality and its intimate interactional relationship with these 'inanimate others', as I called them. Then, I focused extensively on Jung's identification of his Number 2 personality as the Other to his Number 1 personality (Jung, 1961). This was followed by differentiating another three successive phases, which I termed 'the Other-as-Complex' (that is, 'inner others', functioning semi-autonomously within the personality), 'the Other-as-Symbol' (an advanced form of 'inner others' with collective applicability) and culminating in 'the Other-as-Archetype', proposing it as the most radical and complete formulation of Jung's 'problematic of the other', where internal and external Others dialectically interact and interrelate among themselves (Papadopoulos, 1980). I argued that 'the Other-as-archetype represents the pinnacle of Jung's theoretical endeavours as it offers a structuring principle which is also connected with broader cultural and societal perspectives' (Papadopoulos, 2002, p. 170).

Elaborating further on my PhD research, I wrote two chapters on Jung and the Other (Papadopoulos, 1984, 1992), improving some elements of my original thesis; then, in 2002, in my paper 'The Other Other: When the Exotic Other Subjugates the Familiar Other', I introduced the pivotal distinction between two Others in Jung's life and work. My argument was that 'Jung had a genuine adoration for the distant and exotic other whilst he had nothing but contempt for the close and familiar other' (Papadopoulos, 2002, p. 177). Jung is known for being fascinated and for praising the *Fremde*, the cultures and belief systems of people he referred to as 'primitive'. Accordingly, I argued that, in effect, Jung was espousing the doctrine of the 'noble savage' by idealising the 'primitive' people for, supposedly, not being corrupted by our Western rationalistic civilisation, thus supposedly retaining their purity, living close to nature, engaging in meaningful rituals and possessing 'natural wisdom'. While extolling the virtues of such distant, 'primitive' and 'exotic others' (for instance, Far Eastern, African tribal and other similar forms of spirituality), he overlooked and even derided the *Andere*, those people and belief systems right next to him (such as Eastern Christianity) that had precisely the very same ingredients that he valued and praised – actively living sacramental lives and engaging in alive and meaningful rituals.

Needless to say, Jung did not develop on his own these ideas about the 'primitive mind', but he was part of a European tradition influenced by many positions, especially those advanced by Lucien Lévy-Bruhl, who contrasted the 'primitive mind' to the 'Western mind', believing that the former is not using logic to apprehend reality but a *participation mystique*. It should not be forgotten that Jung's thinly disguised 'noble savage' dogma about the 'exotic other' constituted standard Jungian teaching until fairly recently; it was blindly adopted and widely applauded by most Jungians, blissfully unaware not only of its gross erroneousness but also of its dangerous colonial and racist implications.

In 2009, I applied my investigations into the Other in relation to Jung by reflecting on my own preoccupation with researching the Other in South Africa in the 1970s, during the height of the apartheid era and while I was living very vividly the harsh realities of the racist white regime's 'othering' of the 'non-white' populations of the country. In that study, I also pondered over the various forms of 'othering' engendered in the ways Jungian societies behaved and trainings were conducted (Papadopoulos, 2009).

My observations and concerns regarding 'othering' practices at the institutional level in the Jungian professional world were expressed in many contexts, fora and publications, always warning against the 'noble savage' fallacious trap. In particular, these concerns were articulated succinctly in a letter I wrote in the *IAAP Newsletter* in 1991, in relation to the dangers in the way 'established Jungians' related to the new and emerging Jungian professional societies in Eastern Europe and other parts of the world. In the letter, I warned that the pattern of 'us' trying to help 'them', although it contained appropriate and laudable elements, 'may degenerate and get entangled with old familiar scenarios of mercenary, missionary or charitable "help" and patronising colonialism', and I urged that we 'proceed with the necessary caution and genuine mutual respect in a spirit of authentic collegiality' (Papadopoulos, 1991, p. 12).

In 2013, I extended further my previous research on the Other by identifying the 'othering' dynamics in the use of key words that characterise difference in social interactions and theories. Specifically, I focused on the term *ethnic*, concluding that, in fact, it represents another 'index word' that 'carries no clear connotation at all apart from designating an "otherness"'. In effect, *ethnic* would be similar to the word *native*; the 'natives' are usually understood to be the inhabitants of an 'other' foreign land, and they are deemed to be different from 'us', who do not need to be described by anything else than being just 'us'. However, strictly speaking and according to the exact meaning of the word *native*, we are also 'native to our own land' and we are 'ethnic' and 'other' to another group of people (Papadopoulos, 2013, p. 149).

It is instructive that my same research revealed that historically and linguistically, most 'othering' terms (including and in addition to *ethnic*) that are used to characterise groups of people different from us in some respect – for example, *goy, gentile, heathen* – follow three identifiable steps: 'first they are used to characterise any human group, then they tend to be used exclusively for an-other (usually a minority) group, and then they acquire negative, derogatory connotation' (Papadopoulos, 2013, p. 149). This suggests that the moment we begin to focus on differences rather than similarities, when we see another person or a group of people as an Other, it is difficult to prevent the sliding down into pejorative characterisations.

To summarise, my research in this field, spanning more than 50 years, identified and established the heuristic value of the Other in the relation to the psychology of Jung in, at least, four major spheres:

- The Other in Jung's own theory about the structure of the psyche
- The Other in Jung's own life and theoretical development
- The Other in Jung's theories about wider societal phenomena
- The Other as it is used to refer to other people and cultures in theoretical approaches outside the Jungian framework but applied to deepen our understanding of Jungian perspectives.

At the same time, it also revealed several difficulties and paradoxes, including the following:

- **The paradox of reification**: Whereas the Other is a most elusive, nonessentialist and constructivist concept and image (being a counter-index notion), it tends to be objectified, reified and treated as if it were a concrete entity. It is as if our fear of the ungraspable enantiodromically urges us to pin the Other down, thus endangering its very fluidity.

In addition to what I just mentioned, more dangers emerge once ordinary words acquire the status of academic or professional terms, and these have to do with the relationship between nominalisation and reification. *Nominalisation* refers to when, mainly, verbs or adjectives are made into nouns. Whereas nominalisation is appropriate in natural sciences, Michael Billig draws attention to the problems that arise when we introduce it in social sciences because then we 'transform people and their doings into things' (Billig, 2013). The ill effects of nominalisation become particularly evident whenever we speak about feelings. There is a marked difference between saying that 'he feels depressed' and claiming that 'he has depression'. This example shows how nominalisation tends to introduce an ominous and static sense of definitiveness. Comparably, in situations of social interactions whenever the Other is used without any clear qualification, serious complications of perilous reifications may appear and congeal. 'Othering' individuals or groups of people can have severe adverse effects not only on those who are 'othered' but also on those who perform the 'othering'.

- **The danger of ignoring the Other's relationality**: Essentially, the Other is a relational and interactional concept and image, being entirely contingent on a 'this'. Unrelated entities cannot be 'othered'. Yet, this relationality tends to be ignored by over-emphasising the oppositionality of the

Other to the 'this'. Invariably, this leads to overlooking the similarities and connectedness (intrinsic or extrinsic) between 'us' and whose whom we characterise as 'not us' but the Other.

Returning to Jung, one of the main arguments I developed, even in my early researches on the Other, was that the way he conceptualised and utilised the Other included both their antithetical opposition and their supplementary relationship. For example, he understood his No 1 and No 2 personalities as both antithetical and complementary (Papadopoulos, 1980). However, he did not maintain in all contexts this impressively sophisticated understanding of the Other. I would argue that when it came to his theorising of, what he termed, 'primitive man' and 'modern man', he mainly emphasised their incompatibility, idealising the alleged virtues of the 'primitive', that is, the 'exotic other', the *Fremde*, while decrying the 'rationality' of the non-'primitive'.

This book, in effect, follows up, illustrates and develops further my own research. More specifically, it elaborates on aspects of the four major spheres and main paradoxes and dangers that I identified in relation to applying the concept of the Other to Jungian thought and context. In the interim, of course, many worthy studies by eminent authors advanced our thinking about these issues, and the present volume provides an excellent sample of some of them.

Jung emphatically declared that 'Where there is no "other", or it does not yet exist, all possibility of consciousness ceases' (Jung, CW9ii, para. 301). Yet, in his actual work, he did not address with any consistency what he refers to, here, as the 'other'. Moreover, his writings do not reflect the monumental importance that he attributes to the 'other' in this stentorian declaration. By the way, in the German original, he is using *Andere* here, not *Fremde*. And it is this shortcoming that this book attempts to remedy. Not shying away from controversy and critical analyses, this book provides a notable contribution.

References

Billig, M. (2013, 11 July). Social sciences and the noun problem. *The Guardian*.

Jung, C.G. (1951). *The collected works of C.G. Jung: Vol. 9ii. Aion.* (H. Read, M. Fordham, G. Adler & W. McGuire, Eds.). (R. F. C. Hull, Trans.). Princeton University Press.

Jung, C.G. (1961). *Memories, dreams, reflections.* (R. Winston & C. Winston, Trans.). Fontana Press.

Papadopoulos, R.K. (1974). Epistemological considerations of C.G. Jung's psychology: Clinical implications. *Proceedings of the 26th Congress of the South African Psychological Association*, Johannesburg.

Papadopoulos, R.K. (1978). Review of J. Lacan's 'The four fundamental concepts of psychoanalysis'. *Psygram*, *18*, 39–42.

Papadopoulos, R.K. (1979). On developing a training programme in psychotherapy within a university context. *Abstract Book, 11th International Congress of Psychotherapy*, Amsterdam.

Papadopoulos, R.K. (1980). *The dialectic of the Other in the psychology of C.G. Jung: A metatheoretical investigation*. [PhD dissertation]. University of Cape Town.

Papadopoulos, R.K (1984). Jung and the concept of the Other. In R.K. Papadopoulos & G.S. Saayman (Eds.), *Jung in modern perspective*. Wildwood House.

Papadopoulos, R.K. (1991, January). Jung and Eastern Europe. *Newsletter of the IAAP*, 12.

Papadopoulos, R.K. (1992). Jung and the Other. In R.K. Papadopoulos (Ed.), *C.G. Jung: Critical Assessments*. (In four volumes). London and New York: Routledge, pp. 388–426.

Papadopoulos, R.K. (2002). The other other: When the exotic other subjugates the familiar other. *Journal of Analytical Psychology, 47*(2), 163–88.

Papadopoulos, R.K. (2009). Jung and Otherings in South Africa. In P. Bennett (Ed.), *Journeys, encounters: Clinical, communal, cultural*. Daimon Verlag.

Papadopoulos, R.K. (2013). Ethnopsychologische Annäherungen an Überlebende von Katastrophen. Prolegomena zu einer jungianischen Perspektive. *Analytische Psychologie. Zeitschrift für Psychotherapie und Psychanalyse*. Heft 172, 44. Jg., 2, 134–71.

Papadopoulos, R.K. (2021). Therapeutic encounters and interventions outside the consulting room. Challenges in theory and practice. In *Jung and the 'Other': Encounters in depth psychology*. Routledge. https://www.routledge.com/rsc/downloads/Jung_and_the_Other.pdf

Introduction

Sinking like a stone: Activism, analysis and the role of the academy

Andrew Samuels

My story

The organisers of the unique conference on which this book is based will remember how hard it was to make sure it took place in South Africa, fighting both in public and behind the scenes. There was opposition. The reasons I personally was so committed to South Africa were primarily autobiographical, and I want briefly to share them with readers for the first time in public.

Starting in 1967, between school and university (in American terms, between high school and college), I lived in Swaziland (Eswatini today) for over a year, exactly 55 years ago. At that time, the small country, completely surrounded by South Africa, was a British Protectorate. I got a job with the British Colonial Office as a District Officer, complete with ceremonial sword and solar topee (like you can see Jung wearing in the photos of his African trip).

In short order, I was secretly recruited by the African National Congress (ANC), in part because I had been involved with the Anti-Apartheid Movement (AAM) in Britain. I performed certain tasks for the ANC that, as you'd expect, totally contradicted my task as a District Officer. I comprehensively broke the Official Secrets Act. Eventually, I was found out and fired. They threw me out of Swaziland, and when I entered South Africa, I was arrested and flung into Pretoria Central Prison, where Steve Biko, a South African anti-apartheid activist in South Africa in the 1960s and 1970s, was formerly held. Of course, the British had betrayed me.

I stayed in jail for a few weeks, and it was not a pleasant experience. Still, attending a British public (that is private) boarding school prepares one for such ordeals as being kicked, hit and shouted at.

What I am trying to convey is that this country was where I gained whatever understanding I have of the political process and of the necessity of struggle. Hence, I should like to honour my late friends and comrades Henry Malaza and Jerry Dlamini.

But it isn't just the politics that draws me back to South Africa. I still love Kwela and pennywhistle music, drag on rough tobacco roll-ups and even swig cane spirit. *Dagga* (marijuana) is smoked, if available. But I also retain

DOI: 10.4324/9781003223481-1

an aversion to wearing shorts, which I still associate not with an outdoors childhood but with the policemen in Pretoria.

This background led to numerous invitations to work in South Africa as a consultant. One memory worth recounting was meeting Nelson Mandela at a conference on nation building at Rhodes University in Grahamstown. (There was a movement to change the name of the institution in light of the 'Rhodes Must Fall' campaign; however, the university voted to not change it.) I spoke on 'good-enough leadership' as the art of managing failure. He shook my hand afterwards and said with a twinkle in his eye, 'Well, I stayed awake during *your* talk!'

After this passage of personal confession (to use Jung's term), I will now turn to the rest of the introduction. There are three sections: (1) the political turn in Jungian psychology, (2) how the academy is the best critic of the clinic and (3) clinical perspectives on academic research.

The political turn in Jungian psychology

In 2004, in a keynote at the Barcelona Congress of the International Association for Analytical Psychology (IAAP), I said that we had witnessed a 'political turn' in Jungian analysis and psychology. I believed Jung would have silently approved of this development, which has greatly intensified in recent years, given what he wrote in 1946 of 'the analyst's duties as a citizen'.

In the political turn, which has grown in the past 13 years, people seek to see how (and if) depth psychology and Jungian analysis can provide understandings of the political events of the day, coupling the spirit of the depths to the spirit of the times. My own contributions may be found in three of my books (Samuels, 1993, 2001, 2015) and in the co-edited *Analysis and Activism* (Kiehl et al., 2016).

In practical terms, a series of conferences, called 'Analysis and Activism', have been held with the support of the IAAP. The first two were in London and Rome and the third took place in 2017 in Prague. The fourth conference, which took place during the pandemic in 2020, was held online. Readers may note that in the title of this brief introduction, I have reversed the terms so as to write of 'Activism and Analysis'. This is because I have become suspicious and impatient of the incessant depth reflection on the social and political crises of our times that analysts go in for.

Analysts and psychotherapists shy away from action, which all too often is castigated as 'acting out'. Of course, thinking is fine and necessary; I am not in favour of mindlessness. But sometimes we need to recall what Hamlet said in a notable piece of self-criticism:

> Thus conscience does make cowards of us all,
> And thus the native hue of resolution
> Is sicklied o'er with the pale cast of thought,

And enterprises of great pith and moment
With this regard their currents turn awry,
And lose the name of action.

(Act III, Scene 1, ll, pp. 84–89)

Marx was there too, with these words on his monument in Highgate Cemetery in London: 'Philosophers have only interpreted the world in various ways. The point however is to change it'.

The academy is the best critic of the clinic

I propose that the field of Jungian and post-Jungian studies can contribute to the political turn so decisively entered into by our clinical brethren. For, as I said at the first IAJS conference at Essex in 2002, the academy can often function as the best (and friendly) critic of the clinic. So, I've tried to take from Western academic discourses three ideas that might benefit the clinic as it struggles to make its contribution on the social level as well as to the alleviate individual distress:

1. Multidisciplinarity (including intersectionality)
2. *Contemporary* Indigeneity
3. Paying attention to issues of diversity and equality

Multidisciplinarity

In today's Western universities, the talk is constantly of interdisciplinarity, multidisciplinarity and transdisciplinarity. In the human and social sciences, solo performances are increasingly regarded with suspicion. They do not cut the mustard. There are numerous implications of this. One is the development of *intersectionality*, in which we do not split race from gender from socioeconomic class (but without lumping everything together).

Here's a cautionary note, though, with intersectionality in mind. Jungian psychology on its own – or any kind of therapy thinking on its own – is useless when confronting the crises our world is faced with these days. The task is to find people, meaning organisations and movements, with whom to ally ourselves. Let's have an analyst or therapist on every policy committee, but, please God, not a committee of analysts!

Ideally, these partners will be progressive movements and campaigns. They will be interested in social justice, racial, gender and economic equality and climate change. Specific groups might welcome an alliance. For example, refugees, migrants and asylum seekers. Or veterans' groups. Or those working with and on behalf of what we in Britain call 'ethnic minorities'.

Multidisciplinarity and intersectionality are problems for a clinical discipline like Jungian analysis that is, for the most part, esoteric, elitist and proudly indifferent to criticism from within or without (see Samuels, 2017). Individuation is a kind of 'fuck off' to critics who are, allegedly, 'not psychologically minded'. So becoming EXOteric is a tough call for many Jungian analysts. I believe the academy can provide support and sustenance in a renunciation by the analysts of the top table, of their conscious and maybe unconscious focus on the individuation of the 1 per cent.

Instead, academic perspectives suggest to the clinic that it is worth standing up with the materially disadvantaged, especially Indigenous people. This is different from sitting down with educated and adequately funded analysands. In our field, one notable pioneer is Eva Pattis Zoja with her sandplay work in crisis situations.

Clinicians across the board may have to question the milieux in which many of them work, for private practice with a privileged clientele is not politically neutral – which, let me hasten to say, does not make it insignificant. Indeed, therapy may be a politicising experience for some.

Be that as it may, in overall terms, the private practice mode of working has affected depth psychological clinical thinking. Context has driven ideas. Clinicians, suggest this academic perspective, may have to explore why it has taken so long for challenges to be mounted to their automatic preference for the inner world, and the tendency to make 'inner' and 'outer' or 'private' and 'public' into polar opposites.

Here I turn to Achille Mbembe and his book *Critique of Black Reason* (2017). I read Mbembe as issuing a clarion call to the Western clinic, and the Jungian variant of it, in particular: 'The path is clear: on the basis of a critique of the past, we must create a future that is inseparable from the notions of justice, dignity and the *in-common*. ...' (p. 74).

The implication of this is that analysts and therapists need to think more intersectionally about those for whom the right to have rights is refused, those who are told not to move and those who are turned away, deported, expelled. That is to say, the new wretched of the Earth. Those whom Hilary Clinton called 'the despicable' and we call 'the Others'.

Contemporary Indigeneity

The second academic perspective concerns a rather different from the usual revaluing of Indigenous wisdom, especially when it comes to therapeutic work. The paradox of *'contemporary* Indigeneity' is purposeful, with the emphasis on the word *contemporary*. It isn't necessary to look only into Ubuntu, or at Xhosa healers, or Australian Aboriginal healers, or shamans. Sometimes, new ideas crop up in the most unlikely contemporary settings. In today's Africa, there are all kinds of innovative and creative hybrids from which to learn. *Africans are doing their contemporary thing in an African way.*

Here's an example from the mental health field – the 'friendship bench' scheme in Zimbabwe. Therapy on a bench not a couch! (There is a video about the friendship bench scheme here: https://www.theguardian.com/

global-development/video/2017/apr/14/therapy-on-a-bench-grandmas-mental-illness-in-harare-zimbabwe-video)

One in four Zimbabweans suffers from some form of mental illness, but there are only 13 psychiatrists in a country of 16,000,000. A solution had to be found, and it came in the way of a bench and the tradition of respect for African matriarchs. The therapy room is a patch of waste ground, and the therapist's couch a wooden bench under a tree. The therapist is an elderly Zimbabwean woman, in a long brown dress and headscarf. Her patients call her 'Grandmother' when they come along to sit on her bench and discuss their feelings, their depression or other mental health issues. Outside the clinic in Highfield, a poor suburb just south of Zimbabwe's capital Harare, there are lots of grandmothers – trained but unqualified health workers – who take turns on the park bench to hear stories. They listen to the battered wife who has attempted suicide twice, the man who hates women after he became infected with HIV, the unemployed single mother driven to despair by the struggle of raising four children.

The benches are a safe place for people struggling with depression, which in the Shona language is called *kufungisisa,* 'thinking too much'. The grandmothers, all of whom are trained to improve a patient's ability to cope with mental stress, listen and nod, offering only an occasional word of encouragement.

The scheme has been researched and outcome studies performed, and the evidence base is that this works.

I see this project as an illustration of what Frantz Fanon called 'situated thinking'. It arises from a lived experience that was always in motion and in progress. Yes, such a scheme is unstable and changing, but understood a certain way, such praxis smashes, punctures and transforms the legacies of colonialism and racism. It can be 'our' guide received from 'them' through the devastation of our Western present with its global crisis in mental health.

I should like to expand this section on the 'contemporary Indigenous' to say a few words about the global devastation, the impending apocalypse, the environmental crisis, climate change, sustainability and so on. Here, as members of the responsible party, whether they try to deny it or not, ecologically minded Westerners need to pause for a moment. It goes almost without saying that the richer countries ('the North') will be less affected than the poorer countries ('the South'). But the poorer part of even one quite small district in a city like London will also suffer disproportionately, as we saw in the Grenfell Tower fire.

Alongside this, it is also useful to reflect on the ways in which poverty and inequality (global, regional, national and local) inflect and problematise our thinking about Earth. I am far from the first to raise the question of how it can be ethical to insist that people and groups that have never enjoyed the ill-gotten gains of Western capitalism must eschew them in advance. Are they supposed to leapfrog capitalism to enter a new state of political togetherness?

I must ask this next question, disturbing and challenging though it may be: are Indigenous peoples simply required by us liberal Westerners to revert to or remain in traditional ways, whether this is what they want or not? Achille Mbembe is but one key writer on the avoidance of a sentimental return to the past. Following Edward Said (1978) in *Orientalism*, he stresses the patronising and dominating shadow of what looks like admiration for the Other and research into non-Western cultures.

For sure, we need to speak *to* the Other. But do we need to speak quite so much *about* the Other? And maybe we should be ultra-careful when speaking *for* the Other? And let's not forget the Other within the other. I mean the poor within the poor, the dispossessed among the dispossessed – such as the Black poor and working class in relation to the Black monied middle and upper classes worldwide. It is interesting that so many undeveloped countries have agreed to take on their share of what is required by the Paris Accords? Good news. Or is it? Won't the ruling classes of undeveloped countries escape? For there is a privileged 'Northern' element in 'Southern' countries like South Africa. Just as there is, for sure, a 'Southern' element in 'Northern' countries like the US or the UK.

For there are two sides to the coin of this Other. The first is that we in the North and West are engaged in overdue reparation for colonial, heteronormative and neoliberal oppression. This includes the role of the psychological professions in both perpetration and repair.

But the second is that just at the very moment we enter or encounter the world of the Other, we often use the moment to conceal a failure to challenge the power relations, barbarism and inequality of our own Western world.

Recognising that we project a lot (negative or positive) onto other people doesn't amount to much if political and personal behaviour remains much the same. That's why it is so important for Jungian and other schools to twin their analysis of the social and political world with activism in relation to its problems. This is why writers like the psychoanalyst Cornelius Castoriadis and the social theorist Gayatri Spivak refer to 'radical alterity'. This introduces ideas of justice to the discourse.

What we do in relation to the Other and Otherness is too easily positioned as an internal moral and emotional challenge for an individual that smooths away the disruptive and traumatic nature of his or her own times, in his or her own spaces and within his or her personal and intimate relationships.

We might recall that, at the age of 16, the French poet Arthur Rimbaud wrote in a letter, 'Je est un Autre'. The line has become famous. There are many possible translations but, for me, 'I is an Another' will do. At the heart of these few words lies paradox piled upon paradox. If 'I is another', then what is the fate of Otherness and the Other? Doesn't the binary of subject (or self, or I) and Other just collapse under the weight of its own contradictions? Does Rimbaud mean there is no 'I' and no 'another'?

Paying attention to issues of diversity and equality

The third academic perspective concerns the lack of diversity in the professions of psychotherapy and analysis. What can the academy offer in this context?

The question of a lack of diversity on Jungian analysis is a bigger problem than the admittedly significant problem of such a lack in all schools of psychotherapy (see Samuels, 2018). Can anything be done about it? Here are some relevant questions. Where is the evidence that affirmative action or positive discrimination would lower clinical standards? Does reducing or sometimes abandoning the demands for paper qualifications necessarily lead to a lowering of such standards?

The problem is that high standards contribute to patterns of exclusion and inclusion. Universities know about it and worry about it. I am not convinced that the therapy world has fully caught up with the extent of self-created discrimination and prejudice, which, all too often, is based on 'race', ethnicity and culture – as well as money and class.

Clinical perspectives on academic research

As promised the final section of this introduction turns the spotlight back onto the academy, and I want to explore questions of mission and motivation in academic research. After having performed an academic act on the clinic, here's a clinical act performed on the academy.

I always ask my PhD candidates to explain what they see as the social utility of their research. What is it for? What is its meaning? I ask these questions even when the work is (for example) in the arts or religion or clinical process. What is the mission? And then, a further enquiry, what is your motivation for doing this research? I am, of course, thinking of the 'wounded researcher' made famous by Robert Romanyshyn (2013) – but with an added systematic stress on ordinary psychodynamic, developmental self-analysis.

To give a personal example, I have written and researched a lot on the father, with a focus on the benevolent aspects of the father's body for his relationship with his children of all sexes. The problem I was depicting I called 'the dry father', a nice guy, not abusive – but lacking in energy, passion and animation. Why did I develop these ideas?

Well, my father of blessed memory was a good example of the dry father. He was a gentleman in every way. But whatever was missing for me led me to create the notion of the 'dry father' and use it in clinical work. So many patients, male and female, yearned for more paternal passion.

I could give other examples, but this way of thinking, looking for causes, explanations and hints, is typical in the clinic, but not all that prominent in the academy. Maybe that is in the process of changing but I do not know for sure.

A concluding thought

The title of this introduction is drawn from the famous Bob Dylan protest song of the 1960s, 'The times they are a-changin'. Hence, this is a 'protest introduction', full of anger about the state of play in two disciplines that I also love. I think we will sink like a stone if we don't pay attention to disciplines that I also love. I don't claim this is the only way to think about our future. If this introduction suffers from an inflated, prophetic tone, I apologise for it. It has a history in having been invited to give the closing keynote in Cape Town. I wrote it especially for the IAJS conference in Cape Town (2017) because it is time for us, whether in academy or clinic, or in both, to change.

(For those readers who would like to copy what the conference audience did and sing along with Bob, here is the link: https://www.youtube.com/watch?v=JxvVk-r9ut8)

References

Kiehl, E., Saban, M., & Samuels, A. (2016). *Analysis and activism: Social and political contributions of Jungian psychology.* Routledge.

Mbembe, A. (2017). *Critique of African reason.* Duke University Press.

Romanyshyn, R. (2013). *The wounded researcher: Research with soul in mind.* Routledge.

Said, E. (1978). *Orientalism.* Pantheon Books.

Samuels, A. (1993). *The political psyche.* Routledge.

Samuels, A. (2001). *Politics on the vouch: Citizenship and the internal life.* Karnac.

Samuels, A. (2015). *A new therapy for politics?* Karnac.

Samuels, A. (2017). The future of Jungian analysis: Strengths, weaknesses, opportunities, threats ('SWOT'). *Journal of Analytical Psychology, 62*(5), 636–49.

Samuels, A. (2018). Jung and 'Africans': A critical and contemporary review of some of the issues. *International Journal of Jungian Studies, 10*(2), 122–34.

Part I

The transpersonal Other

Dreams, ancestors and the psyche

Jung's fantasies of Africa and the individuation process, and Africa's healing of analytical psychology

Roger Brooke

Jung's transference to Africa and 'non-whites'

The individuation process and the development of consciousness are the central themes of analytical psychology. However, these guiding terms are discussed by Jung and the early generations of his followers in ways that most of us today would find embarrassing. It is not enough to read Jung in the morning and Andrew Samuels or Susan Rowland or Fanny Brewster in the afternoon with happy eclecticism and a fuzzy feeling of being open minded. The shadows in Jung's European view of the world are part of our inheritance too, of whatever colour or ethnicity we might be.

Jung first travelled to Africa in 1920, when he visited Tunisia. He describes a sense of moving backwards in time from the 20th century to the Middle Ages, and he idly wonders how 'these unsuspecting souls' (Jung, 1961, p. 268) will respond to the acceleration of time into modernity. But Jung also imposes a perception that will become familiar and run through his writings. He sees the Arabs as emotional rather than rational, lacking autonomy and closer to nature and childhood. They might have an 'intensity of life' (p. 270), he says, but they are 'prehistoric' (p. 272) and lack what he calls ego consciousness.

We might wonder how Jung could have failed to consider the history of Arab cultural achievements. After all, the people he sees as lacking consciousness invented mathematics, had the world's greatest library in the ancient world and are embedded consciously in linear history, celebrating the lives of Abraham, Jesus and Muhammad. Their culture includes that most highly refined and self-aware mystical tradition, Sufism.

The reason Jung failed to regard Arab culture as containing the self-awareness he calls consciousness might be that whiteness is strangely invisible to itself, but visible in its epistemological hegemony. Whiteness does not imagine itself as one colour among many, but as no-colour. As Hillman wrote in his essay on white supremacy, '*White casts its own shadow ... which as white is indiscernible to consciousness defined in terms of light*' (1986,

DOI: 10.4324/9781003223481-3

p. 38). Whiteness obliterates shades, colours and multiplicity. It underlies the fantasy of purity and is therefore the source of splitting and oppositional thinking. White casts its own white shadow, argues Hillman, dividing the human world simply into white and non-white. From that perspective, Arabs are non-white, and, for the white European Jung, the differences between Arabs, sub-Saharan Black Africans, Native Americans and Asian Indians are all but obliterated from the developmental and psychological prerogatives of whiteness.

This obliteration of the non-white Other was central to the meaning of being white. The invisibility and shadows of Jung's European whiteness have been most of ours if we are white. I grew up in a relatively educated and liberal household in South Africa. My father taught that a measure of a gentleman was how you treated those less powerful or fortunate than yourself. When he became managing director of a mid-sized industrial company nearly 50 years ago, his first order was to rewrite all job descriptions and pay scales free of any reference to colour. He was ahead of his time. Yet even in this atmosphere I was a teenager before I learned that Black people had surnames. When I began reading Jung in late adolescence I learned about the development of consciousness and the spiritual crisis of 'modern man' and about 'archaic man' (1931) and 'primitives' being closer to the unconscious and nature with no conceptual problems at all. I thought I was learning about myself, my culture and Black people when, in fact, I was simply entrenching my projections, dressing them up in Jungian theory. Now that I am an American too, I am going to suggest that there are many white Americans who are no further along in their self-awareness culturally than I was in the mid-1970s.

The invisibility of whiteness remains a challenge for most white people, but back to Jung. He had wanted to find the missing part of his personality, which he thought would be visible in Africa (Jung, 1961, p. 272). However, what was invisible to Jung was not out there in Africa but in Jung's way of seeing. When he was in Tunisia Jung had a dream of an Arab prince. The dream was set in a square mandala-shaped Arabian city with a citadel, or Casbah, in the centre. Jung was on a moat surrounding this centre and keen to see inside the citadel. An Arab prince attacked Jung, trying to knock him down. Then they wrestled, crashed through a railing into the moat, and it then seemed that the prince was trying to drown him. 'No, I thought, this is going too far', writes Jung (p. 271), so he pushes the prince's head under water to subdue him. The scene changes and Jung finds himself in the presence of 'an open book with black letters written in magnificent calligraphy on milky-white parchment' (p. 271). Jung cannot read the Western Chinese script, but he knows that this is his book and that he had written it.

In other words, the book Jung has written – which we can interpret, following Ricoeur (1971/1981) as the narratives and texts that make up Jung's life – is only vaguely familiar to Jung but is also 'foreign' to both Jung and his subdued Arab prince. Jung continues:

> I explained to him that now that I had overcome him he must read the book. But he resisted. I placed my arm around his shoulders and forced him, with a sort of paternal kindness and patience, to read the book. I knew that this was absolutely essential, and at last he yielded.
>
> (Jung, 1961, p. 271)

The colonialism in this dream is unmistakable. The European Jung forces the non-white Other to submit to the narratives that are Jung's own.

Jung's interpretation, even nearly 40 years later, is still an interpretation by an ego in the grip of anxiety. Jung writes that he had experienced an 'unexpectedly violent assault of the unconscious psyche' (1961, p. 273). He also comes to understand this dream as an early indication of his fear of 'going black under the skin' (p. 273), which emerged more directly five years later in East Africa.

What is extraordinary is that Jung understands the dream as coming from the self, but he does not apply his own theory of dreams to his dream. He does not ask how the self might be trying to compensate for the limitations of his ego's view of himself and his world. We might note that there is no good clinical reason for Jung to be so fearful. The mandala image of the self as a squared city with a temple in its centre is highly differentiated and what Jung would have called 'civilised'. It has no bizarre or psychotic features. The dream shows that Jung's self is better structured and contained than his anxious ego, falling through the railings into the moat. Further still, insofar as Jung cannot read the text of what is his own book, we can also say that Jung's self has authorship, symbolic functions and literacy, whereas it is Jung as an ego who is being psychologically illiterate. It does seem that Jung here is victim to his own insight, which is that 'The unconscious mind of man sees correctly even when conscious reason is blind and impotent' (Jung, 1944/1952, CW 12, para. 608).

Jung is surprised at the anxiety in his dream since he had not consciously felt anxious at all. 'On the contrary', he writes,

> I could not help feeling superior because I was reminded at every step of my European nature. That was unavoidable: my being European gave me a certain perspective on these people who were so different from myself and utterly marked me off from them.
>
> (Jung, 1961, p. 273)

However, Jung does also write, 'I became aware of how completely … I was still caught up and imprisoned in the cultural consciousness of the white man' (1961, p. 275).

What this meant in terms of white cultural history became clearer when Jung visited Taos, New Mexico, where he was befriended by an elder, Ochwiay Biano (Mountain Lake). He became Jung's teacher and talked about what he saw as white people's cruel facial features and their restlessness. He pointed out to Jung that white people also thought with their heads instead of their hearts, and the Pueblo Indians thought they were mad. It is worth quoting Jung at length here:

> I fell into a long meditation. For the first time in my life, so it seemed to me, someone had drawn for me a picture of the real white man. It was as though until now I had seen nothing but sentimental, prettified colour prints. This Indian had ... unveiled a truth to which we are blind. I felt arising within me like a shapeless mist something unknown and yet deeply familiar. And out of this mist, image upon image detached itself: first Roman legions smashing into the cities of Gaul, and the keenly incised features of Julius Caesar, Scipio Africanus, and Pompey. I saw the Roman eagle on the North Sea and on the banks of the White Nile. Then I saw St. Augustine transmitting the Christian creed to the Britons on the tips of Roman lances, and Charlemagne's most glorious forced conversions of the heathen; then the pillaging and murdering bands of the Crusading armies. ... Then followed Columbus, Cortes, and the other conquistadors who with fire, sword, torture, and Christianity came down upon even these remote Pueblos, dreaming peacefully in the sun, their Father. I saw, too, the Peoples of the Pacific Islands decimated by firewater, syphilis, and scarlet fever carried in the clothes the missionaries forced on them.
>
> It was enough. What we from our point of view call colonization, missions to the heathen, spread of civilization etc., has another face – the face of a bird of prey seeking with cruel intentness for distant quarry. ... All the eagles and other predatory creatures that adorn our coats of arms seem to me apt psychological representatives of our true nature.
>
> (Jung, 1961, pp. 276–77)

This is Jung's most personal insight into the violence and invisibility of whiteness, but Jung still did not make the mental link that this might be the history written in the book he was forcing the Arab Other to read. In my view, Mountain Lake's lesson was the same lesson Jung might have learned in his Tunisian dream if he had paid more attention to the voice of the Other and less to his own white anxiety.

When Jung visited East Africa in 1925–26 (see Burleson, 2005), he again described the feeling of going back in time, but what happened here was less about white colonial history than about ontology. Jung was moved by the very materiality of the world coming into presence, of the earth's awakening into world as psyche's ground. He describes how his 'liberated psychic forces poured blissfully back to the primeval expanses' (1961, p. 293) and how the calling of consciousness is no less than a calling from the world itself to be brought into being through that human form of being we call consciousness (Brooke, 1991/2015). For Jung, the earth-world came into being as a temple (Jung, 1961, p. 298).

This insight into earth as temple and psyche's sacred ground indicates that Jung's confrontation with his own unconsciousness reaches into the European constitution of identity. For the post-Enlightenment European psychological life has 'withdrawn into the capsule of the head', as he says elsewhere, and mental space is 'a sort of bottle filled with European air' (Jung, 1939, CW 10, para. 988). These expressions describe his experience in India but could just as well describe his experience anywhere that was not Europe or white America.

Jung writes: 'One would surely go under without the insulating glass wall; one would be drowned in all the things which we Europeans have conquered in our imaginations. ... They become formidable realities directly you step beyond the glass wall' (Jung, 1939, CW 10, para. 988). In this evocative passage of living behind a glass barrier, Jung is describing a low-grade chronic, cultural derealization. He admits he feels dreamlike but writes as though it is the Others who are living in the dream, and he interprets his derealization as a cultural achievement of individuating consciousness. It is helpful to understand this when Jung has his next 'African' dream and again panics.

Michael Vannoy Adams (1966) has discussed Jung's seduction and panic in Africa in some detail (see also Brooke, 2008). Jung was enchanted by the young African women, bare breasted and confident in themselves, and he felt himself being seduced – not by them so much as by Africa herself. (Can one say 'herself'? Africa was as much anima as shadow for Jung.) He describes the well-known dream of his Black Chattanooga barber using a hot curling iron to make his hair 'kinky', like Black people's. In his dream Jung could feel the heat of the curling iron and he awoke in terror:

> I took this dream as a warning from the unconscious; it was saying that the primitive was a danger to me. At that time I was obviously all too close to 'going black' ... The only thing I could conclude from this was that my European personality must under all circumstances be preserved intact.
>
> (Jung, 1961, p. 302)

As Brewster recently noted, Jung was afraid of 'becoming *victim* to an African consciousness' (2017, p. 52). As he journeyed northwards down the Nile towards Egypt, moving forwards once again in time toward the modern world, Jung experienced the mythic power of Horus, bringing the divine light of consciousness to humankind and releasing us from 'the darkness of prehistoric times. Thus the journey from the heart of Africa to Egypt became, for me, a kind of drama of the birth of light' (Jung, 1961, p. 302). It was a personal re-enactment of the drama of human, and especially Western, consciousness breaking free from the regressive forces of unconsciousness, darkness and forms of human life almost indistinguishable, in Jung's mind, from nature.

On the other hand, if Jung had applied his own understanding of dreams as compensatory from the self, he would have recognized this barber working on his 'head' with heat as being like an analyst working alchemically, with heat, to effect psychic transformation in an anxious patient, Jung's ego (Adams, 1996). Jung never escapes the dream in order to analyse it. He *reacts* to his dream while in effect still dreaming the dream. He is just as frightened when awake and thinking about his dream as he was when asleep and dreaming. Even when writing *Memories, Dreams, Reflections,* over 30 years later he has, in this regard, still not woken up. He is still dreaming the dream of the educated white European man of the early 20th century, unaware that the African culture he saw was a cultural transference fantasy. It is the transference fantasy that reinforced his emerging theory regarding the development of consciousness and the individuation process. They are the privilege and burden of what Jung calls 'modern man' (Jacobi, 1965/1967), by which he means the white European.

The result is a series of linguistic and imaginal equations that continue to run as the white man's dream through analytical psychology – and not only regarding Africa: white European-non-white Other, light-dark, civilized-primitive, conscious-unconscious, rational-emotional, disembodied-embodied, scientific-superstitious, personal-impersonal, repressed neurotic-paranoid psychotic, individual-collective (*participation mystique*), adultlike-childlike, moral-amoral.

This set of transference fantasies about Africa and blackness provides the set of coordinates regarding Jung's model of the individuation process and the development of consciousness. There seems to have been a reciprocal relationship between his fantasies of Africa and his psychological theory. Each reinforced and was used as evidence for the other. This means that Jung's colonialism remains with us still in the central terms of Jung's developmental theory.

Towards an African healing of analytical psychology

Our task is not so much to analyse Jung as to analyse our own fantasies, both towards people who are culturally the non-white Other and towards our own inner lives. All this leads to the question in the title: What might analytical psychology be like if Jung had allowed himself to be psychically seduced by Africa and had let his dreams of the Arab prince and his Black barber heal his one-sided, anxious ego? How would *we* Jungians think today if Jung had allowed his thoughts, sprouting from his head, to become 'kinky'?

Well, we might be pleased to recognize that analytical psychology would look rather more like post-Jungian psychology today. The field is already moving towards a multicultural imagination, to use Michael Adams's (1996) great phrase; it is reviving *participation mystique* as an indispensable quality of psyche's participatory consciousness rather than as defining it negatively as a form of regressed unconsciousness (Bernstein, 2005, 2014; Colman, 2016; see Winborn, 2014); it is much more interested in psychological hospitality than ego control (Giegerich, 1984; Brooke, 1993); and it is polytheistic rather than monotheistic (Hillman, 1976) and plural in its commitments rather than singular in its fantasies of a self-sufficient, internal 'wholeness' (Samuels, 1989/2016). It is already engaged with politics (Samuels, 1993; Kiehl et al., 2016); social issues, including war and terrorism (Covington et al., 2002; Beebe, 2003; Hillman, 2004); combat trauma (Brooke, 2017); refugees (Papadopoulos, 2016) and the fate of our planet (Bernstein, 2005; Marshall, 2009). It is more self-reflective in terms of the historical context and textual positioning of Jung's writing (Rowland, 2002, 2005). Most importantly, I like to believe that most Jungians today have given up the colonialist humbug about cultural evolution, even if terms such as the development of consciousness have not been critically thought through. More on this presently.

Significantly, this transformation within Jungian thinking has been guided by Jung himself, both in the example of his own personal life in Bollingen and through his alchemical studies. These studies describe processes of dissolution, mixing and transformation into 'substances' that have combined what were previously imagined as opposites. Noting this movement, Marlan (1999) has discussed Jung's alchemical dissolution of the phallocentric and hegemonic image of light, noting deconstructive parallels between Jung and authors such as Derrida and Irigaray. Hillman's writings, which can be understood as a rereading of Jung within Jung's own alchemical and deconstructive logic, all point away from egoic mastery towards a decentred ethic and aesthetic of hospitality towards psychological life (Giegerich, 1984).

In his essay on white supremacy, Hillman points out that Jung's work on alchemy can be seen, like alchemy itself, as a work against whiteness (2004, p. 50). Whiteness and light cannot be images of life. As Jung said in a 1952 interview with Mircea Eliade:

> But in this state of 'whiteness' one does not *live* in the true sense of the word, it is a sort of abstract, ideal state. In order to come alive it must have 'blood', ... the 'redness' of life. ... Blood alone can reanimate a glorious state of consciousness in which the last trace of blackness is dissolved.
>
> (Jung, 1977/1980, pp. 222–23)

It is the alchemical *rubedo,* the reddening of blood, that dissolves the opposites of white and black, transforming them in the direction of an embodied real life. Hillman goes on to say that alchemy's lesson for us is about the materiality and embeddedness of psychic life, in places, with things and in the interiority of our being-in-the-world.

This redemption of Jung's colonialism through alchemy is implied in the historical thrust of his work, which was to reach through the rationalism and materialism of European Enlightenment to a pre-Renaissance sensibility. Interestingly enough, this is, according to Hillman, before the term *white* was ever used to describe Caucasians. In *Memories, Dreams, Reflections* Jung (1961) describes this sensibility as the world of his Number 2 personality, a private world alive and pregnant with meaning, a world from which psychological life is not yet uprooted into the scientific abstractions of his Number 1 personality and idealist philosophy (Brooke, 2000). Unlike all his contemporary psychoanalytic colleagues, Jung understood the historical task of psychology as finding ways for those he called 'modern' to reconnect with sources of meaning that nevertheless remain as a sustaining ground beneath the public assumptions of Western consciousness and the conceit of rationalist philosophy. For all his colonialism and whiteness, Jung seemed to have more affinity with Mountain Lake in New Mexico and with African traditional healers than with his psychoanalytic peers (Brewster, 2017), whose interests were limited to matters of psychodynamics and personal history.

Before moving to the next section, which concerns a rereading of analytical psychology's central terms, I would like to acknowledge the late Augustine Shutte, professor of philosophy at the University of Cape Town, who introduced me to phenomenology as an undergraduate and who wrote a readable little book called *Philosophy for Africa* (Shutte, 1993). He writes, 'I have become convinced that African insights into our humanity can serve as an important corrective to the dominant forms of contemporary European philosophy' (Shutte, 1993, p. 428), including Western humanism, founded as it is on the imperatives of scientific rationalism and individualism. Shutte's main sources of inspiration are Teilhard de Chardin and Leopold Senghor. I would also like to acknowledge the work of the pioneering South African Jungian analyst Dr. Vera Buhrmann (1986), who wrote with great sensitivity about her work with the Xhosa.

What follows is a sketch of how we might understand some of the guiding terms of analytical psychology. My hope is that it will feel familiar to your own experience of Jungian psychology. I shall focus on individuation and the withdrawal of projections, which are intrinsic to the development of consciousness. I shall then briefly discuss object relations theory, which I think has been a mixed contribution – a blessing and a curse – to the Jungian field.

Individuation and *ubuntu*

We might wonder how Jung would have described the individuation process if his starting point had been these words by Archbishop Desmond Tutu (2015): 'My humanity is bound up in yours, for we can only be human together. We are different precisely in order to realize our need of one another'.

The principle here is captured in a Zulu saying, *umuntu ngumuntu ngabantu,* which translates as 'A person is a person through persons'. Shutte (1993, p. vi) makes this the centrepiece of his philosophy for Africa. What persons are and what persons should become – the ontological and the ethical – are mutually implied. The ethical is not merely aspirational but is a determinative constituent of what a person *is.* Such an assumption, common to sub-Saharan cultures (Coetzee & Roux, 1998), offers an important corrective to Jung who only ever discusses the collective as a regressive pull against individuation. Perhaps Jung's Black barber was trying to tell him that the community of persons is both necessary for becoming a person and the home in which one's own personhood is realized.

The most significant African concept for Jung's theory of individuation is the term *ubuntu* (Brooke, 2008). *Ubuntu* defines what it means to become a person, but its development is a task of self-realization requiring the support of others who treat us as persons. It also requires the African virtues Shutte admires. These include personal responsibility, ethical self-knowledge, courage, humility, forgiveness and empathy. The Ghanaian philosopher Kwasi Wiredu writes of this African sensibility as follows:

> Thus conceived a human person is essentially the center of a thick set of concentric circles of obligations and responsibilities matched by rights and privileges revolving around levels of relationships irradiating from the consanguinity of household kith and kin, through ... clan, to the wider circumference of the human family based on the common possession of the divine spark.
>
> (Wiredu, 1992/1998, p. 311)

Ubuntu provides an ethical dimension to the individuation process which always seems conceptually awkward for Jung. *Ubuntu,* which Senghor (1977/2001, 1998) says is the mark of African humanism, is that sense of community which preserves the personal and in which the personal can thrive. It is the animating spirit behind virtues such as hospitality, respect, patience, conviviality, endurance, self-knowledge and sympathy. Within *ubuntu* consciousness, inclusiveness, healing and reconciliation rather than marginalization, blame and punishment are guiding values.

Through *ubuntu* we would imagine individuation as a process of personal growth and transformation within ever-widening circles of identification, from family to friends and classmates, to local community and to the wider society and the world at large. It reaches outwards, towards the stranger and the Other, to the living and even the dead, to our animal cousins and to the wider earth and sky. From infantile dependency to mature spirituality our expanding community is the psychological home in which we become fully persons.

The withdrawal of projections

What, then, of the withdrawal of projections, which are thought to be so central to developing the psychological self-awareness Jungians call consciousness?

In my view, Jung conflated therapeutic insight with Cartesian epistemology. Therapeutically, he recognizes that what we hate or long for in others is often split-off aspects of ourselves. However, he interprets this therapeutic experience of withdrawing projections epistemologically as the return of meaning from the people, things and events of our lives to the inner workings of the psyche or self. It is inevitable that he then bemoans the resultant 'despiritualisation' of nature and the world (see Jung, 1934/1954, CW 9i, para. 54). Jung regards this draining the world of all meaning as the inevitable burden of 'modern man', which leaves him with a sentimental nostalgia for what he imagines are 'primitive' modes of being. In this 'epistemological' form of projection, what we call 'experience' is comprised of mental representations and internally associated meanings. Many of Jung's writings are imprisoned in this epistemological solipsism. For example:

> It is my mind, with its store of images, that gives the world colour and sound; and that supremely real and rational certainty which I call 'experience' is, in its most simple form, an exceedingly complicated structure of mental images. Thus there is in a certain sense, nothing that is directly experienced except the mind itself.
>
> (Jung, 1926, CW 8, para. 623)

Or again:

> We are in truth so wrapped about by psychic images that we cannot penetrate at all the essence of things external to ourselves. All our knowledge consists of the stuff of the psyche which, because it alone is immediate, is superlatively real.
>
> (Jung, 1931, CW 8, para. 680)

A neat little study would be to do a phenomenology of withdrawing projections. We would find that withdrawing projections interpersonally has nothing to do with this epistemological organization of psychic reality. The result would be much closer to David Holt's (1975) wonderful, but seldom noted, reflection from many years ago. If we think of the withdrawal of projections as a visuospatial move of return from being psychologically 'out there' to back 'in here', then the world is indeed drained of meaning. If, however, we imagine the withdrawal of projections as a shift from *speaking* to the world to *listening* to its own soundings, then the world is not abandoned and the meaning is in fact deepened. Is this not what happens when we withdraw projections and see someone as if for the first time? The Other's face appears in a way that deepens our sense of both that person and ourselves as well as the meanings of our relationship. The withdrawal of projections makes available the exteriority of the Other's face (Levinas, 1961/1969). It amounts to an awakening of the Other's presence, of our capacity to hear, of our ethical responsibility and of our own self-understanding as persons – all this as a single occurrence within the structure of being-in-the-world itself. Jung himself implies as much when he writes that:

> As the individual is not just a separate being but by his very existence presupposes a collective relationship, it follows that the process of individuation [and the withdrawal of projections] must lead to more intense and broader collective relationships and not to isolation.
> (Jung, 1921, CW 6, para. 758; see Samuels, 2014, p. 105)

What, then, of the world, if we Jungians listen instead of speak? Jung feared that abandoning his European identity would involve a regression into unconsciousness and tend towards psychosis (see Jung, 1928a,b). On the other hand, Jung (1961) also regarded the ontological awakening of the world as the deepest meaning of human consciousness.

It is appropriate to pause and suggest that Jung was, even here, 'on to something' when, consistent with his Western humanist and rationalist values, he reacted against what he interpreted as the deep levels of superstition in traditional Black African cultures. Significantly, Leopold Senghor of Senegal also sought to integrate scientific rationalism into his overarching 'civilization of the universal' for the same reason, while integrating the humanism of African values. In the shadows of *ubuntu* as an organizing constituent of being human are at least three challenges for which there is support in the writings of Senghor, Wiredu and Shutte:

1. Nepotism, since *ubuntu* too often does not reach beyond one's own, however defined.
2. The loss of the very individual personhood we have been celebrating since the desire for consensus can lead to group think. (Wiredu [1995/1998] has written a passionate plea for nonpartisan politics in Africa for this reason.)

3. If (African) humanism is a total epistemological organization for interpreting the real, it slides towards an anthropomorphism of natural phenomena with sometimes horrible consequences. It is indeed a kind of paranoia when nothing can have any explanation apart from human intelligence and motivations. When human relationships are the source of all meaning then the search for human causes extends too far, assuming malevolent human involvement in natural phenomena such as birth defects, medical illness and natural calamities.

Back to the question: What, then, is an awakening of being, of the earth/world's wild presence without the defensive terror of psychosis and personal oblivion, which Jung imagined? This question invites a phenomenological sketch of the differences between psychotic experience and a much more original awakening of the world in human experience. I hope this might clarify what for Jung remained confused. What becomes clear is that the withdrawal of projections does not remove us from the world but pours us more fully into its wild presence and that this is not at all some sort of return to psychosis.

- Wild presence is liberating; psychotic presence is imprisoning.
- Wild presence has multiple centres of consciousness (Abram, 2010), each living form engaged in its own world of significance (von Uexküll, 1933); the psychotic lives at the centre of the world (Perry, 1976), which is oriented towards him or her in a persecutory way.
- Wild presence offers psyche increasing range, complexity and differentiation; the psychotic's psyche tends to be increasingly narrowed, persecutory and conflated.
- The unseen in wild presence is a place of open enquiry; the unseen for the psychotic is conspiratorial and malevolent.
- Wild presence is sometimes dangerous and can be hostile; the psychotic's world is always so and arranged around oneself.
- The existential wound of an open human heart (Todres, 2005) in the experience of wild presence is a place of vitality and a capacity for wonder, or an experience of the sacred; the open heart for the psychotic is generally inaccessible behind psychotic defences (for example, paranoia and depersonalization).
- Wild presence is a world that is human and more than human; the psychotic's world is rarely more than human unless it is supernatural or religious in an uncanny yet still anthropomorphic sense.

So much for the suggestion that the withdrawal of projections leaves us with a despiritualized and dis-inhabited world, inimitably described by Hillman as 'a slag heap' from which all psyche has been 'extracted' (1973, p. 123). On the contrary, psychological life becomes more deeply embodied, spacious and differentiated.

Object relations and ancestral relations

Given that object relations theory has been integrated into Jungian psychology for over five decades, and for many of us is integral to Jungian psychoanalytic thought and practice, a few critical comments are in order. The aim here is to interpret object relations theory so that what is of value in it can survive the heat of Jung's barber's curling iron.

Object relations theory is about the development of personal identity as it is constituted through the internalization of one's primary relationships. It is further concerned with the ways in which this relational structure shapes one's relationships with others, including the next generation.

The assumption here is that we do indeed, as the Nguni say, become persons through other persons who relate to us as persons (see Redfearn, 1982). Ethics and ontology entwined. Others – our elders – are not most originally those to whom we as already formed persons relate. They are dialectically incorporated into the stuff of our identity. They are as intrinsic to us as our accents. How they relate to us and we to them in those early years are not merely 'important' but are intrinsic to the internal structure of our well-being.

What we call an internal object is the Other's participation in the imaginal structure of our being-in-the-world. This internal object is, of course, also relational in its organisation. Our parents had parents, and so on, back through time. Object relations are thus ancestral relations. Like the gods for Jung, we can say that, evoked or not, ancestors will be present. Whenever we open our mouths to speak our accents reveal the hidden presence of our ancestors.

We need to notice critically what psychoanalysis has done with these ancestral relations. It has made them matters of mind. Our ancestors are no longer real relations mediated within and through our imaginations. We have colonized the imagination by stripping it of its world and making it an internal realm of mental representations and 'symbols'.

A brief story, which I have discussed elsewhere (Brooke, 2009), illustrates the problem. A Xhosa student was discussing his frustration at Jung's notion of symbols, which, he said, seemed to make what was symbolized unreal. At that moment a bee flew in through the window. He asked for a moment's silence because the incoming bee announced the presence of the ancestors. For both of us it was a moment of synchronicity. We then reflected on how the bee in Western thought is 'known' to be merely a biological organism, and that any other significance it might have is 'symbolic', *within the minds* of Xhosa people. But for the Xhosa, the symbolic resonance of the bee is not a matter of mind but of the coming into presence of the ancestral world. It is true that Jung uses the term *symbol* to point to the depth of meaning the bee has for Xhosa people, but the price to pay is that he perpetuates a white Faustian colonialism, claiming the land of bees and flowers and ancestors for our appropriation and white washing it of all meaning. There are no ancestors but only 'symbols'. The term *synchronicity* is rightly Jung's attempt to acknowledge the meaningfulness of the bee itself, but the term betrays the Cartesian dualism it seeks to overcome, so it cannot be entirely successful.

Jungian psychology can offer object relations theory two corrections. The first is to deconstruct it in terms of its historical significance, just as Jung did with Freud's psychoanalysis. Then we can be clearer that what we have theoretically constructed as object relations are ancestral relations. Positively, the essential and creative insight of object relations psychoanalysis is that psychological well-being requires a good relationship with the ancestors. Jungians could not agree more.

The second move we can make is to blow object relations theory's model of mind as mental representation wide open – open into psyche, into that open realm which surrounds and gathers us, in history, language, imagination and in places in which the world shines forth in all its multiplicity.

Conclusion

The following conclusions would not leave most of us now in the Jungian field overwhelmed with anxiety or with heads on fire.

• The notions of individuation and the development of consciousness still have currency, but they have nothing to do with draining the world of meaning, nor with white metaphysics. They have to do with being in the world with an open heart, hospitable to the Other, yet also able to stand and fight when we must. What we call consciousness has many faces and is found in all traditions and cultures. Secular humanism has its investments and defences just as much as any of the religious and spiritual traditions, even as we affirm the wisdom in its ethics and politics. Evoked or not, the gods will be present. Unconsciousness is a fact of life, and none of us escape it (not even by becoming a Jungian – which was my fantasy!).
• Individuation involves the ever-widening and deepening of our relationships with others, from our immediate caregivers to the family and wider community, reaching out in self-awareness to the faces of the Other, to the ancestors we carry, to God if so called, to our nonhuman animal cousins and to our blue planet.

Acknowledgements

Thanks to Sandra Miller, PhD, for her helpful comments on a draft of this chapter. Responsibility for content remains mine.

References

Abram, D. (2010). *Becoming animal: An earthly cosmology.* Pantheon Books.

Adams, M. (1996). *The multicultural imagination: Race, color, and the unconscious.* Routledge.

Beebe, J. (Ed.). (2003). *Terror, violence, and the impulse to destroy.* Diamon Verlag.

Bernstein, J. (2005). *Living in the borderland: The evolution of consciousness and the challenge of healing trauma.* Routledge.

Bernstein, J. (2014). Healing our split: Participation mystique and C.G. Jung. In M. Winborn (Ed.), *Shared realities: Participation mystique and beyond* (pp. 167–185). Fisher King Press.

Brewster, F. (2017). *African Americans and Jungian psychology.* Routledge.

Brooke, R. (1991/2015). *Jung and phenomenology: Classic edition.* Routledge.

Brooke, R. (1993). A coyote barks at Prometheus: Archetypal images of the therapeutic stance. *The Humanistic Psychologist, 21*(1), 51–64.

Brooke, R. (2000). Jung's recollection of the lifeworld. In R. Brooke (Ed.), *Pathways into the Jungian world* (pp. 13–24). Routledge.

Brooke, R. (2008). *Ubuntu* and the individuation process: Towards a multicultural analytical psychology. *Psychological Perspectives, 51*(1), 36–53.

Brooke, R. (2009). The self, the psyche, and the world: A phenomenological interpretation. *Journal of Analytical Psychology, 54*(5), 601–618.

Brooke, R. (2017). An archetypal approach to treating combat post-traumatic stress disorder. In D.L. Downing & J. Mills (Eds.), *Outpatient treatment of psychosis: Psychodynamic approaches to evidence-based practice.* Karnac Books.

Buhrmann, M.V. (1986). *Living in two worlds: Communications between a white healer and her black counterparts.* Chiron.

Burleson, B.W. (2005). *Jung in Africa.* Continuum International Publishing Group.

Coetzee, P.H. & Roux, A.P.J. (1998). *The African philosophy reader.* Routledge.

Colman, W. (2016). *Act and image: The emergence of symbolic imagination.* Spring Journal Books.

Covington, C., Williams, P., Arundale, J., & Knox, J. (Eds). (2002). *Terrorism and war: Unconscious dynamics of political violence.* Karnac Books.

Giegerich, W. (1984). Philemon-Faust-Jung. *Spring*, 107–114.

Hillman, J. (1973). Anima. *Spring,* 97–132.

Hillman, J. (1976). *Revisioning psychology.* Harper and Row.

Hillman, J. (1986). Notes on white supremacy. *Spring, 46*, 29–57.

Hillman, J. (2004). *A terrible love of war.* Penguin Books.

Holt, D. (1975). Projection, presence, profession. *Spring*, 130–144.

Jacobi, J. (1965/1967). *The way of individuation.* (R. Hull, Trans.). Hodder and Stoughton.

Jung, C.G. (1921). *The collected works of C.G. Jung: Vol. 6. Psychological types.* (H. Read, M. Fordham, G. Adler & W. McGuire, Eds.). (R. F. C. Hull, Trans.). Princeton University Press.

Jung, C.G. (1926). Spirit and life. In H. Read, M. Fordham, G. Adler & W. McGuire (Eds.), *The collected works of C.G. Jung: Vol. 8. The structure and dynamics of the psyche* (paras. 601–48). (R. F. C. Hull, Trans.). Princeton University Press.

Jung, C.G. (1928a). Child development and education. In H. Read, M. Fordham, G. Adler & W. McGuire (Eds.), *The collected works of C.G. Jung: Vol. 17. The development of personality* (paras. 47–62). (R. F. C. Hull, Trans.). Princeton University Press.

Jung, C.G. (1928b). On psychic energy. In H. Read, M. Fordham, G. Adler & W. McGuire (Eds.), *The collected works of C.G. Jung: Vol. 8. The structure and dynamics of the psyche* (paras. 1–130). (R. F. C. Hull, Trans.). Princeton University Press.

Jung, C.G. (1931). Basic postulates of analytical psychology. In H. Read, M. Fordham, G. Adler & W. McGuire (Eds.), *The collected works of C.G. Jung: Vol. 8. The structure and dynamics of the psyche* (paras. 649–88). (R. F. C. Hull, Trans.). Princeton University Press.

Jung, C.G. (1934/1954). Archetypes of the collective unconscious. In H. Read, M. Fordham, G. Adler & W. McGuire (Eds.), *The collected works of C.G. Jung: Vol. 9i. The archetypes and the collective unconscious* (paras. 1–110). (R. F. C. Hull, Trans.). Princeton University Press.

Jung, C.G. (1939). The dreamlike world of India. In H. Read, M. Fordham, G. Adler & W. McGuire (Eds.), *The collected works of C.G. Jung: Vol. 10. Civilization in transition* (paras. 515–24). (R. F. C. Hull, Trans.). Princeton University Press.

Jung, C.G. (1944/1952). *The collected works of C.G. Jung: Vol. 12. Psychology and alchemy.* (H. Read, M. Fordham, G. Adler & W. McGuire, Eds.). (R. F. C. Hull, Trans.). Princeton University Press.

Jung, C.G. (1961). *Memories, dreams, reflections.* Random House.

Jung, C.G. (1977/1980). *C.G. Jung Speaking.* (W. McGuire & R.F.C. Hull, Eds.). Pan Books.

Kiehl, E., Saban, M. & Samuels, A. (Eds.). (2016). *Analysis and activism: Social and political contributions of Jungian psychology.* Routledge.

Levinas, E. (1961/1969). *Totality and infinity.* (Alphonso Lingis, Trans.). Duquesne University Press.

Marlan, S. (1999). The metaphor of light and its deconstruction in Jung's alchemical vision. In R. Brooke (Ed.), *Pathways into the Jungian world.* Routledge.

Marshall, J. (Ed.). (2009). *Depth psychology, disorder, and climate change.* Jung Downunder Books. C.G. Jung Society of Sydney.

Papadopoulos, R. (2016). Therapeutic encounters and interventions outside the consulting room: Challenges in theory and practice. In E. Kiehl, M. Saban, & A. Samuels (Eds.), *Analysis and activism: Social and political contributions of Jungian psychology* (pp. 11–20). Routledge.

Perry, J.W. (1976). *Roots of renewal in myth and madness.* San Francisco, CA: Jossey-Bass.

Redfearn, J.W.T. (1982). When are things persons and persons things? *Journal of Analytical Psychology, 27*(3), 215–37.

Ricoeur, P. (1971/1981). The model of the text: Meaningful action considered as text. In *Hermeneutics and the human sciences* (pp. 197–221). (J. Thompson, Trans). Cambridge University Press.

Rowland, S. (2002). *Jung: a feminist revision.* Blackwell.

Rowland, S. (2005). *Jung as a writer.* Routledge.

Samuels, A. (1989/2016). *The plural psyche: Personality, morality, and the father.* Routledge.

Samuels, A. (1993). *The political psyche.* Routledge.

Samuels, A. (2014). Appraising the role of the individual in political and social change processes: Jung, Camus, and the question of personal responsibility – possibilities and impossibilities of 'making a difference'. *Psychotherapy and Politics International, 12*(2), 99–110.

Senghor, L. (1977/2001). Negritude and modernity or negritude as a humanism for the twentieth century. In R. Bernasconi (Ed.), *Race*. Blackwell.

Senghor, L. (1998). Negritude and African socialism. In P.H Coetzee & A.P.J. Roux (Eds.), *The African philosophy reader* (pp. 438–48). Routledge.

Shutte, A. (1993). *Philosophy for Africa*. Marquette University Press.

Todres, L. (2005). Freedom-wound: Towards the embodiment of human openness in Daseinsanalytic therapy. In D. Martino (Ed.), *Daseinsanalysis. The Twenty-Second Annual Symposium of the Silverman Phenomenology Center*. The Simon Silverman Phenomenology Center.

Tutu, D. (2015, 7 October). 10 pieces of wisdom from Desmund Tutu on his birthday. Desmund Tutu Peace Foundation. Retrieved from http://www.tutufoundationusa.org/2015/10/07/10-pieces-of-wisdom-from-desmund-tutu-on-his-birthday

von Uexküll, J. (1933/2010). *A foray into the world of animals and humans*. (J.D. O'Neil, Trans.). University of Minnesota Press.

Winborn, M. (Ed.). (2014). *Shared realities: Participation mystique and beyond*. Fisher King Press.

Wiredu, K. (1992/1998). The moral foundations of an African culture. In P.H. Coetzee & A.P.J. Roux (Eds.), *The African philosophy reader* (pp. 306–16). Routledge.

Wiredu, K. (1995/1998). Democracy and consensus in traditional African politics: A plea for a nonparty polity. In P.H. Coetzee & A.P.J. Roux (Eds.), *The African philosophy reader* (pp. 374–82). Routledge.

Chapter 2

The spectre and its movement

The dynamic of intra- and transgenerational influence

Stephani Stephens

> *Everyday life is haunted by implicit 'others' who supposedly live outside the ordinary, the everyday.*
> Ben Highmore, The Everyday Life Reader (2002, p. 1)

The spectre and the mark

The word *spectre* is inherently complex, derived from the Latin root words *specere* and *spectare*, which both mean 'to watch'. The association of the words is compelling in that it raises the not so obvious question as to *who* exactly is doing the watching. Does the derivation speak to the ability to perceive an apparition? Or rather does it raise the possibility that a presence is watching us? The word *spectre* is quite different from the word *apparition*, which indicates an appearance, and thus, the activity seems to be one sided: we see; we take in; we attempt to recognise an apparition. With a spectre, the idea of watching leaves open the possibility of an engagement on both parts, from both sides.

A similar sense of ambiguity is no less evident when Jung describes it in *The Red Book*:

> Once you have seen the chaos, look at your face: you saw more than death and the grave, you saw beyond and your face bears the mark of one who has seen chaos and yet was a man. Many cross over, but they do not see the chaos; however the chaos sees them, stares at them, and imprints its features on them. And they are marked forever.
> (2009, p. 299, n. 198)

The chaos can be understood as the cacophony of the unconscious, the troubled and unsettled content of the past or previous generations as well as the 'Unanswered, Unresolved, and Unredeemed' (Jung & Jaffé, 1961/1995, p. 217). And it can be interpreted as the dead, reaching beyond the grave as spectres of an unconscious ready to engage those who are ready not only to look but also to see.

DOI: 10.4324/9781003223481-4

The suggestion, here, is that the spectre establishes this engagement. Like its derivative sibling the spectator, the spectre forms a relationship as the *Other* and proceeds to work often unknowingly and yet sometimes in conjunction with the psyche. Those who have experienced this chaos in the beyond are distinguished from even the dead who reside there. What Jung emphasises is that after such an encounter, there is a discernible quality, a difference, detected by both the living individual and the dead themselves.[1]

Examining Jung's experiences with spectres, apparitions, ghosts and spirits is crucial to apprehending his relationship with his own unconscious experience and his subsequent psychological understanding. In turn, this helps highlight the dynamic of a collective unconscious of the past that might be instrumental in making us who we are in the present, with obvious implications for who we will be in the future.

Jungian Sam Kimbles proposes that 'intergenerational processes are manifested as phantom narratives that provide structure, representation and continuity for unresolved or unworked-thorough grief and violence that occurred in a prior historical cultural context that continues into the present' (2014, p. 21). Although Kimbles uses the phantasm concept to represent how cultural complexes exist historically and, at times, resist change, at play is the idea that the spectre exhibits agency; it serves a functional role in engagement.

Jung appears to encounter the chaos as part of the terrain of the unconscious. And this chaos looks to be wanting. Spectres have looked upon Jung and have identified him as among the living, that is 'a man' amid their unconscious venue. As a result, chaos has 'imprint[ed] its features'; it has left a mark. Jung, who has journeyed beyond consciousness, will always be recognised as having done so by its inhabitants.

There is no going back for Jung; there is no unseeing. He becomes marked as someone who not only has taken the journey (like a long list of predecessors: Inanna, Gilgamesh, Orpheus, Odysseus, Aeneas, Theseus and Hercules) but also has undertaken to accept what he has seen. We find a similar indication of this identifying mark in the ancient Orphic Mysteries. After initiates experienced a quality of immortality, they were forever changed. The word *Brimo* was used as a password, recorded on funerary tablets, as one of the words the soul repeated to prove it was an initiate and entitled to enter the Elysian Fields (D'Este & Rankine, 2009, pp. 171–72). The word indicated that the initiate had spent a lifetime as a knower of the beyond, of the chaos, and would therefore manage differently, perhaps more knowledgeably, fluidly, but definitely recognise when their final arrival into the afterlife occurred.

The dynamic at play

Where chaos makes its mark, Jung, in turn, acknowledges the dead, and this is the first part of the dynamic of intra- and transgenerational influence.

This ability to respond to the spectre is what sets the dynamic in motion and is where the 'Unanswered, Unresolved, and Unredeemed' become operational. Jung warns several times in 'Liber Secundus' of the treacherous risks of ignoring spectres: 'Do you think that the dead do not exist because you have devised the impossibility of immortality?' (2009, pp. 297b–98a).[2] In a sense, Jung warns us: just because you don't believe in the dead doesn't mean they aren't there. In fact, he encourages: 'put your ear to that wall and you will hear the rustling of their procession' (p. 296a).

In one sense the spectre, by standing outside time/place, serves as a placeholder to a present that has refused to move to the future until a reconciliation is complete.

The spectre acts as Other by occupying a space in the psyche with whom there is a relationship, possibly genetic or even emotional. This space accommodates a theme in which the opportunity to engage arises. There are subtle messages, intrusions, uninvited visions and behaviours that appear 'out of nowhere'. Sounds we cannot discern, unexplained aromas that take us far from where we are, a touch or sensation that we cannot explain. Compulsion and repetition beg attention and just might be the spectre knocking at the door of consciousness.

A drawing out occurs such that the theme incites intense focus and action while the spectre's role serves as the issue at hand, a space in which a looping of thought occurs until a reconciliation is complete. Relief occurs when, as in Jung's case, the spectre is acknowledged in its own right as either interloper or agent. As Mark Wolynn, director of The Family Constellation Institute, notes, 'Though we're not exactly certain how an ancestor's unfinished business takes root inside us, it appears to bring relief when such a link is made conscious' (2016, p. 55).

Examples

A few examples here demonstrate this dynamic at work. These are not exclusive, and certainly there are a myriad of ways that the past moves in to occupy our present to varied affect. The first example shows the spectre of the past influencing the present or how the Other can lodge in the psyche and mould and steer action. Although this example is of intragenerational influence, the dynamic is engaged in a similar manner as transgenerational influence and is useful to see played out.

The Australian book and film *Lion* tells the story of Saroo Brierley who was adopted by an Australian family at age five after unexpectedly and tragically becoming separated from his biological family in India. As an adult, Brierley is thrown into emotional chaos as he begins to remember the time when the separation occurred. He recalls that he, along with his older teenage brother Guddu, went to look for food, and Saroo became tired and so asked to wait on a train platform bench where he fell asleep. The last words from his brother were 'Just sit down and don't move. I'll come back in a little while and we can find somewhere to sleep the night' (Brierley, 2013, p. 28). But the very young Brierley, upon waking, sees he is alone, feels scared and goes in search of his brother. He boards a train, falls asleep and is taken literally thousands of miles away from the bench, his family and the life he knows. As an adult he becomes consumed and haunted by this separation and begins to search for the circumstances and story that led him to his adoption and his current life. What we learn when the adult Brierley finally locates his Indian family (with the extraordinary help of Google Earth) is that his brother Guddu also did not return home that night. After meeting his mother and sister after those 25 years, he asks after Guddu and learns he was killed perhaps that same night, likely by a train, leaving Brierley wondering if on that night Guddu searched for him frantically and perhaps this was the cause of his death (p. 186).

In one central respect, Brierley's story is Guddu's story. Perhaps Guddu's purpose is to set right what he was unable to do in life, and thus, he does so in death. In the film, we learn that Brierley hears his mother and brother often calling his name, and his grip on his life slowly begins to unravel. It is this missing piece that sits in Brierley's psyche and spurs him to search for his family. We can imagine Guddu keeping a promise to bring Brierley home, and this drives Brierley to search and search until he finds his village in India. The reunion of family is deeply healing for Brierley himself, but the reunion is Guddu's as well, and what is left is a sense of having come full circle. Thus, if we understand the Other to assist in unresolved questions, here might be an example of Guddu, with Brierley's willingness, healing them both by guiding Brierley back home.

In *Red Book* terms, Guddu has put a mark, his mark on Brierley, and unknowingly Brierley can do nothing but search obsessively for his family of origin. The mark works like a puzzle-piece-sized space that also fits the same psychic shape/wound that Brierley holds, and when they arrive at resolution these puzzle pieces each dissolve into a wholeness for them both. The end of Brierley and Guddu's story foreseeably sees them both at peace. As Jung reflects, 'Inner peace and contentment depend in large measure upon whether or not the historical family which is inherent in the individual can be harmonised with the ephemeral conditions of the present' (Jung & Jaffé, 1961/1995, p. 264).

A further example derives from ancient literature and addresses how the inclusion of the Other in one's exploration of the present can influence the course of future events. Aeneas, the protagonist of Virgil's *Aeneid*, is a typical hero. At the end of the Trojan War, he escapes the burning Troy with his father and son and the remaining survivors of the attack by the Greeks. He wanders many years and has many adventures, but these are difficult times and particularly for a hero destined to found a great nation that will become Rome. He is fated to do this, but this does not make it easy. He has suffered the loss of his wife, Creusa; his city, Troy; his lover, Dido; and now most recently during the journey his father, Anchises. He is lost and has come to the end of his physical and emotional reserves. He simply does not know what to do next.

The deceased Anchises appears to him in ghostly form and encourages him to journey to the underworld: 'seek, my son, a meeting with me there' (Virgil, 1972, ll. 732–33) ... 'then you will learn of your whole race' (l. 737). Aeneas meets the Sibyl who assists him in preparation. Here, Aeneas not only sees his past, including a painful attempt at an exchange with Dido, but Anchises also shows him his future and, more importantly, what his future will ensure; the deeds of his successors are paraded regally as evidence of a long and prosperous people that will unfold if Aeneas fulfils his fate. Anchises stresses how important the completion of Aeneas's journey is because his progeny will found a wondrous city that will be known for future ages. This visitation and vision of the future shores up Aeneas for the necessary impending hardships that he will inevitably endure; the difference is now he understands his destiny.

Only when Aeneas acknowledges Anchises's intervention, does the integrity of Anchises's efforts solidify and his movement from present to future become apparent. Anchises's role shifts from a ghostly spectre beseeching Aeneas to partake in the visions of his future to that of an ancestor stepping into his own rightful place in the lineage of Aeneas's fate.

Once Aeneas questions his life, this leaves a psychic opening for Anchises to assist, his spectral form emerging as a result of Aeneas's intense self-reflection. We might say about Aeneas what James Hollis describes: '*we are not our history*; ultimately, *we are what wishes to enter the world through us*, though to underestimate the power of that history as an invisible player in the choices of daily life is a grave error' (2013, p. 53).

The contemporary Guddu and the ancient Anchises are spectral presences who assist the living, and the living respond. Brierley, although driven, might be unaware of the question that Guddu's presence raises, but he is lost and therefore open to the guidance that will bring resolution to his pain. Aeneas is equally lost and yet is fully aware of Anchises but not of his own future. Thus, he accepts the deceased Anchises's guidance as well as the visions he facilitates. This confirms for Aeneas his destiny and the hardships he has suffered in order to fulfil his fate.

Abraham and Torok

When we talk about how the spectre occupies the psychic space of remaining and succeeding generations, we find people who are oftentimes unaware of the influence they are living under. Freudians Nicolas Abraham and Maria Torok discovered in several of their clients the entombing of a secret, an unmourned loss or an ancestor representing the secret, into the unconscious of a descendent. The translator and editor of Abraham and Torok's essays, Nicholas Rand, explains the idea of the phantom and the crypt: 'here symptoms do not spring from the individual's own life experiences but from someone else's psychic conflicts, traumas or secrets' (Abraham & Torok, 1994, p. 166).

The patient unwittingly serves as host to a story from a previous generation. In an almost occult manner, the phantom literally haunts and the patient remains unknowingly complicit in keeping this secret hidden. Often in analysis, to a trained ear, the Other can be heard representing its position through symptoms or repetitive expressions. Torok suggests, 'This means that when people say "I" they might in fact be referring to something quite different from their own identity..., *a phantom* ... is acting, a phantom is speaking' (Abraham & Torok, 1994, pp. 179–80).

Torok stresses instead of the traditional emphasis on identifying a repression, a far different question should be addressed: 'What is the nature of the phantom returning to haunt?' (Abraham & Torok, 1994, p. 180). In other words, what does the phantom want? Psychoanalyst Louise Demers clarifies Torok's concept: 'The cryptophores through an occult incorporative process, become hosts to these unmourned deceased, the latter having developed a parasitical relationship to them' (1993, p. 32). Both Brierley and Aeneas experience the agitation that forces them to look, and when they do, they see. There, in the form of a spectre, is the answer looking at and seeing them.

A further example of how this dynamic occurs is discussed not only by Abraham but also in the work of Anne Ancelin Schützenberger in *The Ancestor Syndrome:*

[The] patient was a geology lover. Every Sunday he went out looking for stones, collecting them and breaking them. He also chased butterflies, caught them and stuffed them in a jar of cyanide before pinning them up ... The man felt very uncomfortable and sought counseling ... He went to see Abraham, who had the idea of exploring the man's family, researching information going back several generations. He learned that this man had a grandfather ... who nobody mentions. ...[he] had been suspected of bank robbery ... [and] sentenced to forced labor, to 'break rocks' and then he had been executed in the gas chamber ... what does our man do on weekends? A lover of geology, he 'breaks rocks,' and catches butterflies and proceeds to kill them in a can of cyanide'.

(1998, p. 47)

The implication is that the secret of the grandfather's exploits was encrypted by the grandson who had not known his family's history. As a result, his actions were, in part, dictated by his grandfather, the phantom. The crypt, the unconscious psychic space housing the phantom, keeps hidden its secrets from the inheritor. Jungian Alessandra Cavalli describes more specifically this dynamic. She makes note of Gerson's idea of 'the dead third' being a result of 'an enduring presence of an absence ...'. This dead third, 'made of undigested facts which create annihilation anxieties, shadows like a ghost the development of the second generation who creates an attachment to it. It is this attachment that the third generation seems to absorb into their selves' (2012, p. 601).

Considering Jung's personal history, there were plenty of inherited secrets on both sides of his family. His paternal grandfather with his medical bent and his maternal grandfather with his paranormal interests, each offers a possibility of an inherited phantom lodged in Jung's psyche.[3] Well known were Paul Jung's unresolved Christian faith and Jung's mother's mediumistic abilities, both of which could be considered phantoms prompting issues to be explored and addressed. And could Jung's break with Freud literally have cracked open the crypt and unleashed the throngs of dead whom Jung encountered throughout his confrontation? Those whose emergence and presence posed the questions, 'What will you do about us? How are you going to explain us, the dead?'

The presence of Jung's ancestors can be considered the spectres of the 'Unanswered, Unresolved, and Unredeemed' dead (Jung & Jaffé, 1961/1995, p. 217; Shamdasani, 2008, p. 26). In Jung's case, the crypt then looks to hold the secret of the dead's existence *at the outset*. Perhaps the crypt housed generations of Jung's dead awaiting an invitation to be defined and understood within a psychological landscape that only he was able to define.

Rand further suggests:

> We should engage in this unveiling and understanding of the former existence of the dead not because we may want to appease them or prevent them from perpetrating their nocturnal pranks, but because unsuspected, the dead continue to lead a devastating psychic half-life in us.
>
> (Abraham & Torok, 1994, p. 167)

James Hollis adds a further dimension to such importance when he addresses 'the fact that in daily life we slip easily between worlds and are seldom conscious of how often we are serving both at the same time' (2013, p. 87).

Considering 'the phantom's periodic and compulsive return ... works like a ventriloquist, like a stranger within the subjects' own mental topography' (Abraham & Torok, 1994, p. 173)[4], could Jung's fascination with mummification and his verbal slip in conversation with Freud when he said 'mummies' but meant bog men have been such a phantom at work? (Jung & Jaffé, 1961/1995, p. 180). Psychologist Annie Rogers claims, 'listen instead for the unsayable, which is everywhere, in speech, in enactments, in dreams, and in the body' (cited in Wolynn, 2016, p. 56). This would point to the very nature of a secret being quite different from what we have considered traditionally: we don't keep secrets or hide them; we live them.

One of the most compelling results of the phantom is the possibility that 'though manifest in one individual's psyche, the phantom eventually leads to the psychoanalysis in absentia of several generations through symptoms of the descendent' (Abraham & Torok, 1994, p. 168). Could this be, as Shamdasani has suggested, what prompted Jung to affirm 'a striking reversal' of the spiritualist understanding of the day, which would see him in service *to* the dead as opposed to the living seeking information *from* the dead? (Shamdasani, 2008, p. 19). Having recognised the spectre in the chaos, this seemed to oblige Jung to 'know' the questions that the dead posed as well as the answers, which only he was able to provide on their behalf. This step, or arrival point, would see Jung being 'together with' his dead and see him arriving later in life, at the Tower where his 'ancestor's souls are sustained by the atmosphere of the house' (Jung & Jaffé, 1961/1995, p. 265).

Additional thoughts

Epigenetic research has found the effects of trauma being passed down and detectable to the grand offspring generation. Possibly, our experience of trauma when not encountered first-hand can be inherited:

> Case in point: many young people born after 1994 in Rwanda, too young to have witnessed the senseless killings of approximately 800,000 people, experience the same symptoms of posttraumatic stress as those who witnessed and survived the brutality. The young Rwandans report feelings of intense anxiety and obsessive visions similar to the horrors that occurred before they were born.
>
> (Wolynn, 2016, p. 33)

This raises a question: what do you call a memory that you have never experienced? This places the psychic terrain in uncomfortable proximity to the biographical history of the Other. This could also mean that experience of visual products from the body could very well be access to others' stories, from previous generations, similar to having a download of an ancestor's events accessible. What would this look like exactly? I can't help but be reminded of the scene in *Star Wars* when Princess Leia emerges out of R2D2 with an animated message for Obi Wan and Luke. The message is from the past, but crucially relevant to the present moment, and helps steer a future direction. After the message is delivered and recognised for its relevance, Princess Leia in her holographic splendour simply dissolves.

In this respect a discerning principle might need to be developed to help us understand whether the stories we experience as active imaginations occur within the realm of our own bodies and psyches. Or if, like Brierley and Aeneas, these stories and spaces of unresolved issues invite spectres to step in because they too need to be healed in order to take their places as ancestors. They emerge in the same role they've literally left off. In this respect, by addressing their family stories, they finish their own, tying off the narrative thread that is their contribution to their lineage.

In conclusion

Finally, I must ask: Does this type of presence or intrusion by the spectre suggest haunting? Are Brierley and Aeneas in a sense haunted? Was Jung haunted? The answers depend at which stage and to what degree they consciously interacted with the spectre.

From Jung's perspective haunting is specific and conditional:

> While you mock them one of them stands behind you, panting from rage and despair at the fact that your stupor does not attend to him. He besieges you in sleepless nights, sometimes he takes hold of you in an illness, sometimes he crosses your intentions. He makes you overbearing and greedy, he pricks your longing for everything ... he devours your success in discord. He accompanies you as your evil spirit, to whom you can grant no release.
>
> (Jung, 2009, p. 296a)

While there is no acknowledgement, the spectre's presence adds pressure and intrusion. But with Jung, the seeing and acceptance of the Other initiates engagement and begins to address that question that both Torok and Hollis raise: why have you come? This ushers movement with the spectre to the rightful place of resolution.

To face our fears and frailties is, in essence, to face our ancestors, directly and courageously. To look at their lives, efforts, loves and lost secrets and to reconcile these with our own is part of *our* work. In this sense a calibration between lifetimes and lives' histories unfolds and a natural healing occurs within the realm of 'knowing' that then permits generations to build their lives on a platform of their own choosing. Acknowledgement is the key to accepting that quite possibly 'I am my ancestors' wildest dream'.[5]

Notes

1 Jung uses the word 'mark' several times in his personal material to describe an experience of just such discernment. On each occasion, the mark indicates the ability to be recognised by or soon to be attributed to the venue of the unconscious. The term appears in the garden party dream of his sister and a lady who was going to die (Jung & Jaffé, 1961/1995, p. 334), is implicit during the vision of his physician in 'primal form' (p. 324), and in a letter to Kristine Mann on February 1, 1945, when Jung says, 'I will not last too long any more, I am marked' (Jung, 1992, p. 61).
2 The quote preceding this line: 'What the ancients did for their dead! You seem to believe that you can absolve yourself from the care of the dead, and from the

work that they so greatly demand, since what is dead is past. You excuse yourself from disbelief in the immortality of the soul'.

3 Jung's grandfather, who had been arrested for student protests, had to leave Germany upon his release from prison because he could not find employment, resulting in the relocation of Jung's family to Switzerland. Jung's other grandfather was a Freemason, a society with secret initiations. There was plenty of secret fodder to suggest Abraham and Torok's concept was applicable to Jung (Bair, 2003, p. 13).

4 The repetition or word pattern interjection by the phantom points to itself and can serve as a method to resolution. Interestingly the analytic work of Roger Woolger (1998) fundamentally rests on identifying repetitive phrases that have their origin in the unconscious, but in Woolger's experience, these seem to be oriented in a past-life incarnation of the individual.

5 Brandan Odums, Studio Be, http://bmike.com/project/studio-be/.

References

Abraham, N., & Torok, M. (1994). *The shell and the kernel* (N. Rand, Ed.). University of Chicago Press.

Bair, D. (2003). *Jung: A biography*. Back Bay Books.

Brierley, S. (2013). *Lion*. Penguin Random House.

Cavalli, A. (2012). Transgenerational transmission of indigestible facts: From trauma, deadly ghosts, and mental voids to meaning-making interpretations. *Journal of Analytical Psychology*, 57, 597–614. https://doi.org/10.1111/j.1468-5922.2012.02005.x

Demers, L. (1993). Intergenerational grief: Who's mourning whom? *Canadian Journal of Psychoanalysis*, 1(1), 27–40.

D'Este, S., & Rankine, D. (2009). *Hekate liminal rites: A study of the rituals, magic and symbols of the torch-bearing Triple Goddess of the Crossroads*. BM Avalonia.

Highmore, B. (Ed.). (2002). *The everyday life reader*. Routledge.

Hollis, J. (2013). *Hauntings: Dispelling the ghosts who run our lives*. Chiron.

Jung, C.G. (1992). *Letters: 1906–1950, Vol. 1*. Princeton University Press.

Jung, C.G. (2009). *The red book: Liber novus* (S. Shamdasani, Ed.). (Mark Kyburz, S. Shamdasani & J. Peck, Trans.). W.W. Norton & Co.

Jung, C.G., & Jaffé, A. (1961/1995). *Memories, dreams, reflections* (R. Winston & C. Winston Trans.). Fontana.

Kimbles, S. (2014). *Phantom narratives: The unseen contributions of culture to psyche*. Rowman and Littlefield.

Shamdasani, S. (2008). The boundless expanse: Jung's reflections on death and life. *Quadrant*, 38(1), 9–30.

Schützenberger, A.A. (1998). *The ancestor syndrome: Transgenerational psychotherapy and the hidden links in the family tree*. Routledge.

Wolynn, M. (2016). *It didn't start with you: How inherited family trauma shapes who we are and how to end the cycle*. Viking.

Woolger, R. (1998). *Other lives, other selves: A Jungian psychotherapist discovers past lives*. Bantam Books.

Virgil. (1972). *The Aeneid of Virgil, books 1–6*. (R.D. Williams, Ed.). St. Martin's Press.

Chapter 3

Satan's mouth or font of magic

What is it about the anus?

Marybeth Carter

> *I saw something lying on the ground. I looked closer and realized it was a cockroach, which sprang to life and scrambled up my leg. The roach entered my rectum. I scratched wildly at my anus, trying to remove it. I could not get the cockroach out of me.*

Over the years, patients have brought dreams to therapy with images of the anus and rectum, such as this dream about the cockroach. Male and female dreamers often feel shame about these images in their dreams – so much so that they can hardly tell me the details of what occurred. No doubt, these images have personal meaning for each dreamer and even for me as the analyst in the *temenos* with them. However, as these images have continued to emerge over months and years, I've questioned the solely negative associations about the anus and rectum that the dreamers and the larger therapeutic community often resort to in relation to these images. In Jungian analysis, the analyst helps by expounding on possible connections of the dream images to the mythological and archetypal realms. I researched the images and discovered that the anus and rectum can be archetypal symbols with unique psychological and psychosocial significance as a site of psychic coniunctio. These positive associations are psychologically powerful and allow for a spectrum of possibility for the advancement towards psychic wholeness.

The dreams

In some male patients' dreams, they are attempting or completing anal intercourse with girlfriends. In other dreams, women discover their boyfriends having anal intercourse with other women. Other scenarios depict cockroaches scampering up the dreamers' legs, through their anuses and into their rectums. The dreamers respond with disgust and frantic attempts to claw out the cockroaches. One dream, a mother made tamales in the kitchen and cooked them in her vagina. Shocked by this cooking method,

DOI: 10.4324/9781003223481-5

the dreamer was even more horrified when his younger brother shoved a tamale into his rectum, saying, 'That's the way we cook the tamales'! All the dreamers denied interest in anal sex. Each of the male dreamers felt the need to explore the possibility of being gay and concluded they were not. The female patients found the images of their boyfriends having anal sex with others disturbing and felt feelings of betrayal. These individuals' conscious responses to this unconscious material are filled with horror, betrayal and shame. Yet how are these reactions not only representations of the individuals' attitudes but also of the overlay of cultural complexes that are steeped in shame-invoking psychoanalytic theories? Alternatively, what are some positive meanings of dream images of the anus and a conjoining in the rectum from a depth-psychological perspective?

One-sided vs. whole

One approach to interpreting anal-rectum dream images is through Freud's psychosocial stages based on anatomical parts of the body. Each must be successfully traversed to develop into a mature adult. The *anal stage* is the child's relationship to the bowels and the sphincter muscles concomitant with the ability to hold and let go. Freud theorized that the parental stance of encouragement or shaming towards the child during the anal stage creates psychological capacities that range from the highly creative to the pathological, such as the development of the 'anal personality'.

If there is incomplete or malformed development at any of the stages, Freud postulated that individuals regress emotionally and behaviourally to the psychological challenges of that stage. It is the work of analysis to guide individuals to sublimate the instinctual dynamics to become more mature adults. Freud wrote, 'Through the overcoming of these resistances, the patient's mental life is permanently changed, is raised to a higher level of development and remains protected against a fresh possibility of falling ill [to depression, hysteria or other mental illness]' (Freud, 1916–17; as cited in Fonagy, 2000, p. 620).

Jung challenged Freud's focus on resistance and regression as one-sided (Jung, 1966, para. 199). He insisted that Freud's theory, which focused on repression related to undeveloped childhood stages, was problematic because it was an 'attempt to connect such an unconscious product (symptoms) with the past, [and] its value to the individual in the present may be lost' (Samuels, 1985, p. 135). Jung's emphasis was not only on the unhealthy psyche that needs healing, as Freud's focus was, but also on the entire psyche in both its healthy and unhealthy aspects as a functioning dynamic system. Jung's emphasis *on what might be lost* shifts Jungian psychology from the past to the present and, ultimately, towards futurity and the prospective movement of individuation. Although there may be an aspect of the psychological explained by the reductive approach, it cannot be the *sole* explanation: 'The psyche is not *just* the one or the other [sick or healthy], nor for that matter both together. It is *also* what it has made and will make out of them' (Jung, 1966, para. 67). The presence of symptoms and images as symbols and the meaning from them are what is important to the individual in their present state of being.

Jung advocated that *Eros* is a more essential theoretical explanation of the psyche. *Eros* gives rise to meaning from the images and symptoms that emerge from the movement – or lack of movement – by the libido. The transmutation of the libidinal propels psychic dynamism towards wholeness (Samuels, 1985). *Eros* generated through the vitality of the libido transforms an individual's psyche that is now 'not only something evolved but also continually evolving and creative' (1971, CW 6, para. 717). The interpretation of dream images of a union, or coniunctio, in the rectum could be viewed as a meaningful representation of the dreamer's current psychic development. The union of the energic images is propelling the individual towards wholeness from their current level of consciousness – not back to their former developmental stage. In this way, Jung's *Eros* theory, related to libido, symbol and union (*coniunctio*) along with the emergence of the 'third' – that something more – demands a different attitude towards the symbols that emerge from the unconscious and a process that considers the positive potential of the libido-filled image. Because this movement of libido is neutral, not only sexual as Freud theorized, the rectum, as well as the mouth, the vagina or other body parts are squarely in psychological territory when they become a receptacle for a potential coniunctio.

Transformational unions

An example of a coniunctio with an unexpected body part is in Orthodox Christianity's teaching that the conception of Christ was through the ear of the Virgin Mary (Sanidopoulos, 2017). That the union took place in her ear was necessary for the retention of the belief in her divinity. It also emphasizes faith in the word of God for believers because the pregnancy does not follow the usual biological means of impregnation. Clearly, this is an example of how some images spontaneously arise from the collective unconscious, 'from [that] deep level of the psyche' (Frey-Rohn, 1974, p. 56). Two dialectical images join and have symbolic and archetypal power with the potential to transform. The psyche can constellate a dialectical union with any two images, such as the wind and an ear, a penis and a rectum or any other bodily orifices as receptacles for potential coniunctio, if one represents the conscious attitude and the other the content from the unconscious.

The dream journal of filmmaker Federico Fellini contains images that illustrate dialectical union via anal coniunctio in sketches he made of two dreams. He sketched one of the images from a dream he had on 25 March 1975 that depicted a voluptuous naked woman, 'L', an anima symbol for

Fellini. In the dream, 'L' arrived on a beach near Fellini's birthplace, where a tiny war was happening. Using her hands, she separated her buttocks, and out of her rectum came the head and body of King Vittorio Emanuele the Third, who, for 46 years as King of Italy, led them through two world wars (Fellini, 2020, pp. ii/38–9). This dream coniunctio, of the rectum and the King, helped Fellini's inner daemon transform from projections onto actresses to 'his creative daemon, to assist him in his artistic expression' (Wojtkowski, 2017, p. 10). Prior to the dream of 'L' on the beach, there is an earlier dream entitled 'The Ass of "Secrecy"', in which Fellini is confronted with the depths of shadow in a dream woman's ass that is illuminated by a candle (Wojtkowski, 2017, p. 55). 'What light does an ass emit? Is it a representation of anal consciousness?' (p. 56). In the early 1960s, Fellini had begun working with Ernst Bernhard, a Jungian analyst, who recommended that he keep a dream journal and read Jung. Rather than an obsession with fantasies projected onto actresses, Fellini's creativity further emerged with the insights gained about 'anima and animus, the role of archetypes and the collective unconscious' from Jungian psychology (Fellini, n.d.). His surge of creativity is exemplified in the dream he had of 'L' on the beach with the king's release. In these ways, as depicted in his dreams that included images of the ass and the dark depths of the anus, the anima emerged as the new ruling principle as well as a 'new order of the psyche' within Fellini, where he begins to work in concert with her, shifting him towards being more directive in subsequent dreams and his artform (p. 58). The tiny war in the 'L' beach dream, which could be the tension of the opposites of his consciousness and the unconscious contents, transforms into a new consciousness resulting in a more resilient egoic structure. In these ways, Fellini's dream sketches exemplify how creative people live, think and imagine in transgressive ways that are as audacious as a coniunctio in the anus giving birth to a new level of consciousness and creativity.

Satan's mouth and dirty cockroaches

Dream images of the anus and a conjoining in the rectum, especially of a penis in the rectum, evoke a potentially transformative numinosity. This is because the penis, anus and rectum are primordial archetypal symbols (Scott, 1966; Literski, 2021). Biologists have discovered 'that anal openings first appeared around 550 million years ago, around the time of the first worm-like creatures' (Westreich, 2021). Allan (2016) pointed out that the anus has utopian potential. It is not exclusive to one gender, sexual orientation, 'one sex, [or] to one type of body' (p. 27). Furthermore, research has not found an evolutionary preference for the mouth to have primacy over the anus. Some creatures use the same opening to take in food and expel waste. During gestation, some creatures first create the anus and then the mouth. Others create the mouth and then the anus is formed, while still others create the anus and the mouth at the same time. Humans create a primitive mouth; then four weeks later, they form a primitive anus. For some creatures, such as the sea cucumber, 'the anus serves as a second mouth … [and is] rhythmically inflated with seawater via the anus, and [is] considered to have respiratory and excretory functions' (Jaeckle & Strathmann, 2013). Thus, for the sea cucumber, both its mouth *and* its anus breathe. In these various ways, the anus and the rectum have a close relationship in the alimentary canal, some shared functionality and a long-standing history. They have numinous qualities because of their archetypal nature within the collective unconscious.

Despite these incredible facts about the anus and rectum, along with their archetypal qualities, the dominant Western cultural associations to the anus and the buttocks are ones of forbidden contact and filth. Allan (2016) confirmed this association:

> The anus is a key part of the human body, a remarkably complex organ that has significant symbolic potential, not least because of the numerous ways in which we have desperately tried to keep it repressed. It is also the organ that most makes many of us rather uncomfortable because of its alignment with abjection, dirtiness, shame, and, in our homophobic culture, male homosexuality … This observation that the anus is gay – rightly or wrongly – does not quite make sense. After all, it seems to be fair enough to suggest the obvious: we all have one.
>
> (p. 27)

Everyone has an anus, and gay men are not the only ones who enjoy engaging in anal sex, though it is cast as the *sine qua non* of male homosexuality. In their complex relationship with homosexuality, both Freud and Jung (with some exceptions) paired homosexuality and homosexual sex with a lack of mature development. They promoted heterosexism and posited sex with the opposite gender by inserting the penis into the vagina as the ultimate in psychological development. This supremacy of heterosexism was advanced even though, in cultures worldwide, there is historical evidence of persons with many genders and many expressions of sexual orientation.

For centuries, sexual orientation and gender expression have been under siege. One of the many condemnations of the diversity of sexual expression was when the 'European missionaries and colonists, upon encountering indigenous two-spirit persons in North America, imposed the derogatory label of berdache (i.e., sodomite) upon them and engaged in a campaign of extermination' (Williams, 1986; Literski, 2021). In the 1600s, this extermination campaign extended to women accused of being witches and working with the devil as part of their witchcraft. The exterminators insisted that even the devil has an anus called 'Satan's mouth'. In Europe and the United States, those who practised non-Christian religions or herbalism, even successful community members, were accused of being witches and attacked.

A fantastical lie was created called the 'kiss of shame' (*osculum infame*), an illustration of which is in Francesco Maria Guazzo's *Compendium Maleficarum* in 1608 CE (ARAS record 5GT.244; *The Book of Symbols*, 2010, p. 364). The *Kiss of Shame* depicts a woman, who is supposedly a witch, eagerly kissing the devil's anus. This imagery was a weapon to accuse and humiliate women, instil compliance and create revulsion towards those in what might be called, in modern parlance, alternative communities. This imagery is a sad commentary on patriarchal culture.

The cockroach is another archetypal image that is reviled by our culture. The word *cockroach* can also be pondered given its combination of the words 'cock' and 'roach', which reveals another way of becoming aware of phallic symbolism evoked by the unconscious for consideration by a dreamer. Dream cockroaches crawl up the body through the anus and enter the dreamers' rectums. Like associations to the anus, negative scatological associations are often given to cockroaches. Cockroaches are associated with the 'bowels of the earth', the 'criminal element' of nature and the fear of the chthonic aspect of the 'Great Mother's "underside" of witchcraft and destruction' (*The Book of Symbols*, 2010, p. 224). This is despite the World Health Organization (WHO) review in 2008, which concluded that 'definitive evidence that cockroaches are vectors for human disease is still lacking' (Ray, 2018).

Protective spirits and font of magic

In addition to these negative associations with cockroaches, the cockroach can have positive associations such as 'a protective spirit ensuring good fortune, a mentor of heroic adaptation to everything from merely onerous circumstances to nuclear upheaval, an emblem of continuity and an embodiment of the tough, survivalist spirit of those culturally treated like vermin' (*Book of Symbols*, 2010, p. 224). Despite Western culture's disgust, the cockroach is a food source for some people. For instance, Madagascar Hissing Cockroaches 'have a taste and texture like greasy chicken' (Martin, n.d.). Ecologically, the cockroach provides the vital function of producing compost from the leaves and droppings from trees. With these polarities of meaning, the cockroach can be viewed as not only a symbol of regression but also a symbol of creative aspects, good fortune and potentiality. These positive associations should also be considered if a cockroach enters a rectum during a dream.

Neumann (1973) wrote extensively about the positive aspects of the anus, bowels and digestive system – the organs that comprise the alimentary canal. He viewed the anus as representing the unconscious through the chthonic aspect versus the mouth and head as the conscious aspect. The anus, in his view, was as integral a part of the primal relationship as the mouth. Together they form a mother-infant oneness in a person's early life that he called the *alimentary ouroboros*. He proposed that upon the separation of the infant from the mother-infant oneness, a psychological polarization occurred when the child began to stand, creating distance from the anal end of the pole, which results in negativity and filth-filled associations. The separation between the head and the butt redirects the child's focus away from the anal area and its smells. In this way, the problematic negative association with the anus begins.

> Neither the smells nor substances connected with the anal zone are disgusting in any primary sense; this disgust is cultivated, quite consistently to be sure, by the patriarchal world which stresses everything 'upper', spiritual and nonsensuous and rejects everything that is 'lower', bodily and earthy.
>
> (Neumann, 1973, pp. 125–6)

Neumann (1973) asserted that our sense of smell contains vestiges of the chthonic symbolism of the anal pole. Unlike dogs, we may not be greeting each other by sniffing our behinds, but we still use our 'psychic' noses when we want to assess someone in these contemporary times. For instance, the word *distrust* is often interchanged with the phrase 'I smell a rat' (*Thesaurus.Plus*, n.d.). We 'smell' or sense someone. We distrust a person if we 'can't smell them' – or if we can't suss them out. We utilize this psychic knowing to assess whether it is okay to trust or whether we are in danger (Neumann, 1973). Distrust, danger and trust are also closely related to magic through the conjoining of 'smell, air, and spirit' (Neumann, 1973, p. 125). Vestiges of magic transform from child's play to superstitious beliefs and paganistic practices in later life. Jung (1959) stated that 'the ancients did not know of the existence of the psyche, so not being able to call anything psychic, they used the word magic' (p. 71). These connections are closely related to the primal relationship at birth when the anal pole is positively integrated; then they are lost as we age. Notably, Neumann advocated that not just as a child *but also in adult life*, we should keep a connection to the anal aspect and not relegate it only to the act of defecation or the oneness with the mother.

Neumann viewed this lost connection to the 'earthly world' as the source of humanity's oppressive stance towards the feminine and the archetypal energies related to the Great Mother, which has, in turn, split modern humans from vital psychological aspects of ourselves and alienated us from our earthly aspect. He thought that the loss of connection to the feminine that projects a negative stance towards the anal area creates fear about the dynamic of its symbolism. Instead of a cause for fear, he viewed the symbolism of the anal pole as related to wholeness because of its association with the archetypal energies of the feminine and the oneness first known through the mother-child alimentary ouroboros. From this perspective, the anal-rectal dream images and the objects that enter them could be viewed as nudging dreamers towards a more integrated relationship with the feminine, bringing healing and renewal. The dreamers' reactions of shame might be the defeat of the ego when confronted with the numinous qualities of these feminine-oriented images.

Additional positive interpretations of the anal aspects lie in shamanism and mythology, where the bowels of the earth and the human body are associated with transformation and rebirth (Neumann, 1973). This association is especially relevant because the shamanic process is often cited as a model for Jungian analysis and the individuation process. Neumann hailed the alimentary ouroboros as connected to 'the highest levels of spiritual life' and as related to 'creation and transformation' (1973, p. 37). Related to spirituality and transformation are the lives of shamans. In his book *Shamanism*, Eliade (1964) wrote multiple accounts of shamanic initiates undergoing dismemberment and having their bowels removed as essential to a spiritual transformation. An old shaman or spirit helper will commonly place a crystal or an animal part, such as a snake's head, inside the initiate's body during the initiation process, which parallels the cockroaches entering the rectums of dreamers. The shamanic initiate is given healing skills from these animal parts and then is 'reborn', complete with a 'renewal of the organs', including new bowels (Eliade, 1964, pp. 47–5; 108). For the Ngadju Dyak people of Borneo, the shamans (basir) serve as intermediaries between the earth and the sky because they 'combine in their own person the feminine element (earth) and the masculine element (sky)' (p. 352). A coniunctio in the rectum, including the penetration by a cockroach, might enliven dormant and ancient archetypal spiritual qualities to assist dreamers in their individuation process. The shamanic initiation and Neumann's theories provide opportunities to connect positive healthy meanings, not only regressive unhealthy meanings, to the phenomenological emergence of anal and rectal images in dreams.

Even earlier than Neumann's association of the nose, magic and the earth with the anus and rectum is the face of a Babylonian mythological being from the 2nd century BCE (or earlier) called Humbaba (also known as Huwawa). Humbaba's face is a 'continuous line of entrails' (ARAS). It would not be too far of a stretch to conclude that embedded in Humbaba's face is an anus, or possibly that his face is an anus. The mask of Humbaba was used to divine the omens when the entrails of sacrificed animals were examined. It was considered prescient when the animal's intestines were wound in their body in a way that mirrored Humbaba's face. A relationship between divination and intestines parallels Neumann's writings about magic and the nether region. Other associations to Neumann's theories lie in the 'Epic of Gilgamesh', where Humbaba is assigned to guard the cedar forest. In this tale, this intestinal being is connected with Nature, reinforcing Neumann's point about the anal pole's association with the chthonic underworld, the feminine and the Great Mother.

Thus in the first phase of the primal relationship the anal pole is positively integrated, but later on it becomes the object of a moral devaluation and exclusion stemming from the symbolic hostility of the sky-heaven world to the earthly world.

(Neumann, 1973, p. 126)

Understood from this perspective, a dream about a union in the rectum might be trying to evoke the archetypal energies of the intestinal region and the possibility that good fortune lies ahead or a greater connection with Nature and the feminine needs to occur. This amplification of the symbol of the nether region is quite an alternative to the symbolism of the image of Satan's mouth.

What might be lost

Humbaba, shamans, cockroaches as protective spirits and the nose that senses the anal pole and intuits magic – these examples are positive, powerful symbols that can amplify the dream images of the anus. They reveal how dream images of a union in the rectum can bring a prospective dynamism by moving an individual towards wholeness. To provide these images and their individuation-inducing power with psychological significance, Jung's admonition must be kept in mind that the coniunctio is representative of the psyche's message about the dreamer's present situation *and the potential* of *something more emerging*. A coniunctio should not be collapsed into *only* an interpretation of reductive psychosocial stages. Too often it is – or it is intimated that it is, merely a minor *coniunctio* rather than a powerful, alchemically numinous union in the *rectal temenos*.

Collapsing into one-sidedness is partially due to the tendency to conflate. Like Jung, who often conflated 'gender into bodily sex' (Rowland, 2002, p. 45), there is a similar tendency to conflate dream images and behaviours related to the anus or a union in the rectum to anal personalities that are not fully developed or to stereotypes about homosexuality. This conflation can also occur when an association to the alchemical turning 'shit into gold' (alluding to the alchemical process of turning base metals into gold) is made. Turning 'shit into gold' is a dynamic movement of something created *after* a coniunctio has occurred – but first the analytic focus should be on making a full range of associations to the symbolism of the union. A tamale cooked in the rectum might represent necessary nutritive and generative energy to empower the individual and the power of cultural connection. For instance, tamales are made of corn (maize), which has significant symbolic and cultural meaning related to the Aztec goddess Chicomecóatl.

> Chicomecóatl, (Nahuatl: 'Seven Snakes') also called Xilonen ('Young Maize-Ear Doll', Aztec goddess of sustenance and, hence, of corn (maize), [is] one of the most ancient and important goddesses in the Valley of Mexico. The number seven in her name is associated with luck

and generative power. She was often portrayed as the consort of the corn god, Centéotl. Chicomecóatl is depicted in Aztec documents with her body and face painted red, wearing a distinctive rectangular head-dress or pleated fan of red paper. She is similarly represented in sculpture, often holding a double ear of corn in each hand.

(Editors of the *Encyclopaedia Britannica, 2020*)

A coniunctio of a tamale in the rectum associated with the feminine aspects of the goddess Chicomecóatl might bring fertile generative energies to a conscious attitude that is fatigued or stagnated. This association contrasts to the interpretation of the alchemical turning of shit into gold, or Freud's anal theories, which have become the predominant analytical views whenever the nether region appears in images or therapeutic content. Interpreting in *only* these latter ways of reduction and stereotypes causes the 'something more' that Jung insisted is vital to health and wholeness to be lost. What a waste!

Since it is easy to fall into reductive approaches or stereotypes in relation to dream material when the content includes images of the anal region of the body, we might instead reflect on our biases. Some questions listed in an ARAS entry are helpful to support the deepening approach that Jung advocated when working with anal-rectum images. This entry describes the 'kiss of shame' and then asks several questions to help bring consciousness to personal attitudes and prejudices:

How do I ... secretly despise in the night of my unconsciousness the goatlike [devil as the goat] process of nature? How do I find it difficult to 'kiss' my earthy 'backside'? Am I willing to embrace the difficult modern problem of the terrible 'backside' of God? Am I willing to risk the accusation of having imparted the 'kiss of shame'?

(ARAS record 5GT.244)

As Neumann proposed, the nether region is not an area to outgrow and leave behind. This transgressive body area is filled with archetypal symbolism and essential instinctual knowledge. Jungians welcome the transgressive because it can lead to wholeness. The union of the vertical pole with the anal pole *remains the foundation of our existence even after our consciousness [has] grown independent [of the mother]* (Neuman, 1977, p. 33; italics added). In other words, images of the anus are not just about regressive childhood issues or homosexuality. Homosexuality, which the American Psychiatric Association in 1973 adopted as a valid, healthy form of sexual and relationship expression, must be decoupled from concepts of immature or incomplete development that make it too easy to engage in (unconscious) heterosexist interpretations and viewpoints.

Contemplating these questions from the ARAS entry about the dream images of the anus and a coniunctio in the rectum will help access the dialectical nature of the images and foster the tension that can lead to greater consciousness, creativity and transformation. Acknowledging the presence of the other – the polar opposite of the ego's attitude – that has shown itself through symbolic images to join with the conscious attitude will help set the stage for the constellation of the transcendent function and the union that is engendered.

Employing Jung's recommendation to hold the tension of the opposites to create the coniunctio induces the emergence of that 'something more' that brings new levels of consciousness while resolving neuroses and trauma. His focus on the wholeness of the psyche furthers individuation instead of lapsing into stereotypes or only resorting to reductive theory, which induces shame, humiliation and even death from the dominant paradigm of fear and loathing related to the anus and rectum. Like other forms of uninvited control of the human body by others, negative attitudes about the anus and punishments related to it are, in fact, anti-feminine, anti-receptive and anti-coniunctio. Refashioning our thinking about the nether region to include its role in coniunctio experiences that lead to psychic wholeness will increase the psychological power of this symbolism.

References

Allan, J. (2016). *Reading from behind: A cultural analysis of the anus.* University of Regina Press.

The Editors of Encyclopaedia Britannica. (2020, April 2). Chicomecóatl. *Encyclopaedia Britannica.* https://www.britannica.com/topic/Chicomecoatl

Eliade, M. (1964). *Shamanism: Archaic rites of ecstasy.* Princeton University Press.

Fellini, F. (2020). *The book of dreams.* (S. Toffetti, ed.). (A. Maines, Trans.). Rizzoli.

Fellini, F. (n.d.). *Wikipedia.* Retrieved 20 June 2022, from https://en.wikipedia.org/wiki/Federico_Fellini

Fonagy, P. (2000). The outcome of psychoanalysis: The hope of a future. *The Psychologist. 13*(12), 620–23.

Frey-Rohn, L. (1974). *From Freud to Jung: A comparative study of the psychology of the unconscious.* (F.E. Engreen & E.K. Engreen, Trans.). C.P. Putnam's Sons.

Jaeckle, W.B., & Strathmann, R. (2013). The anus as a second mouth: anal suspension feeding by an oral deposit-feeding sea cucumber. *Invertebrate Biology, 132,* 62–68. https://doi.org/10.1111/ivb.12009

Jung, C.G. (1959). ETH Lecture XI. In Jung, C.G., Welsh, E. & Hannah, B. (Eds.). *Modern psychology: October 1938–March 1940: The process of individuation: 3. Eastern texts. 4. Exercitia spiritualia of Saint Ignatius of Loyola.* K. Schippert & Company.

Jung, C.G. (1966). On the psychology of the unconscious. In H. Read, M. Fordham, G. Adler & W. McGuire (Eds.), *The collected works of C.G. Jung: Vol. 7. Two essays on analytical psychology.* (R. F. C. Hull, trans.). Princeton University Press. (Original work published 1917)

Jung, C.G. (1971). *The collected works of C.G. Jung: Vol. 6. Psychological types.* (H. Read, M. Fordham, G. Adler & W. McGuire, Eds.) (R. F. C. Hull, trans.). Princeton University Press. (Original work published 1921)

Literski, N.S. (2021). Defacing Dionysus: The fabrication of an anti-transgender myth. *Psychological Perspectives, 64*, 360–68. https://doi.org/10.1080/00332925.2021.1996137

Martin, D. (n.d.). List of edible insects. *Girl meets bug: Edible insects: The Ecological alternative.* https://edibug.wordpress.com/list-of-edible-insects/

Neumann, E. (1973). *The child.* (R. Manheim, Trans.). Shambhala.

Ray, C. (2018, 8 August). Do cockroaches carry diseases? *New York Times.* https://www.nytimes.com/2018/08/03/science/cockroach-diseases.html

Rowland, S. (2002). *Jung: A feminist revision.* Polity Press.

Samuels, A. (1985). *Jung and the post-Jungians.* Routledge.

Sanidopoulos, J. (2017, 25, May). The conception of Christ through the ear of the Virgin Mary. *Orthodox Christianity Then and Now.* https://www.johnsanidopoulos.com/2017/03/the-conception-of-christ-through-ear-of.html

Scott, G.R. (1966). *Phallic worship: A history of sex and sex rites in relation to the religions of all races from antiquity to the present day.* Luxor Press.

The Archive for Research in Archetypal Symbolism. ARAS record 5GT.244.

The Archive for Research in Archetypal Symbolism. (2010). *The book of symbols: Reflections on archetypal images.* Taschen.

Thesaurus.Plus (n.d.). Distrust/Smell a rat. In *Thesaurus.Plus.* Retrieved 29 March 2022, from https://thesaurus.plus/related/distrust/smell_a_rat

Westreich, L. (2021, 8 September). Which came first, the butt or the mouth? New research gives an answer. *Massive.* https://massivesci.com/articles/blastopore-anus-butt-month-mouth-evolution/9/8/2021

Williams, W.L. (1986). *The spirit and the flesh: Sexual diversity in American Indian culture.* Beacon Press.

Wojtkowski, S. (2017, 18 December). Fellini and the giantess: Individuation of the monster. *ARAS Connections,* Issue 4. http://aras.org/articles/federico-fellini-and-giantess-individuation-monster

Chapter 4

My kinky shadow

The poetics of the sadomasochistic Other

Douglas Thomas

According to the Oxford English Dictionary, the term *BDSM* appeared in the early 1990s as an abbreviation for bondage and discipline, domination and submission and sadism-masochism. It has since become a catch-all phrase to describe a wide range of behaviours, activities and relationships that involve some combination of sexuality, eroticism and role-playing, often including a consensual unequal power dynamic, more accurately referred to as an *authority exchange* (C. Shahbaz, personal communication, 15 June 2017). The other popular slang term for a wide range of unconventional sexual interests is *kink*, or *kinky* in its original adjectival form. Cultural references to these practices abound with iconic images of handcuffs, ropes, riding crops and leather accoutrements (Barker et al., 2007). Such activities and relationships appear across all sexual and affectional orientations, all gender identities and a broad range of social, racial and ethnic groups (Shahbaz & Chirinos, 2017).

Roughly a century before the term BDSM entered the vernacular, Richard von Krafft-Ebing (2011) published *Psychopathia Sexualis* in 1886 as a forensic reference book. Widely regarded as a landmark in psychiatric writing, its author popularized the terms *sadism* and *masochism* based on the historical lives and fictional writings of the Marquis de Sade and Leopold von Sacher-Masoch. Widely regarded as a landmark text, the author's inclusion of sadomasochism and other sexual practices that currently fall under the BDSM rubric established them as sexual pathologies, a view perpetuated by Freud (2000), who dubbed sadomasochism 'the most common and the most significant of all the perversions' (p. 23). This view went largely unchallenged by mental health practitioners and theorists until recently (Barker et al., 2007).

Despite the historical tendency of the mental health field to marginalize BDSM and kink as perverted and deviant, there appears to be a growing interest and enthusiasm for this form of psycho-sexual exploration among the collective. The runaway success of E.L. James's *Fifty Shades of Grey* trilogy is one striking example, having sold 125 million copies worldwide, and the movie based on the first book having grossed more than 500

DOI: 10.4324/9781003223481-6

million dollars (Stedman, 2015). At the same time, members of the BDSM community have sharply criticized the franchise as misrepresenting the modern fully consensual version of these relationships (Marcus, 2015). The question remains how many people practice BDSM or take an interest in some aspect of it. In 1993, *The Janus Report on Sexual Behavior* estimated that up to 14 per cent of men and 11 per cent of women in the United States engaged in some form of BDSM behaviour. More recently, Christian Joyal and Julie Carpentier's (2016) rigorous study with 1,040 subjects selected from the general population in Canada found that 45.6 per cent of their sample expressed interest in at least one paraphilic behaviour as defined by the DSM-5 and 33.9 per cent had engaged in such behaviours at least once. The authors persuasively question why sexual behaviours that are statistically neither atypical nor unusual should still be labelled anomalous and paraphilic.

During this same period in which research has found an increase in public acceptance and curiosity towards BDSM and kink, the American Psychiatric Association (APA) has also softened its diagnostic stance. The DSM-5 (2013) now makes a clear distinction between paraphilias and the paraphilic disorders. The manual states, 'A paraphilia by itself does not necessarily justify or require clinical intervention' (APA, 2013, p. 686). It goes on to say, 'The majority of individuals who are active in community networks that practice sadistic and masochistic behaviors do not express any dissatisfaction with their sexual interests, and their behavior would not meet DSM-5 criteria for sexual sadism disorder' (p. 697). Caroline Shahbaz and Peter Chirinos (2017) have reviewed over 20 years of research that supports this update by the APA: 'BDSM practitioners generally tend to have a higher level of self-esteem; are healthier than the average person; have better than average communication skills, imagination, and self-awareness; and are capable of undergoing insightful reflection during psychotherapy' (Shahbaz & Chirinos, 2017, p. 25). Despite this research data and the important move towards a more open and affirming attitude by the mental health field, reports of stigma, therapeutic bias and inadequate care remain a common complaint by practitioners of BDSM when they seek therapeutic services (Kolmes et al., 2006; Barker et al., 2007; Lawrence & Love-Crowell, 2008; Shahbaz & Chirinos, 2017).

This disparity between changing social attitudes towards BDSM and an undereducated therapeutic community does not improve when one considers the field of analytical psychology. An online search of journal and research articles on the EBSCO research database yields 1,771 matches for the topic of BDSM, yet there are no matches when the words 'Jung', 'Jungian' or 'analytical psychology' are added to the query. Apart from important contributions a generation ago from Lyn Cowan (1982) and Thomas Moore (1990) on masochism and sadism, respectively, Pamela Power's (2014) insightful essay is one of the few recent examples of Jungians contributing to the psychological discussion of BDSM, even though the extravagant sexual imagination of this area of human experience seems like a natural topic of enquiry for Jungian thought.

More than the attitudinal shift in the collective or the evidence calling for greater awareness and sensitivity among therapists, what arouses curiosity from a Jungian perspective is the pronounced tendency to pathologize, marginalize and ignore the kinks that come into the consulting room with patients. This tendency appears to be part of a larger pattern noted by Edward Santana (2017), in which Jungian practitioners avoid issues of sex and sexuality as clinical issues, despite Jung having made significant contributions to understanding human sexuality from a depth perspective, as James Hillman posited back in 1960:

> The step that Jung took has still to be taken by many even now. Jung saw that instinct has an imaginal aspect, a mythic factor, and that therefore the sexual is also an activity of the imagination, a psychological expression; the sexual is a way the soul speaks.
>
> (p. 141)

The tendency of Jungians to neglect the logos of the soul in patients' sexual lives becomes more ironic when BDSM is part of the erotic landscape. If a patient were to share a dream involving imprisonment in a dungeon or tying a beautiful youth to a tree, a Jungian analyst would likely greet these images with enthusiasm, noticing the dynamic archetypal themes on display. Are the mythopoetic elements of these images any less vital when they appear as part of a couple's consensual sex play?

Consider this passage from Guy Baldwin's book *SlaveCraft* (2004), which describes the intimate bond that develops between a modern-day BDSM slave and his Master, who share an extreme authority exchange:

> The more He [the Master] demands from me, the deeper down into the Sea of Surrender i drift. If He should push the limits of my current capabilities, my descent stops at that point, and i remain suspended at that depth. But if He continues to push me, i take that as a sign that He wants me to go deeper and i use my internal slave tools to dissolve my resistance and continue my descent. If He continues, before long, i shall find myself slowly settling to the very bottom of the Sea of Surrender, a place i have come to call the Great Deep.
>
> ... my internal experience at such times is one of a limitless, resonant joy enveloping me, sometimes quietly, other times vibrantly. All words, all thoughts, are swept away, and i am so very peaceful inside. And, in the distance, i can sometimes hear the deep, low-pitched, undulating sounds of what a slave buddy of mine calls, The Roaring Void.
>
> (pp. 63–4; reprinted with permission from the author)

This account resembles what Jungian thinkers refer to as a numinous experience and an encounter with the archetype of the Self. Lionel Corbett's description of the numinous and its psychological value is surprisingly compatible with the preceding description of deep submission:

> We feel stunned, astonished, and filled with wonder because we have been addressed by something uncanny, not of our ordinary world, something very difficult to put into words. We may be cowed by the experience because its sheer force overpowers us, making us feel very small. Or we may feel entranced, captivated, and transported. Contact with the numinosum ... may also produce a profound sense of union or oneness with the world and with other people.
>
> (2007, pp. 12–3)

Both of these descriptions are consistent with reports from other practitioners of BDSM, some who have described transcendent transformative experiences through their sessions (Mains, 1984; Beckmann, 2008; Sagarin et al., 2009). Jungian psychology could support such experiences as part of a person's individuation process, recognizing, as Henri Ellenberger (1970) does, that numinous feelings signal the presence of deeper transformative archetypal energies (p. 706). What is it then that prevents Jungians from understanding the practice of BDSM and kink within the framework of Jung's model?

The spectre of the Other and Jung's formulation of the syzygy offer a possible answer to this question. In multiple aspects BDSM involves an encounter with the archetypal Other. Shahbaz and Chirinos (2017) discuss the dark counter-cultural aspects of BDSM as congruent with Jung's conceptualization of the shadow. On the interpersonal level, many of the negotiated relationships in BDSM exaggerate the sense of otherness between the partners through the extreme imbalance of authority and control. As an individual reaches deep within the personal psyche to embody that which is archetypally dominant or submissive, they encounter the Other, the complementary polarity, embodied in the partner. It is, in fact, a conscious consensual engagement with otherness that characterizes BDSM activities, making the phenomenology of differentness explicit, overt and valued.

One example of this intensification of intent and consent around the conscious enactment of otherness is the development of a contract between people entering into a long-term or continuous BDSM relationship, such as Dom/me and sub, which both people sign (Shahbaz & Chirinos, 2017). Such contracts typically stipulate how partners will handle specific protocols, communication, conflict resolution, decision-making and limitations and boundaries of the relationship. Part of what distinguishes the modern movement is the importance of open communication and dialogue, safety precautions and the essential respect accorded to each practitioner. This is apparent in the use of terms such as 'safe, sane, and consensual' (Stein,

2000), or 'risk aware consensual kink' (Switch, 2017), which commonly appear in introductory literature about BDSM. The attention given to creating a dynamic of trust, candour and open communication between partners illustrates how the Other is consciously acknowledged and valued.

In contrast to the phenomenology of conscious otherness that characterizes BDSM, the shadow aspect of the Other also appears in the consulting room when clinicians experience discomfort in the presence of a kinky patient. The natural tendency is to resolve such feelings of discomfort by distancing oneself from that which is Other and casting a pathologizing eye on the patient's activities. Shahbaz and Chirinos (2017) developed the concept of 'othering', originally formulated by Edward Said (1979) in his work with Palestinians, to delineate the social and clinical marginalization of BDSM and kink communities. Von Krafft-Ebing's (2011) legacy can serve as a professional validation of the clinician's dis-ease, which could also be termed *kinkophobia* (Baldwin & Bean, 1993). The power of a diagnostic label can become an apotropaic gesture for clinicians, serving as a barrier against our deeper fascination with our own proclivities for cruelty, ugliness, humiliation and violence. This clinical situation offers a nuanced illustration of Jung's famous declaration: 'The gods have become diseases' (1957/1983, CW 13, para. 54). That which the clinician views as pathological in a patient's presentation may also be where the gods of the archetypal unconscious have been forced into hiding. Cowan (1982) concurs in acknowledging what is at once both counter-cultural and divine in the deep psychology of masochism:

> Masochism carries a radical anti-ego message: there are gods in our sickness who relieve us of the tedious and boring demand for good feeling; there are gods who, in the worst moments of torment and humiliation, remind us that we are, emphatically and constitutionally, *not okay*.
> (p. 31; emphasis in original)

Suddenly two possibilities appear simultaneously: to view kink as sick and twisted and at the same time to see its transcendent possibilities for healing and transformation. Let us imagine kink as a living symbol of the deep psyche.

This potential for the psyche to hold pairs together in dialectic tension lies at the heart of Jung's formulation of the syzygy, that divine marriage, which he originally referenced in regard to anima and animus (Jung, 1978/1951, CW 9ii). Hillman (1985) asserts that the notion of pairing in tandems is more compatible with the polymorphous nature of the psyche than is the classical concept of opposition. In fact, a pair of opposites is only one possible configuration of a tandem:

> To imagine in pairs and couples is to think mythologically. Mythical thinking connects pairs into tandems rather than separating them into

opposites. ... Opposites lend themselves to very few kinds of description: contradictories, contraries, complementaries, negations—formal
and logical. Tandems, however, like brothers or enemies or traders or
lovers show endless varieties of styles. Tandems favor intercourse—
innumerable positions.

(p. 173)

As a concept, the tension of the opposites connotes both an inherent incompatibility and a dynamic antagonism between elements. This is apparent
in Jung's description of the play between conscious and unconscious as a
fight: 'Conscious and unconscious do not make a whole when one of them is
suppressed and injured by the other. If they must contend, let it at least be
a fair fight with equal rights on both sides' (1939/1990, CW 9i, para. 522). In
contrast to the antagonism implicit in the tension of the opposites, a tandem
connotes two figures in perpetual relationship with each other, exploring a
range of contrasting possibilities.

This suggests that the Other as it constellates in BDSM is always operating in relationship with another figure designated as its dialectical coun-
terpart rather than its opposite. In BDSM, there is no Dom/me without a
sub, no Master without a slave; the Other cannot be rejected or expelled
without breaking the syzygy and collapsing the archetypal potential of the
scene. Even if a scene involves more than two people, roles are clearly defined, protocols are established and the authority exchange becomes a col-
laborative construction of a conscious Other (Shahbaz, 2012). For some, this
is the essence of BDSM's psychological value: the consensual exchange of
authority and control occurring within an established container facilitates
the emergence of a syzygy between Dominant and submissive. In such a
configuration, opposition is no longer experienced as a threat or a problem;
an unconscious value split between good and bad does not occur. Rather,
the conscious Other is indispensable to the pursuit of pleasure and growth.

In psychotherapy, a similar situation constellates between the figures of
patient and analyst, as they exist not in opposition so much as in tandem
as a syzygy of archetypal potential, a therapeutic pair. There is no analyst
without an analysand, and the two pass through a range of contrasting relational attitudes in the protracted course of the therapeutic encounter. In
fact, the similarities between BDSM and psychotherapy are more significant
than one might easily admit. Adolf Guggenbühl-Craig (1971) famously de-
lineated the potent and sometimes sinister forces at work in the helping professions. The practice of obtaining the informed consent of the patient prior
to initiating treatment is, in part, to safeguard against the sadomasochistic
potential of the relationship to go awry, just as the consensual contract in
BDSM is a safeguard against the potential for physical abuse and trauma.

The restrictions of a time-limited therapeutic hour, the imposition and humiliation of a fee for the service, which some patients regard as the obligation

to pay for a relationship, the imperatives of self-disclosure and stripping away defences as well as the necessity of enduring probing questions and painful truths about one's own nature, all bear the archetypal imprint of a sadomasochistic syzygy between patient and analyst that thrives as an unconscious dynamic. Hence, without recognizing the influence of an archetype of sadomasochism per se, the profession has recognized the value of analysis as part of analytic training and the imperative of astute supervision and consultation to acknowledge and address the dynamic presence of these shadowy impulses. BDSM and kink acknowledge and affirm the enduring presence of such deep impulses in the human psyche both to inflict and to endure humiliation and suffering in relationship with others. Kink communities have developed ethical practices to contain, explore and integrate the transgressive aspects of our nature, aspects that both Moore (1990) and Cowan (1982) have recognized as necessities of the soul itself. 'We need … to recognize the soul-need in its downward movement, and the passion and need in its extremity. Masochism is a natural product of soul, ready and needing to bring forward its own vision and its own cure' (Cowan, 1982, p. 33). It is this soul-centred approach to understanding the practices of BDSM that affords a unique opportunity for Jungian thinkers to support a greater understanding and appreciation for the unconventional passions of this marginalized community.

The spectre of the Other and the tandem of the syzygy both find expression in the conscious consensual practices of BDSM as well as in the less comfortable hidden aspects of the therapeutic relationship. Analytical psychology offers a powerful repertoire of concepts to understand and affirm the value of these darker necessities of the soul. Jung's strongly held opinion, expressed in *The Psychology of the Transference* (1946/1985, CW 16), was that the therapeutic relationship had to become a real human relationship for psychological transformation to occur. The alchemical symbolism of the *Rosarium Philosophorum*, which depicts the progression of a king and queen passing from the polite conventions of a formal relationship to the naked truth of two beings stripped of social artifice, served as his preferred metaphor for the therapeutic process of developing an authentic human relationship based on the objective reality of the psyche. In the therapeutic encounter, both people are changed, Jung said. When an analyst neglects or turns away from the sadomasochistic aspects of the therapeutic relationship, the encounter with the naked truth of who the two people truly are in their deeper nature is forestalled or shunned. When an analyst interprets the pleasure and meaning a patient finds in the creative consensual exploration of BDSM as a pathological perversion, the Other is unconsciously split from the inner reality of the practitioner and projected on to the patient as a problem in need of a cure. The syzygy of the therapeutic relationship collapses, and the naked truth of who the two people are remains concealed behind the guise of professional correctness. Psychological transformation, as Jung imagined it, is not able to occur under these conditions. What is called for is a recollecting of pathologized projections by the analyst and an engagement with the mythic and archetypal dimensions of the psyche that give sado-masochism and kink a depth of meaning as a sexual logos of the soul. This mythopoetic aspect of our sexuality is what Hillman was referencing when he said, 'The step that Jung took has still to be taken by many even now' (1960, p. 141). Jung's ability to find the gods at work in the instincts of our sexual lives remains an unfulfilled promise of his pioneering work.

The capacity to find the mythopoetic at work in our instinctual lives in-volves the creative function of the psyche and its expression through play in the broader cultural sense of the word. Johan Huizinga (2014) has developed the concept of play as a basis for culture, tying its significance to the devel-opment of metaphor and poetic thought as well as ritual as an expression of the collective mythic imagination. Huizinga's insights into the essential elements of play provide a useful bridge between 'the step that Jung took' (Hillman, 1960, p. 141) and the call for a deeper psychological appreciation of the modern practice of BDSM. It is striking how the author's phenomeno-logical reduction of play illuminates the ludic aspect of BDSM. He describes play in its essential characteristics: it is voluntary and free; it occurs outside of so-called ordinary or real life; its locality and duration are secluded and limited; it creates order ('into an imperfect world and into the confusion of life it brings a temporary, a limited perfection' [Huizinga, 2014, p. 10]); it involves tension; it has rules that are clear and binding; it enjoys an air of secrecy (pp. 8–12).

Each of these characteristics finds prominent expression in the activities of BDSM: the emphasis on consent makes it an activity that is voluntary and free; practitioners observe a clear transition into BDSM activities as a domain set apart from so-called ordinary life; activities occur in designated secluded locations often referred to as 'play spaces', in which 'scenes' are enacted within a temporal boundary; order exists through the designation of specific roles and the performance of tasks associated with each role; tension occurs through the exploration of boundaries and limitations, in-cluding the transgressive nature of that which is counter-cultural; rules are present as part of negotiated exchanges of power and authority, including limits and safe words, expectations and punishment; the subversive pleas-ure in the secretive aspect of having a hidden yet profoundly meaningful dimension to one's life can be part of the appeal of BDSM and kink. Some may argue that the time-limited characteristic of play does not always per-tain to BDSM. The deeply felt enduring sense of identity as a Dominant or submissive can motivate some practitioners to structure their lives around those identities (Shahbaz & Chirinos, 2017). This can lead to the establish-ment of a household that supports what is called a 24–7 living arrangement, in which protocols of dominance and submission are permanently in place. However, even within such situations, time spent within the household is set apart from other aspects of a person's life and the more intense power exchange activities that take place within a dungeon or playroom occur for a time-limited period. It is not overly surprising that Huizinga's characteristics of play find robust expression in BDSM and kink, but what is perhaps less obvious is the mythopoetic or meaning-making aspect of play that is also relevant to these activities.

Huizinga (2014) finds the characteristics of play at work in some of our most earnest and sacred activities, including law and politics, warfare and religious rituals and festivals. Play for Huizinga is something that reaches beyond its popular associations with frivolity and caprice, although play characteristics are undeniably present in our lighter moments of mirth. They are also present in the mythopoetic function of the psyche, that deep impulse to bring order and meaning to the rhythms of nature at work within us and around us through imaginative representation in story and metaphor. Through play we represent our experience of the numinous. I have already noted the correspondence between BDSM activities and numinous experience. Here that correspondence deepens through the function of play in the world of alternative sexualities. It is this ludic aspect of BDSM that introduces the meaning-making function of *poiesis*, the layering of meaning that occurs as a syzygy between the imaginative possibilities of what one is and what one is not. The embodiment of the conscious Other becomes a shadow play.

With BDSM as it has developed over the past quarter century, the psyche appears to have discovered a poetics of sadomasochism, thereby creating a psychological container with the potential for self-discovery, personal growth and transformation via the sexual imagination. Like all forms of *poiesis*, these relationships foster the creation and layering of symbolic meaning. In such an imaginal space, the soul finds value in suffering. Suffering becomes important and necessary, and it is greeted with intentionality and consent. This brings to mind Hillman's (1975) notion of pathologizing as one of the primary innate expressive modes of the soul, in contrast to the historical characterization of sadomasochism as a disease. 'Were we able to discover its psychological necessity, pathologizing would no longer be wrong or right, but merely necessary, involving purposes which we have misperceived and values which must present themselves necessarily in a distorted form' (Hillman, 1975, p. 57). By pathologizing BDSM and kink, the field of psychology turns the numinous pathos of suffering into a pathologized Other, a projection of one's own shadow, that is ostensibly in need of a cure. And this fantasy of cure involves a rejection or sublimation of that which is unwanted and labelled as diseased.

Professional perspectives are evolving as social attitudes toward BDSM and kink change, such that a new paradigm could emerge in which the kinky sadomasochistic Other is no longer an opposite concealed in the analyst's shadow, but rather a mysterious twin in a dialectical syzygy paired with the conscious personality. This presentation of new possibilities merits further attention. *Poiesis* invites play in the broader hermeneutic sense of the word (Palmer, 1969), and the opportunity to play with the potential of the sadistic and masochistic aspects of our own nature honours a fuller and more deeply engaged relationship with the Other in ourselves and in the world.

References

American Psychiatric Association. (2013). *Diagnostic and statistical manual of mental disorders* (5th ed.). Author.

Baldwin, G. (2004). *SlaveCraft: Roadmaps for erotic servitude*. Daedalus.

Baldwin, G., & Bean, J.W. (1993). *Ties that bind: The SM/leather/fetish/erotic style: Issues, commentaries and advice*. Daedalus.

Barker, M., Iantaffi, A., & Gupta, C. (2007). Kinky clients, kinky counselling? The challenges and potentials of BDSM. In L. Moon (Ed.), *Feeling queer or queer feelings: Radical approaches to counselling sex, sexualities and genders* (pp. 106–24). Routledge.

BDSM *n*. (2013, June). *Oxford English Dictionary Online* (draft ed.). Oxford University Press. Retrieved from https://www.oed.com/view/Entry/14168#eid289098363

Beckmann, A. (2008). The 'bodily' practices of consensual 'SM', spirituality and 'transcendence'. In D. Langdridge & M. Barker (Eds.), *Safe, sane, and consensual: Contemporary perspectives on sadomasochism* (pp. 98–118). Palgrave MacMillan.

Corbett, L. (2007). *Psyche and the sacred*. Spring Journal Books.

Cowan, L. (1982). *Masochism: A Jungian view*. Spring Publications.

Ellenberger, H. (1970). *The discovery of the unconscious*. Basic Books.

Freud, S. (2000). *Three essays on the theory of sexuality*. Basic Books.

Guggenbühl-Craig, A. (1971). *Power in the helping professions*. Spring Publications.

Hillman, J. (1960). *The myth of analysis: Three essays in archetypal psychology*. Northwestern University Press.

Hillman, J. (1975). *Re-visioning psychology*. HarperCollins.

Hillman, J. (1985). *Anima: An anatomy of a personified notion*. Spring Publications.

Huizinga, J. (2014). *Homo ludens: A study of the play-element in culture*. Martino Fine Books.

Janus, S.S., & Janus, C.L. (1993). *The Janus report on sexual behavior*. John Wiley & Sons.

Joyal, C.C., & Carpentier, J. (2016). The prevalence of paraphilic interests and behaviors in the general population: A provincial survey. *The Journal of Sex Research, 54*(2), 161–71. doi: 10.1080/00224499.2016.1139034

Jung, C.G. (1978). *The collected works of C.G. Jung: Vol. 9ii. Aion*. (R.F.C. Hull, Trans.). (H. Read, M. Fordham, & G. Adler, Eds.). Princeton University. (Original work published 1951)

Jung, C.G. (1983). Commentary on 'The Secret of the Golden Flower'. In H. Read, M. Fordham, & G. Adler (Eds.), *The collected works of C.G. Jung: Vol. 13. Alchemical studies* (pp. 1–56). (R.F.C. Hull, Trans.). Princeton University. (Original work published in 1938)

Jung, C.G. (1985). The psychology of the transference. In H. Read, M. Fordham, & G. Adler (Eds.), *The collected works of C.G. Jung: Vol. 16. The practice of psychotherapy* (pp. 163–326). (R.F.C. Hull, Trans.). Princeton University. (Original work published in 1946)

Jung, C.G. (1990). Conscious, unconscious and individuation. In H. Read, M. Fordham, & G. Adler (Eds.), *The collected works of C.G. Jung: Vol. 9i. The archetypes and the collective unconscious* (pp. 275–89). (R.F.C. Hull, Trans.). Princeton University. (Original work published in 1939)

Kolmes, K., Stock, W., & Moser, C. (2006). Investigating bias in psychotherapy with BDSM clients. In P. Kleinplatz, & C. Moser (Eds.), *Sadomasochism: Powerful pleasures* (pp. 301–24). Haworth Press.

Lawrence, A.A., & Love-Crowell, J. (2008). Psychotherapists' experience with clients who engage in consensual sadomasochism: A qualitative study. *Journal of Sex & Marital Therapy, 34*(1), 67–85. https://doi.org/10.1080/00926230701620936

Mains, G. (1984). *Urban aboriginals*. Daedalus.

Marcus, S. (2015, February 16). 'Fifty Shades of Grey' isn't a movie about BDSM, and that's a problem. *Huffington Post*. Retrieved from http://www.huffingtonpost.com

Moore, T. (1990). *Dark Eros: The imagination of sadism*. Spring Publications.

Palmer, R.E. (1969). *Hermeneutics*. Northwestern University Press.

Power, P. (2014). Negative coniunctio: Envy and sadomasochism in analysis. In M. Winborn (Ed.), *Shared realities: Participation mystique and beyond* (pp. 33–50). Fisher King Press.

Sagarin, B.J., Cutler, B., Cutler, N., Lawler-Sagarin, K.A., & Matuszewich, L. (2009). Hormonal changes and couple bonding in consensual sadomasochistic activity. *Archives of Sexual Behavior, 38,* 186–200.

Said, E.W. (1979). *Orientalism*. Vintage Books.

Santana, E. (2017). *Jung and sex: Revisioning the treatment of sexual issues*. Routledge.

Shahbaz, C. (2012). Kinkophobia. Harmful psychiatric diagnosis: A call to action. *Paper given at Psychologists for Social Responsibility conference*, Washington, DC.

Shahbaz, C., & Chirinos, P. (2017). *Becoming a kink aware therapist*. Routledge.

Stedman, A. (2015, June 10). 'Fifty Shades' spinoff 'Grey' copy reportedly stolen from publisher. *Variety*. Retrieved from http://variety.com

Stein, D. (2000). Safe, sane, consensual. *Leather Leadership Conference Library*. Retrieved from http://www.leatherleadership.org/library/safesanestein.htm

Switch, G. (2017). Origin of RACK: RACK vs. SSC. Ambrosio's BDSM Site. https://www.evilmonk.org/a/rack.cfm

Von Krafft-Ebing, R. (2011). *Psychopathia sexualis*. Arcade Publishing.

Chapter 5

The white lion as symbol of the archetype of the Self and the cannibalisation of the Self in canned hunting

Denise Grobbelaar

> *Have we forgotten*
> *that wilderness is not a place,*
> *but a pattern of soul*
> *where every tree, every bird and beast*
> *is a soul maker?*

Ian McCallum, 'Wilderness'

I was standing naked outside a stadium. I was completely invisible to the leaving concertgoers. Out of nowhere a white lioness walked up and embraced me, standing on her hind legs. She gazed directly into my eyes with immense love and acceptance. I have never felt such deep belonging. She nudged me onto her back. I wrapped my arms around her as I lay down, and she touched my arm with her paw to reassure me.

I believe this was what C.G. Jung would have referred to as a 'big dream'. In retrospect, I recognise that this was a numinous encounter with this magnificent creature in dreamtime. It left me awestruck and inspired. This personal dream from July 2013, long before I even knew of the existence of white lions (Figure 5.1), provided the seed for this paper.

Ecological perspective and human's alienation from nature

Humans are destroying the beauty of nature and decimating its majestic animals, such as the white lions, for unconscious and egotistical reasons. A lack of reverence for the natural world as well as the absence of a meaningful connection to nature is at the root of the devastation all around us. I propose that the lion, and the white lion, in particular, is a symbol of the Jungian concept of the Self. Furthermore, our interconnectedness with nature is an integral part of the archetype of the Self.

C.G. Jung saw our relationship with nature and all nonhuman Others as essential to the development of consciousness and wholeness (Sabini, 2001). He linked the loss of our mystical identity and the de-spiritualisation of

DOI: 10.4324/9781003223481-7

Figure 5.1 Matsieng (© Global White Lion Protection Trust)

nature with the atrophy of our phylogenetic roots, or survival instincts, which have fallen back into the unconscious psyche. In the 'civilization process, we have increasingly divided our consciousness from the deeper instinctive strata of the human psyche' (Jung, 1964, p. 36). Jung believed the malaise of modern society to be a consequence of an alienation from the two-million-year-old human being in us all, our archaic original nature.

Meredith Sabini (2001) believes we have placed an artificial boundary between ourselves and other life forms, the nonhuman world, thus denying the interconnectedness that was always an important aspect among the so-called primitive people, providing them with a deep sense of belonging.

This estrangement from an emotional participation in nature has resulted in a fatal dissociation from the more instinctual aspects of our psyche. In *Memories, Dreams, Reflections* (1962, pp. 247–53), Jung described a visit to the United States where he met with Native Americans of New Mexico. Through his conversations with Ochwiay Biano, he realised that our poverty lies in our over-reliance on reason and rational consciousness. We are unable to recognise our impoverishment, but Jung understood that Ochwiay Biano's sense of himself as a son of the sun was cosmologically meaningful, giving him a proper 'place in the great process of being' (Sabini, 2001, p. 49).

> Our ancient contact with nature has gone and with it has gone a profound mental energy that this symbolic action supplied. Thunder is no longer the voice of an angry god ... No river contains a spirit ... no snake the embodiment of wisdom, no mountain cave the home of a great demon. No voices now speak to man from stones, plants and animals, nor does he speak to them thinking they can hear. His contact with nature has gone, and with it has gone the profound emotional energy that this symbolic connection supplied.
>
> (Jung & Von Franz, 1964, p. 85)

Since most modern people no longer believe in the old gods of nature, how can we re-establish such a connection? Western society's overvaluing of the development of left-brain rational consciousness – the result of the industrial and cultural revolutions – has led to a devaluing and disconnection from the right-brain's 'irrational' intuitive aspects of the psyche (McGilchrist, 2010). These include aspects such as receptivity, resonance and interconnectedness. A fundamental erroneous assumption of modern humans is that consciousness and intelligence only lie within human beings, not also in animals, plants, microbes and the elements. I agree with Meredith Sabini that the Earth has a soul – that there is an organising intelligence within nature.

Ian McCallum, an inspirational ecologist and Jungian analyst who has a profound love and passion for nature and the wilderness, refers to a brain-environment link in his book *Ecological Intelligence* and sees our environment as a dynamic extension of the psyche. In agreement with philosophers Pierre Teilhard de Chardin and Karl Popper, he feels the human psyche exists not only within, but also 'out there' (2005, p. 137). If we were receptive to and aware of this connection, it could engender a deep sense of belonging in our species. He explains that human beings exist within what he calls a 'mindfield' of intelligence, information and influence (not confined to the human sphere) that we could potentially access (p. 85). Similarly, Jung stated, 'Nature is an incomparable guide if you know how to follow her' (1973, p. 283; quoted in Sabini, 2001, p. 136).

During May 2018, I was privileged to walk the Imfolozi Wilderness trail with McCallum. The Imfolozi trail was pioneered by Dr. Ian Player and Magqubu Ntombela, who, having recognised the fundamental necessity for people to connect with the natural world, founded the *Wilderness Leadership School* in 1957. They understood the profoundly transformative power of a journey into the wilderness and sleeping under the stars, that it could be a deep experience of our connection to nature and a journey into ourselves. We hiked through an area abundant with wild animals, following the natural animals' paths while Ian guided us to see nature in all its aspects as a reflection of the archetype of the Self. More specifically, he offered us the opportunity to be in resonance with the surroundings.

I had a numinous experience one night while I stood guard alone, listening to the faint sound of a lion roaring in the distance. My task was to maintain the campfire to keep the wild animals at a distance and be on the lookout for any approaching predators. After patrolling the path leading into our campsite, a path regularly used by animals, the scene that awaited me as I walked back to the fire evoked an archetypal energy. I experienced a felt sense of connection to all the ancestors, stretching back to the beginning of humanity, to all those who had walked a similar path towards that unique scene for millennia before me. From the utter darkness of the shadowy night our small fire appeared with the silhouette of a seemingly ancient tree behind it and above the tree, the glittering Milky Way. This engendered within me a sense of awe and belonging – a sense of being embedded in the world around me. In a moment of expanded consciousness, I understood that I was not alone. We are not alone. We are the memory of those who will come after us, and we are the dream of those who came before us. We are life itself, and nature is our sacred vessel.

According to transpersonal psychotherapists Zana Marovic and Mazvita Machinga (2017), in writing on African cosmology and shamanic tradition, African and other indigenous belief systems see the human psyche as whole and nondualistic, both containing and being embedded in relationships with Others – people, ancestors, descendants, society, animals, nature, the cosmos as well as the spiritual and transpersonal realms. This fundamental interconnectedness between self and Others broadens the idea of what it means to be a human being – in contrast to the Western individualistic view. This holistic view is captured in the South African concept of *Ubuntu,* meaning a person is only a person through Others, giving priority to the interdependence of relationships as an embodiment of our humanity (Bùhrmann, 1984). It is precisely this interconnected relationship with nature that many of us have lost.

Jung's archetype of the Self

Jung's archetype of the Self denotes the regulating centre of the psyche. It is an archetype of wholeness, a transpersonal power that transcends the ego. 'The Self is not only the center, but also the whole circumference which embraces both conscious and unconscious; it is the center of this totality, just as the ego is the center of consciousness' (Jung, 1953/1970, CW 12, para. 44). The archetype of the Self refers to *psychic totality,* namely, the integration of opposites insofar as it holds the tension between opposing forces rather than their merging into undifferentiated form. To integrate the opposites, we must bring into consciousness the darker side of our nature or the previously denied shadow aspects that reside in the unconscious. According to Edward Edinger, the archetype of the Self can be described as follows: 'wholeness, totality, the union of opposites, the central generative point ... the central source of life energy, the fountain of our being ...' (1972, p. 4). Experiences of the Self possess a numinosity, characteristic of religious revelations. Hence, Jung believed there was no essential difference between the Self as an experiential, psychological reality and the traditional concept of a supreme deity. For Jung, the psychological construct of the Self expresses

> an unknowable essence which we cannot grasp as such, since by definition it transcends our powers of comprehension. It might equally be called 'the God within us'. The beginnings of our whole psychic life seem to be inextricably rooted in this point, and all our highest and ultimate purposes seem to be striving toward it.
>
> (1928/1971, CW 7, para. 399)

According to McCallum, the Self is 'the organizing survival force of nature within each individual' (2005, p. 85). I understand McCallum's definition to mean the archetype of the Self within each human being is a manifestation of the interconnected and interdependent universal life energy that flows within and between all living creatures. This idea is sketched in more detail by Marie-Louise von Franz. Von Franz uses the metaphor of a 'nuclear atom', with its miniscule nucleus at the centre, as an analogy of the Self's centrality in our psyche:

> The Self is often symbolized as an animal, representing our instinctive nature and its connectedness with one's surroundings ... This relation of the Self to all surrounding nature and even the cosmos probably comes from the fact that the 'nuclear atom' of our psyche is somehow woven into the whole world, both outer and inner. All the higher manifestations of life are somehow tuned to the surrounding space-time continuum. Animals, for example, have their own special foods, their particular home-building materials, and their definite territories, to all of which their instinctive patterns are exactly tuned and adapted. Time rhythms also play their part: We have only to think of the fact that most grass-eating animals have their young at precisely the time of year when the grass is richest and most abundant.
>
> (Jung & Von Franz, 1964, p. 220)

I propose that the lion, as an 'ordering principle' in the natural order of life on Earth, its association with the sun and its deep rootedness as a motif of both the collective conscious and unconscious make it an appropriate symbol of the Self. I will clarify my proposition that white lions are an even more pertinent symbol of the Self by elaborating on the phenomenon of the white lion itself, the significance of white in colour symbolism and the importance of white animals in spiritual traditions around the world.

The lion as symbol of the archetype of the Self

Throughout the ages lions have held a special place as significant symbols for humans – from the earliest cave paintings to the gods of ancient Egypt and, more recently, as representing both religious and state power. From the dawn of civilisation there has been a special relationship between humans and lions. The earliest recorded depictions of lions date back 40,000 years and are found in Palaeolithic cave paintings and ivory-carved figurines from ancient cultures. The most famous of these is the zoomorphic (animal-shaped) *Löwenmensch* (translated as 'Lion-human'), a lion-headed ivory figurine (see Figure 5.2) from Hohlenstein-Stadel, Germany (40,000 BCE). Other examples are an ivory carving of a lion's head from Vogelherd Cave in the Swabian Jura in Southwestern Germany from the Aurignacian culture (40,000 BCE); cave paintings of lions in the Chauvet Cave in the Ardèche region of Southern France (32,000 BCE) and the cave paintings of Lascaux in Southwestern France (15,000 BCE).

Most of the world's great patriarchal religions have revered the lion and equated their spiritual founders to the lion. In Hinduism, *Narasimha,* the incarnation of Vishnu, is worshiped as 'Lion God' (Guirand, 1968). The Bhagavad Gita describes Krishna as 'a lion among wild creatures'; Christ is referred to as 'The Lion of Judah' and the Buddha is 'The Lion of the Shakyas' (Tucker, 2001). The adage 'Lion's Roar' signifies the echoing of Buddha's teachings to the four corners of the world, thus representing enlightenment (Campbell, 1959).

The Great Goddess is associated with lions or other big cats in many early cultures. The Anatolian goddess Cybele is depicted driving a chariot drawn by lions or shown sitting on a throne flanked by lions. Other examples are the Greek goddess Rhea, who is also depicted sitting on a throne flanked by lions, and the Hindu deity Durga, who is frequently depicted riding a lion or tiger. The lion as depicted on the inner city gate of Babylon was the symbol of the Mesopotamian goddess Ishtar, who later was identified with the Sumerian goddess Inanna. She was also depicted standing on the back of two lions. Freya from Germanic lore rides a chariot pulled by two cats.

Many ancient cultures considered the lion to be an embodiment of the God image in its association as a sacred solar animal symbol (Cirlot, 1962). For example, the Egyptian goddess Sekhmet, who is represented as a woman

Figure 5.2 The Löwenmensch figurine after restoration in 2013 (By Dagmar Hollmann – Own work, CC BY-SA 3.0)

with the head of a lioness, is often depicted with the sun disk on her head, as was the Sun God, Ra (Graves, 1968). The lion-sun motif has also been a powerful mythological symbol in Iran since Mesopotamian times – and was depicted in the state flag until 1980 (Farrokh, 2009).

The most famous and mysterious lion relic is the Great Sphinx, a remnant of ancient Egypt. The sphinx form was an important ancient Egyptian symbol, associated with the lion-headed solar goddess, Sekhmet

(Figure 5.3), one of the oldest and most powerful deities in ancient Egypt (Guirand, 1968). She was the goddess of war and destruction, but she was also the goddess of healing. This is an example of how the opposites are contained in a specific archetypal image – Sekhmet was a symbol of both destruction and renewal, ultimately in the service of restoring rightful order (Tucker, 2001).

Within mythologies and cultural narratives around the world, lions are often portrayed as guardians and protectors of good. Numerous ancient cities and temples contain an abundance of lion sculptures, often as gate guardians, such as the Lion Gate of Ancient Mycenae in modern-day Greece; the Lion of Babylon from the Mesopotamian culture, which is now modern-day Iraq; and the city gates from the Hittite empire, now modern-day Turkey (Sutherland, 2017). In China, in the Forbidden City in Beijing, two lion statues guard almost every doorway as the Chinese believed that lions protected humans from evil spirits (Chen, 2018). Snow lions, featured on the Tibetan flag, are mythical creatures important in the Tibetan culture, as they are regarded as protector entities in Buddhism (Beer, 2003).

Similarly, in African mythology, the protective role of lions is depicted in this myth told by Credo Mutwa, a well-known South African shaman:

> The Earth Mother asked the Exiled Lion, Imbudebingile, to send down great carnivores to the earth – lions, leopards and wild cats – to protect human kind from negative entities. Man was too scared to live with the lions, so he chose the wild cats to tame and live with him in his houses.
>
> (Tucker, 2001, p. 212)

The word for *lion* used by the first indigenous people of South Africa, the San, is *Tsau* (Tucker, 2001). *Tsau* not only refers to the physical form of a lion, but also embodies the essence of a lion, the archetypal energy or spirit of the lion. According to Mutwa, *Tsau* translates as 'Star Beast' (p. 209). He believes *Tsau* to be a sacred word and, according to the 'Great Knowledge' of the *sanusis* (the highest order of indigenous South African shamans), invoking it is seen as calling on an elemental force.

According to Linda Tucker, founder and CEO of the Global White Lion Protection Trust, whose work has delivered LionHearted Leadership to humanity, as apex predators lions are viewed as true guardians of land and ecological balance. Like the Self in the human psyche, they could be equated to an ordering principle in nature. The theory of tropic cascades argues that *apex* or *alpha predators* (animals at the top of the food chain), such as lions, are critical to healthy ecosystems and to the maintenance of biodiversity (Lindeman, 1942). Ecosystems are believed, in part, to be ruled from the top of the food chain – the highest trophic level – as the presence of a predator affects the behaviour of prey, who seek safer pastures when a predator is present. This, in turn, affects plant life as plants' growth patterns are directly affected by the grazing behaviour of herbivores. Even the flow of rivers may be affected, which was clearly demonstrated by the reintroduction of wolves into Yellowstone National Park in the United States (Fraser, 2011). Over-population of deer and elk, due to the lack of natural predators, had led to over-grazing and defoliation, which caused erosion, reshaping the landscape. Once the wolves were reintroduced, the herbivores avoided areas where they could be easily hunted and the vegetation in these areas regenerated. The thriving plant life stabilised riverbanks and stemmed erosion, which changed the course of streams and rivers.

Symbolically speaking, an apex predator such as the lion can be seen as having metaphorically ingested and metabolised all of creation, including the sun. Alchemy aptly mirrors this metaphor in its image of the green lion. In the natural food chain, apex predators consume herbivores – their natural prey. In so doing they indirectly consume the herbivores' food source, namely, plants, which absorb sunlight via the process of photosynthesis. As the centre of our solar system, the sun is the source of all life. 'At the mythic level the sun and lion are interchangeable symbols' (Tucker, 2001, p. 257).

White lions and African mythology

The first reported sighting of a white lion by a European dates back to 1938, but it was only in 1975 that Chris McBride (1977), an animal biologist, officially verified their existence through photographic evidence in his book *The White Lions of the Timbavati*. White lions, like other sacred white animals around the world, are not albino animals. The white lion is a colour variant of the tawny African lion, with their colour being the result of a recessive gene, a rare phenotype, called *leucism* (Tucker, 2001).

White lion mythology has been part of oral African tradition for centuries. White lions have great spiritual significance for the indigenous people of the Timbavati, which is in the northeast region of South Africa adjacent to Kruger National Park and is the only place in the world where white lions naturally live. Timbavati was identified as a sacred site by the earlier African kings, and the name in *Shangaan,* the language of the local people, means 'the river of stars' as well as 'the place the star lions came down from the heavens' (Tucker, 2001). In the local legend of the Shangaan people, a special white lion cub was born when a shining star fell to Earth during the reign of Queen Numbi, the Rain Queen, over 400 years ago (Tucker, 2001, pp. 120–3). The Shangaan people believe the white lions to be star beings that came down from the heavens to herald a new era for humanity and the Earth.

An important aspect of white lion mythology is the belief held by African lion shamans that white lions were the first animals to be created and that they will be the last to roar at the end of time (Tucker, 2001). The lands of Timbavati lie on the *Nile meridian,* the longitudinal meridian 31 degrees east of the Greenwich meridian. It is also referred to as *Zep Tepi*, translated as 'the beginning of time' (Tucker, 2001, pp. 231–4). According to the 'Great Knowledge' accessed by Sangomas, or African shamans, there is a direct association between this longitudinal meridian and the emergence of life on the planet. If one follows the Nile meridian north, it runs straight through the ruins of Great Zimbabwe, the massive megalithic site associated with lion lore, and then leads directly to the Great Sphinx of Ancient Egypt. Is this only coincidence or could it be greatly significant in terms of the spiritual value and meaning of white lions?

African elders regard white lions as the most sacred animal in Africa. Credo Mutwa taught that the white lions of Timbavati (see Figures 5.4 and 5.5) symbolise the eternal essence of African wisdom and have an important and crucial message for humanity (Tucker, 2001). According to prophecies, their presence calls for an awakening of consciousness and for true ethical leadership. It is also believed that the message of the white lions constitutes a warning against humanity's unrestricted, excessive consumption of nature, which desecrates natural law.

White lions are believed to be direct messengers of the divine and symbolic of the consciousness of the original Source or Creator (Tucker, 2001). They are ancestral bringers of light that will lead us to an inner connection to our highest self.

Figure 5.4 Zukhara (© Global White Lion Protection Trust)

Figure 5.5 Close-up of Nebu (© Global White Lion Protection Trust)

The significance of the colour white

From primitive societies to the great Greek thinkers Plato and Aristotle to Christian tradition and mythologies around the world, the colour white has been associated with light, brightness, goodness (in a non-moralistic sense), innocence, purity (as in the virgin bride wearing white), divinity, illumination, openheartedness, harmony, beauty, peace, joy, happiness and health (Cirlot, 1962; Bentz, 1977). 'Light is traditionally equated with Spirit ... Its whiteness alludes to just such a synthesis of the All ... the significance of emanation from the "Centre", for light is also the creative force, cosmic energy ...' (Cirlot, 1962, p. 187).

Dominique Zahan, who wrote on colour symbolism in Africa, equates white to a mystical union with God that takes place during initiation rituals in many African customs where initiates are painted with white clay and a white goat is slaughtered. This union with God is not a separation from community, but a sense of a deeper integration, presence and connectedness. "'There is no union with God", a Bambara would say, "without the world we live in'" (Zahan, 1977, p. 77).

In alchemy's great work, or *Magnum Opus*, a process symbolic of spiritual evolution (turning lead into gold), white (the albedo phase) denotes 'an indication of the success of the first part of the *Magnum Opus* which has been achieved after a purification process of subjective and inner evils, which we may call "private"' (Cirlot, 1962, p. 1). The albedo phase is interpreted as the initiation of dialogue between conscious and unconscious elements in order to bring clarity through the integration of opposites and thereby recover the original purity (or wholeness) and receptiveness of the soul to ultimately receive the divine Spirit (Burckhardt, 1967, pp. 183–9). The great work can be equated to Jung's individuation process (psychological development through enquiry and self-reflection), with the proper relationship to the archetype of the Self being the goal – where the ego in relationship to the Self is analogous to the Earth revolving round the sun (Jung, 1928/1971, CW 7, para. 405).

Colour symbolism supports my hypothesis that the colour white is a significant aspect of the archetype of the Self. Edinger describes white as a colour of primal wholeness, which is a principal characteristic of the archetype of the Self:

> Whiteness is described as symbolizing the impersonal, infinite, eternal undefined vastness that lies behind the personal, particular, concrete and ordinary phenomena of everyday life. It is the original undifferentiated whole before it has been refracted – dismembered as it were – into its particular component parts. It is the infinite and impersonal that has never been subjected to the personalizing process, that is the process which incarnates the eternal forms in personal, particular manifestations.
>
> (1995, p. 83)

Sacred white animals

White animals hold important meaning in the mythologies of many cultures; they are often considered sacred, and it is forbidden to hunt them (Edinger, 1995). Examples of sacred white animals are the white dog of the Iroquois; the Kermode spirit bear, a white variant of the North American black bear found in British Columbia's Great Bear Rainforest; the white elephant from Southeast Asian cultures and the white buffalo from the myths of the First Nations of America (Bates, 2014). The birth of a white animal is considered an omen in many cultures around the world, a message from the Great Spirit and a forewarning of powerful but necessary change (King, 2015). They are believed to be messengers of hope, peace and harmony among all people and restoration of balance with the natural world (King, 2015). Arthurian, Hungarian and Sumerian legends refer to white animals, frequently a white stag, which often led individuals to battle or new lands and had magical properties. These white animals directed people to a potential challenge that could assist them on their journey of individuation.

Edinger (1995), in his analysis of Melville's *Moby-Dick* as an expression of the transpersonal spirit world and the archetypal psyche, understands the white whale as the archetype of the Self or a God-image. The significance of Moby-Dick, according to Edinger, is that he represents the collective, eternal immortal soul or essence of the whale as a species. Its sacredness is represented by its whiteness and to hunt it is sacrilegious.

Hunting mythology: the sacred hunt and 'canned hunting'

There was a time when the hunt was considered sacred and was conducted in a deeply respectful and religious manner (Campbell, 1959, 1988). This perspective is reflected in the myths, legends, rituals and traditions of various peoples around the world, for example, the seal hunt of the Inuit, the buffalo hunt of the Blackfoot Native Americans and, more locally for me, the hunts of the First People of South Africa, the Khoi-San. Joseph Campbell (1959) said these myths made it clear that, for these hunters, the hunt involved an aspect of a deity being sacrificed as the animal. Ian McCallum states that 'Hunting, then, was also a symbolic act' (2005, p. 207), imbued with meaning. Rituals were performed by shamans before the hunt to identify the animal to be killed. These rituals involved dressing in the hides of animals with specific headdresses and entering a 'Dreaming State', while also experiencing a visionary journey where the shaman would intentionally enter into an identification with the animal (Campbell, 1988, pp. xix–xx). It was the responsibility of the hunter to hunt and kill that specific animal in an honourable and respectful manner and to show appropriate gratitude. It was believed that there was a soul exchange between the hunter and hunted. An example of this reverent attitude towards the spirit of the animal is reflected in Campbell's description of the buffalo hunt of the Blackfoot Native (First Nations) Americans:

> Where the animal rites are properly celebrated by the people, there is a magical, wonderful accord between the beasts and those who have to hunt them. The buffalo dance, properly performed, insures that the

creatures slaughtered shall be giving only their bodies, not their essence, not their lives. And so they will live again, or rather, live on; and
will be there to return the following season. The hunt itself, therefore, is
a rite of sacrifice, sacred, and not a rawly secular affair.

(1959, p. 293)

The hunt in its traditional form – on-the-ground fair-chase hunting,
where you match your wits with those of the animal through knowledge,
instinct, skill and stealth – involves a close relationship with animals and
nature (Eaton, n.d.). American environmentalist and wildlife conservation-
ist Randall Eaton (n.d.) said the hunter must be extremely alert and present, immersed in the environment, with acute perception of the aliveness of
all he perceives, knowing when and where to move, exercising patience and
being conscious of the importance of silence and the art of stillness. For
Eaton this increased awareness, consciousness and presence is a powerful
rite of passage. He sees it as a transformative experience strongly bonding
humans to nature, developing wisdom and heart intelligence as opposed to
ego-intelligence. He emphasises that we very much need the wisdom and
humility, seen in traditional hunting societies, of the 'proper relationship'
to the 'nonhuman Other'. Eaton in no way condones the hunting of lions or
trophy hunting.

In contrast to my previous description of a hunter, picture this: lions bred
in captivity, cubs taken from their mothers as early as a few days old, often
hand-reared or used in the cub-petting tourism industry to habituate them
to people (Barkham, 2013). These tame lions are released into fenced-in confined areas, from which there is no escape, and where they are easily tracked
down, guaranteeing the hunter a kill. These 'hunters' pay up to $50,000 per
'hunt' for a slaughtered lion. However, there is no hunting involved here.
Today both white and tawny lions are bred commercially in the 'canned
hunting' industry in South Africa (Tucker, 2001). The documentary *Blood
Lions: Bred for the Bullet* (2015) gives a full account of this trade, which
many South Africans consider despicable and shameful.

This travesty of the sacred hunt, where lions are killed for trophies in
organised fenced-in enclosures offering them no escape, illustrates spiritual
poverty, the absence of self-reflection, blunted feelings, detachment from
and a lack of respect for nature in humans who are removed from any meaningful relationship with nature. To genuinely embody the powerful energy
represented by lions requires deep self-awareness, mindfulness, empathy
and a recognition of Spirit in all living things. Lion energy is not for sale.
Real greatness requires stewardship, not domination and most definitely
not slaughter. This sad caricature of the sacredness and meaning of the hunt
as practised by our ancestors is a misguided attempt to bolster unconscious
feelings of inferiority.

The lion is the ultimate power animal – a beautiful, majestic creature whose name, nature and image we have used through the millennia as symbols of strength, divinity, royalty, dignity, wisdom, courage, justice, authority and grace. Yet we find ourselves in the 21st century, in a so-called civilised world, with lions being gunned down for the sake of ego satisfaction – for the sake of a trophy on a wall. Do these so-called hunters somehow believe that through this indiscriminate slaughter they can claim the lion's power for themselves? The Khoi-San people, for instance, never hunted lions because they understood the human-lion interaction as a fundamental aspect of shamanism, and they revered the lion as the great hunter (Tucker, 2001, p. 54). In the pre-colonial time of the African Zulu Kings, wanton and indiscriminate hunting was not permitted and transgressors would be severely punished if they killed a protected animal (Player, 1997).

Modern humans are asleep, egotistical, disconnected from their own natural instincts as well as from nature and all nonhuman Others. Or are we possibly simply infected by *Wetiko* – a cannibalistic spirit? *Wetiko* is a concept that author Paul Levy (2013) borrowed from the wisdom of the First Nations of North America. *Wetiko*, or *Windingo*, refers to a state of cannibalistic, insatiable greed and selfish, excessive consumption with no regard for others, which leads to the decimation of natural resources and life systems on Earth. According to Paul Levy, *Wetiko* is a negative manifestation of an archetype that is part of the human psyche, a demonic force or pathogenic virus that convinces its host that it is logical and righteous to devour resources necessary for life, including cannibalising the life-force of Others, human and nonhuman. He states that *Wetiko* disturbs people's ability to see themselves as an integral, interdependent and interconnected part of the environment so important to our ancestors and tribal communities. It is this false separation of self from nature, and in my opinion, from the archetypal Self, that makes this cannibalism rather than simple indiscriminate slaughter. The 'canned hunting' of lions depicts a cannibalising of the Self where the ego has been usurped by the negative, devouring archetypal energy of *Wetiko*.

This false separation from the archetypal Self as implied in the concept of *Wetiko* mirrors the primordial drama of the *accursed hunter*. In one version of the myth of 'The Infernal Hunt', humans are doomed to an 'endless chase' when their attention is easily distracted from their God and they fall prey to possession by the archetype of the accursed hunter (Cirlot, 1962, p. 154). This myth demonstrates how humans perpetually chase transitory worldly objects with an insatiable urge, 'a blind outward activity', instead of 'contemplative activity' (such as Jung's individuation process), never realising that that which is hunted in the world is actually a seeking of the Self or 'the centre' that is within (Cirlot, 1962, p. 366):

> This is clearly a case of a symbol for a 'limiting situation', that is, of a falling away from the centre ... towards the endlessly turning periphery

of the wheel of phenomena: unending because self-delusion is a perpetual incitement to the sterile urge of the pursuit of worldly things.

(p. 154)

Jung elaborated on this idea:

> The man whose interests are all outside is never satisfied with what is necessary, but is perpetually hankering after something more and better which, true to his bias, he always seeks outside himself … The externalization of life turns to incurable suffering, because no one can understand why he should suffer from himself. No one wonders at his insatiability, but regards it as his lawful right, never thinking that the one-sidedness of his psychic diet leads in the end to the gravest disturbances of equilibrium. That is the sickness of Western man, and he will not rest until he has infected the whole world with his greedy restlessness.
>
> (1936/1970, CW 11, para. 962)

Are some humans possessed by the archetype of *Wetiko* or in the grips of the *accursed hunter*? It would be easy to project these negative archetypes onto the 'canned hunting industry' and other perceived atrocious figures in our world, but much more difficult to look at our own role as consumers and the way, directly or indirectly, we contribute to the destruction of our ecosystem. Humanity is devouring the planet's resources at a rate faster than nature's capacity to regenerate, and this consumption is beyond a sustainable level (Watts, 2018).

Conclusion

Known for his work in saving the white Rhino, Ian Player wrote of how the indigenous Zulu game guards taught him to live with the greatest respect in the animal and natural world. One of the many lessons Ian Player learned from Magqubu, his life-long Zulu friend and colleague, is that 'If you live well with the animal world, then you live well within yourself' (1997, p. 185). He understood why animals were seen as brothers and described his own experience with animals as follows: 'Their presence activated archetypal forces within the psyche, and at times I felt I was moving in another dimension' (p. 65). Player is insistent that indigenous knowledge is crucial to our modern society, and we are at risk of losing the spiritual wisdom engendered by a profound connection to land and animals.

My mentor Graham Saayman, who shared his unique dream appreciation method with me and who introduced me to the white lions, helped birth the ideas for this paper in our initial dialogues. He wrote that honouring our world and nature is an essential respectful attitude that we humans need to cultivate (Saayman 2007). Further, in his realisation through an instructional dream of the shamanic truth that the two worlds are actually one, he states that to in any way damage this temporal world in which we live is 'to deface the template of the Eternal' (220). He writes that the First People had protocols and covenants, incarnating the value of respectful interactions with nature which, in turn, constituted an honouring of the inner realms of spirit.

A pivotal question is how to nurture an ethically responsible and mindful relationship with nature? In his foreword to Neumann's *Depth Psychology and the New Ethic* (1949), James Yandell referred to the ecological perspective of a 'recognition of the wholeness of the earth and its vulnerable interdependence of parts and processes' as an apt model for the integrated 'whole' human psyche. This ecological consciousness may also be a necessary condition for the continued existence of the natural world.

A beautiful numinous dream and subsequently two visits to the Timbavati, heartlands of the white lions (Figure 5.6), led me down this path of exploration. Through my journey I became aware of the real plight of the white lions as well as of lions in general. This paper is my lion's roar in defence of their right to walk this Earth, not be turned into trophies. In my exploration of the significance and symbolism of the white lion, I equated it with Jung's concept of the Self. I also believe that hunting animals in the wild was once a sacred ritualistic act of reverence towards the animal in the context of a respectful relationship with nature. Since we have disconnected from nature,

Figure 5.6 Nebu (© Global White Lion Protection Trust)

hunting no longer carries this numinosity. In exploring the symbolism of the white lion, I arrived at the significant conclusion that canned hunting of this magnificent creature is nothing less than a desecration and cannibalisation of the Self.

Wilderness interwoven with humankind's ancient lived experiences and evolutionary leaps, as an archetypal pattern of the soul, constitutes the bedrock of our consciousness. Nature is sacred and invaluable to the overall well-being of human beings. When we destroy nature and the nonhuman Other, we in essence destroy ourselves. As Linda Tucker's teacher, Maria Xhosa, said, *'Loko u dlaya ngala yo basa u dlaya tiko'* ['If you kill a white lion, you kill the world'] (Tucker, 2001, p. 33). The white lion as symbol of the Self calls us to consciousness of ecological balance and the imperative of a proper relationship with the Self as embodied in the natural world and the nonhuman Other.

Acknowledgements

I would like to thank Professor Graham Saayman, honorary member of the Southern African Association of Jungian Analysts, for his expert advice, guidance, inspiration and encouragement in this endeavour, but most importantly for introducing me to the white lions through his 'Waking Dream Retreats'. Also inspirational has been Ian McCallum and his love and passion for nature and the wilderness, as well as his most generous permission for the use of the extract from his poem 'Wilderness'. Many thanks to Linda Tucker and her partner, lion ecologist Jason A. Turner, whose pioneering conservation efforts have restored the white lions to their ancestral heartlands, now declared a *Sacred Natural Site* by the ASSEGAIA Alliance. I am deeply indebted to them both for the unforgettable and for life-changing encounters with the white lions of the Timbavati.

References

Barkham, P. (2013, 3 June). 'Canned hunting': The lions bred for slaughter. *The Guardian*. Retrieved from https://www.theguardian.com/environment/2013/jun/03/canned-hunting-lions-bred-slaughter

Bates, M. (2014, 11 February). Special albinos and unusually white animals. *National Geographic*. Retrieved from https://blog.nationalgeographic.org/2014/02/11/pictures-special-albinos-and-unusually-white- animals/

Beer, R. (2003). *The handbook of Tibetan Buddhist symbols*. Shambhala Publications.

Benz, E. (1977). Color in Christian visionary experience. In K. Ottman (Ed.), *Color symbolism: Eranos lectures*. Spring Publications.

Bùhrmann, V. (1984). *Living in two worlds: Conversation between a white healer and her Black counterparts*. Human and Rousseau.

Burckhardt, T. (1967). *Alchemy: science of the cosmos – science of the soul*. Penguin Books.

Campbell, J. (1959). *The masks of God: Primitive mythology.* Viking Press.

Campbell, J. (1988). *Historical atlas of world mythology: Vol. I. The way of the animal powers part II: Mythologies of the great hunt.* Harper & Row.

Chen, Y. (2018, 17 March). Chinese guardian stone lions. *Way of China.* Retrieved from https://wayof china.com/culture/chinese-guardian-stone-lions/

Chevallier, N. (Director Camera) & Young B. (Director Script) (2015). *Blood lions: Bred for the bullet* [Documentary Film]. D. Cohen, P. Hankinson, & J. Nathan (Producers). I. Michler (Consultant). A. Venter (Executive Producer). Hilton: Wildlands & Regulus Vision.

Cirlot, J.E. (1962). *A dictionary of symbols.* Routledge.

Eaton, R. (n.d.). Hunting as rite of passage. Retrieved from http://www.randalleaton.com

Edinger, E.F. (1972). *Ego and archetype: Individuation and the religious function of the psyche.* Penguin.

Edinger, E.F. (1995). *Melville's Moby-Dick: An American nekyia.* Inner City Books.

Farrokh, K. (2009, 14 August). The lion and the sun motif of Iran: A brief analysis. Dr. Kaveh Farrokh website. Retrieved from http://kavehfarrokh.com/news/the-lion-and-the-sun-motif-of-iran-a-brief-analysis/

Fraser, C. (2011, 15 September). The crucial role of predators: A new perspective on ecology. *Yale Environment 360.* Retrieved from https://e360.yale.edu/features/the_crucial_role_of_predators_a_new_perspective_on_ecology

Guirand, F. (Ed.). (1968). *New Larousse encyclopedia of mythology.* Hamlyn.

Jung, C.G. (1928/1971). The relations between the ego and the unconscious. In H. Read, M. Fordham, G. Adler & W. McGuire (Eds.), *The collected works of C.G. Jung: Vol. 7. Two essays in analytical psychology.* (R. F. C. Hull, Trans.). Princeton University Press.

Jung, C.G. (1936/1970). Yoga and the West. In H. Read, M. Fordham, G. Adler & W. McGuire (Eds.), *The collected works of C.G. Jung: Vol. 11. Psychology and religion: West and East.* (R. F. C. Hull, Trans.). Princeton University Press.

Jung, C.G. (1953/1970). Introduction to the religious and psychological problems of alchemy. In H. Read, M. Fordham, G. Adler & W. McGuire (Eds.), *The collected works of C.G. Jung: Vol. 12. Psychology and alchemy.* (R. F. C. Hull, Trans.). Princeton University Press.

Jung, C.G. (1962). *Memories, dreams, reflections.* (A. Jaffé, Ed.). Random House.

Jung, C.G. (1973). *Letters: Vol. 1, 1906–1950.* Princeton University Press.

Jung, C.G., & von Franz, M.-L. (1964). *Man and his symbols.* Dell Publishing Co.

King, S.A. (2015). The sacred white animals of prophecy. *Animal Dreaming.* Retrieved from http://animaldream ing.com/animal-info/white-animal-prophecy/

Levy, P. (2013). *Dispelling Wetiko: Breaking the curse of evil.* North Atlantic Books.

Lindeman, R.L. (1942). The trophic-dynamic aspect of ecology. *Ecology, 23,* 399–418.

Marovic, Z., & Machinga, M.M. (2017). African shamanic knowledge and transpersonal psychology: Spirits and healing in dialogue. *The Journal of Transpersonal Psychology, 49*(1), 31–44.

McBride, C. (1977). *The white lions of the Timbavati.* Paddington Press.

McCallum, I. (2005). *Ecological intelligence: Rediscovering ourselves in nature.* Africa Geographic.

McGilchrist, I. (2010). *The master and his emissary: The divided brain and the making of the Western world.* Yale University Press.

Neumann, E. (1949). *Depth psychology and the new ethic.* Shambhala Publications.

Player, I. (1997). *Zululand wilderness: Shadow and soul.* David Philip Publishers.

Saayman, G.S. (2007). *Hunting with the heart: A vision quest to spiritual emergence.* Kima Global Publishers.

Sabini, M. (Ed.). (2002). *The earth has a soul: The nature writings of C.G. Jung.* North Atlantic Books.

Sutherland, A. (2017, 10 October). The majestic lion: ancient symbol of power and royalty found world-wide. *Ancient Pages.* http://www.ancientpages.com/2017/10/10/the-majestic-lion-ancient-symbol-of-power-and-royalty-found-world-wide/

Tucker, L. (2001). *Mystery of the white lions: Children of the sun god.* Npenvu Press.

Watts, J. (2018, 23 July). Earth's resources consumed in ever greater destructive volumes. *The Guardian.* Retrieved from https://amp.theguardian.com/environment/2018/jul/23/earths-resources-consumed-in-ever-greater-destructive-volumes

Zahan, D. (1977). White, red and black: Colour symbolism in Black Africa. In K. Ottmann (Ed.), *Color symbolism: Eranos lectures.* Spring Publications.

Part II

Sociopolitical lives of otherness

Pain and possibility

Chapter 6

In remembrance and celebration of Other

Fanny Brewster

We have just survived

following Remi Raji's 'My Country is Bereaved'

Those of us descendants of Yemanjá
Her waters bear us through the depths of waves
Carry us on wooden planks
Stand us on the boards of auctions
while white voices rattle our worth in a foreign tongue.
We have just survived
the days of dirt, hoed and raked
through the fields of cotton whiteness
bearing us forward one day,
one hundred days
one hundred years
another hundred years.
We have just survived
the bullwhip
the rope
the gun
as our eyes look back
always to our Motherland.
The last drop of us Diaspora
we are washed
beyond imagination
and into our blackness.
We take breath now
from the howling winds
sent across the waters.

Fanny Brewster

When African slaves arrived on American soil, they brought with them the essence of a rich African heritage. We descendants have for centuries struggled,

DOI: 10.4324/9781003223481-9

succeeded and sometimes failed in laying claim to the vitality of this heritage. Though we have been separated by time and the painful remembrance of what became of us once we travelled across the waters, we are always psychically in search of our African Other. Not the socially constructed imposed Other but the one to which we belong in remembrance and reverence.

It may be difficult for those not of an Africanist lineage not only to understand but also to save the psychic space needed for understanding, the life of those whose ancestors were caught in the darkness of African American slavery and its aftermath. Recently, in a seminar I was conducting, a woman felt that I was giving too much weight to the history of African Americans as former slaves and its psychological effects on the African Diaspora. I felt as if she wanted me to move on – those are my words. She actually used the word forward ... to move forward. I wish it were that simple. Jung, in his 1930 paper 'The Complications of American Psychology', in which he just barely mentions what I have called a 'racial complex', notes how difficult it is for Americans – Black and white – to sort through our cultural differences (1930/1968, CW 10). He notes these differences are there but provides no answers for how to resolve them. I believe that this work has been left to us. Our work as 21st-century Jungians is not any less difficult than it was for Jung to consider in the 1930s.

In considering this quote from Jung:

> It has always seemed to me that I had to answer questions which fate had posed to my forefathers, and which had not yet been answered, or as if I had to complete, or perhaps continue, things which previous ages had left unfinished.
>
> (Jung, 1989, p. 233)

I must ask: What are the unanswered questions that fate had posed to my forefathers? And I would include mothers. The questions that came to me have developed from Jung's question and involve a second round of questions that relate very much to being of Black African descent.

Some of my own questions include the following:

- How can we, as the African Diaspora, know, learn and accept our true selves in the face of the construction of a false Other that was created in service of white America's social, economic and political needs?
- What do we do with our rage, anguish and sorrow to overcome the historical trauma we have experienced?
- Where do we go to nourish our souls?
- When will we be able to claim those lost parts of ourselves?
- Who can love us for who we are?

I believe some possible answers to these questions bring us to remembrance of an African Other, our foreparents who crossed the Atlantic as slaves and those who remained on the African continent. The oral tradition that was essentially an aspect of African life continues to live on in African American language. Ebonics, with its black speech rhythms, consonant sounds and patterns, is linguistically based on Western African languages.

African American healers and midwives, those from slavery times who took care of our African descendants to those of this 21st century, are practitioners of Traditional Healing Practices. These practices have evolved from a belief in organic root-based healing combined with the language of spirituality. As a child growing up in South Carolina, my childhood was full of experiences of a grandmother who practised healing from this Africanist tradition. In fact, my father's mother was the midwife at my own birth in her home. Women served as midwives to daughters and daughters-in-law, as was the case for my mother, because it was a natural part of our African American lives. It wasn't only because of existing racism in public facilities such as hospitals that provided less or no quality care to African Americans; we did it because it was the way of our African tradition.

Another way in which African Americans re-created our African lives was through building communities that duplicated our ancestral villages. Yes, we were excluded by whites from living in certain neighbourhoods from the very early days of American slavery. But this segregation, although intentional on the part of those who felt we were unworthy of living in close contact due to our skin colour, only deepened our conscious, and perhaps unconscious, efforts to re-create the villages we had lost decades and centuries ago: neighbourhoods like Bedford-Stuyvesant in Brooklyn, New York; neighbourhoods in Atlanta, Georgia; Greenwood in Tulsa, Oklahoma, which was destroyed by a white race riot in 1921. Rosewood, Florida, was the location of a flourishing close-knit African American community following emancipation from slavery.

The idea that we live together only because banks red-lined us and forced us into certain neighbourhoods does not acknowledge our desire to be with one another in community. This lack of acknowledgement keeps us eternally as the object – the Other in a relationship of Opposites that dismisses our kinship and relatedness as a people. It ignores the communities we built that included our businesses, homes and most of all our neighbours and families.

As Jung spoke of the African huts he once saw and wanted to model in his creation of Bollingen, might we not consider that African Americans may have an even stronger unconscious and conscious drive for such a home? Being with one another in community helps us remember where we are from as Original People.

The celebration of our own Africanist Other as descendants of African slaves includes strength, a will for life and freedom, blessings of intellect, creativity and soul. These are just a few of the qualities we possess and claim in a celebration of having an Africanist lineage. African Americans survived one of the worse genocidal periods in Western history. We have lived through centuries of being bred for the survival of a white Other who proclaimed us to be weak of mind – only worthy of serving as physical labour. Our will for life and our fight for freedom – even today – speak to our need for celebration of this incredible accomplishment.

African Americans have invented everything from gas masks – Garrett Morgan in 1912 – to the Laserphaco Probe used for the removal of eye cataracts – Dr. Patricia Bath in 1986. In the field of American psychology, African Americans have long borne the weight of being considered intellectually poor. This projection onto us as a poorly functioning Black Other has coloured every aspect of the historical relations between whites and Blacks in America. We have had to fight for our children to receive a quality education in public schools and not be relegated to Special Education classrooms. It is not the lack of intelligence that has contributed to poorly educated African American children but rather a racist history in which African Americans were thought and taught as Other, as if we were inferior in intelligence. Our capacity to overcome the falsehood of this harmful bias is a tremendous cause of celebration.

Our creativity has been boundless. We invented a new form of music – Jazz. We lived, cried and danced the Blues. As our African descendants emerged from under the yoke of slavery, the spiritual music they had sung as slaves evolved into a highly stylized form of Gospel and the Blues. The passionate music of our African forefathers and their creative call has produced a response in African Americans that continues today in our dance and music. Hip hop thrives around the world.

African Americans continue to live their spiritual and religious practices with rituals oftentimes based on African philosophical beliefs. Voudon is, of course, an excellent example. In the area of religion, Africanist people have continued to be enriched and empowered in a most significant manner. I remember when soul became such a popular word in the 1960s and how many African Americans wondered why it had taken so long for so many 'Others' to discover they had soul!

How ironic since much of the basis for the European invasion into Africa – the foundation for the economic exploitation of Africanist people – was the falsehood that Africans were soul-less and required saving. The use of Christian missionaries and religious propaganda sought to capture the spirit of Africans along with their bodies. As Africans lost their villages and their lives, their descendants found a new common language through spirit that lived, grew and was celebrated in the church communities of African Americans.

The truth of our African Diaspora is that we reflect the best of our African forefathers and foremothers. We have lived through and extended the strength of our ancestors who lived and survived on the African earth. We were the plantation growers who took care of feeding millions during and after the years of slavery. We nurtured one another and fed one another through sharing ways of survival so that members of the African Diaspora could be here today. We must remember and celebrate what they painfully held out to us through the centuries – the art of survival under the most inhumane circumstances.

We must celebrate the African American women circles that created Sojourner Truth, Harriet Tubman and Mary Bethune. These women brought us through slavery and educated us in the deepest understanding of the African tradition that we are one together for each other. We do not exist in the unconscious way of a participation mystique but rather in our choosing to create a life together because we are kin. In this kinship we may have lost one another through the tragic interruption of our destinies through American slavery, but we remain joined together through our Africanist roots and our archetypal DNA. It has taken the last 100 years or so for those of Africanist lineage to be able to openly claim and accept with pride the connections we African Americans have to the African Motherland. We must continue to be awake to ways in which we can maintain this connection.

Our struggle is not over. I believe it continues with recognizing the need for discovery, looking to do as Jung said – 'to complete or perhaps continue things which previous ages had left unfinished' (1989, p. 233).

We must de-construct the mythological Black 'Other' created by another. We must work to remember our Africanist roots in our language, thoughts and actions. How best to do this? How do we live as our own selves, claiming subjectivity and completing what our foreparents left unfinished? We who are members of the African Diaspora must consider 400 years of racist oppression in completing the tasks that remain.

The woman who sat in my group seminar feels I need to move forward. African Americans do not need to move forward; we do not need to move away from our collective historical trauma – an African Holocaust. What she cannot see is that this trauma has helped forge us into the people we are today. We have cause to remember and celebrate our existence. We do not need to hold shame or guilt as if we own these things because they have been projected onto us in our role as cultural scapegoats. We are the creators of mythology and the givers of rhythm. Our work is to remember the place of our first given birth – the African Motherland.

We must resist being only the constructed, mythological Other of another. We must remember and learn the traditions, stories, dreams and healing of our ancestors. Our existence does not take life away from another. In the current state of American politics, some would have us believe that we take away from the glory or beauty of that which is America when we insist on ourselves and our history being seen and heard. We of the African Diaspora are a part of the glory and beauty that created and is America.

I believe, as members of the African Diaspora, we must remember to bring forth and celebrate our African ancestry, as Langston Hughes, the great African American poet, does in his poem 'The Negro Speaks of Rivers'. In this way we continue to live, honouring the unanswered questions of our foreparents. Our horizon extends into the past from the lives of our ancestors and into the future of our descendants yet to be born. We honour and celebrate our past and the future of our Africanist lineage.

Metal

We are together
holding one another
in the darkness
that has become
our lives
strangers before
now we are one
setting ourselves as buffers
against the storm that has overtaken us
Ogun's iron at our feet
strengthens our blood
We live this life
and continue as
our ancestors
more than one visible life
captured in one time
one place
we are many
known and still unseen
those yet to come
We have become the chain
so others will survive
this journey

References

Hughes, L. (1921). The Negro speaks of rivers. In *The crisis: A record of the darker races.* (A. Rampersad, Ed.). NAACP. https://en.wikisource.org/wiki/The_Negro_Speaks_of_Rivers {PD-old-50-US}.

Jung, C.G. (1930/1968). The complications of American psychology. In H. Read, M. Fordham, G. Adler & W. McGuire (Eds.), *The complete works of C.G. Jung: Vol. 10. Civilization in transition.* (R. F. C. Hull, Trans.). Princeton University Press.

Jung, C.G. (1989). *Memories, dreams, reflections* (A. Jaffé, Ed.). (R. & C. Winston, Trans.). Vintage.

Chapter 7

Encountering the Other

The white shadow

Karen H. Naifeh

My own confrontation with my cultural shadow began in 1963 when I started dating my husband-to-be, an Arab-American. I was born in Texas to second- and third-generation Northern European Americans, but I grew up in the army. Because my family moved around a lot, I was not as deeply embedded in the cultural values of one place as I might otherwise have been, although I was certainly embedded in the cultural values of the military. But the army was integrated, which meant that the army schools I attended and the military housing I lived in were all integrated, unlike the situation in most of the United States during my childhood. I took for granted going to school with and living near people of colour, and we children all played together. Still, there was a belief system of superiority/inferiority in the background. Back in Texas racism was far more prominent, but I spent relatively little time there until I was 16. My family was not overtly racist, and I observed them treating individuals of other ethnic backgrounds respectfully. However, there was an underlying rule that 'you are nice to them, but you don't socialize with them, and you certainly don't marry them'.

I went to college at the University of Texas at Austin, where I met my Lebanese American husband. My immediate family had no problem with my dating a man of colour, but I remember feeling a sense of fear and dread about potentially being shamed, derogated and even ostracised by my white Texas community. I was also so deeply in love that I couldn't imagine giving him up; I remember just giving over to the love, accepting that the white community might see me as 'tainted' and deciding not to worry about the reaction of others. Then I experienced discrimination from another quarter, as his family was totally opposed to the marriage, wanting him to marry a Lebanese girl, not a white girl. I experienced considerable ostracism and shaming, from his mother primarily. I felt erased by her. It was a very painful and harrowing time for me. Thankfully our marriage made it through that ordeal.

My next big lesson regarding the Other came in 1967 from Mickey Leland, a Black activist in Houston with whom my husband and I became colleagues and friends. Mickey was on fire with the civil rights movement; he

DOI: 10.4324/9781003223481-10

was a force to be reckoned with and knowing him changed me. He insisted we learn about racism, oppression and a new way of being in a multicultural world. He was the first person to confront me about my unconscious racism and about what I recognise today as my white privilege; I began to wake up to what was going on regarding race in the United States.

More recently, growth has come from being on the supervisory faculty at the Women's Therapy Center in Berkeley, California, a relational psychody-namic, social justice–oriented internship programme where I've been since 2011. That is where I began to confront systematically my own more uncon-scious racial micro-aggressive beliefs and actions and to become more fully aware of my white privilege and white fragility. I found that the more I could stay with my discomfort and shame, the freer I felt. And I became more open to hearing people of colour talk about their experiences; I could let it 'sink in'; I could tolerate hearing their truth. The result was an expansion in my sense of well-being and peace. My greater openness to the suffering of other groups due to white privilege and institutional oppression and my awareness of the negative impact of these forces even on white people are the impetus for this chapter. I am writing now in the conviction that Jungian psychology may offer a way to move forward a process of increasing white resilience, thereby helping to make inroads into entrenched societal racism.

Fanny Brewster, an African American Jungian analyst, in her book *African Americans and Jungian Psychology: Leaving the Shadows* (2017), names shadow phenomena at work in maintaining racial bias in the United States. Brewster also discusses Jung's cultural shadow as it manifested in his writ-ings about Africans and African Americans and the impact of that on us as analytical psychologists: 'Jung's failure to deepen his theoretical conversa-tion regarding race, culture, and conscious awareness in these areas, that is, beyond his own theory of the collective unconscious, has left the practice of American Jungian psychology regarding African Americans and race with-out direction' (2013, p. 71).

Despite Jung's encounter with the spirit of the depths that he described in *The Red Book* and his reverence for other cultures, he remained very much a man held by the spirit of the times in which he lived. Eurocentrism, even unconscious patronising racism, is evident in Jung's writings, as seen in his many comments about the African cultures, people of African heritage and 'primitives' in general. From our perspective in the 21st century, we can see Jung's unconscious bias, whereas he seemed blind to it.

Here, I am focused on the impact of the spirit of the times on *us*. Do we who identify as white unconsciously express attitudes, writings and actions that are offensive to the Other? There are embedded forms of racism, and thereby oppression, that members of the dominant group learn not to see, to keep in the shadows. Further, what forces keep unconscious racial bias alive and active in our societies? One answer lies in a culture's shadow and the polarisations along the lines of culture and race that have existed since our country's founding that have contributed to the cultural unconsciousness white people harbour in their shadow. A central tenet of bringing culture's shadow into consciousness is understanding the creation and maintenance of the sense of Other in the psyche.

Robin DiAngelo, a white American psychologist working to increase awareness of white privilege, writes:

> White people in North America live in a social environment that pro-tects and insulates them from race-based stress. This insulated environ-ment ... builds white expectations for racial comfort while at the same time lowering the ability to tolerate racial stress, leading to ... White Fragility ... a state in which even a minimum amount of racial stress be-comes intolerable, triggering a range of defensive moves, ... [including expression of] anger, fear, and guilt, and behaviors such as argumenta-tion, silence, and leaving the stress-inducing situation. ... Whites have not had to build the cognitive or affective skills or develop the stamina that would allow for constructive engagement across racial divides.
>
> (2011, pp. 54, 55)

Here is an example from her article:

> I am a white woman. I am standing beside a black woman. We are fac-ing a group of white people who are seated in front of us. We are in their workplace, and have been hired by their employer to lead them in a dialogue about race. The room is filled with tension and charged with hostility. I have just presented a definition of racism that includes the acknowledgment that whites hold social and institutional power over people of color. A white man is pounding his fist on the table. His face is red and he is furious. As he pounds he yells, 'White people have been discriminated against for 25 years'! I look around the room and see 40 employed people, all white. There are no people of color in this workplace. Something is happening here, and it isn't based in the racial reality of the workplace. I am feeling unnerved by this man's discon-nection with that reality, and his lack of sensitivity to the impact this is having on my cofacilitator, the only person of color in the room. Why is this white man so angry? Why is he being so careless about the impact of his anger? Why are all the other white people either sitting in silent agreement with him or tuning out? We have, after all, only articulated a definition of racism.
>
> (pp. 54–5)

Something about white peoples' reaction to what DiAngelo calls 'race-based stress' seems to evoke a much larger reaction than an individual's response to confronting his or her own shadow. In the invitation to put ourselves in the shoes of people of colour, white people may begin to apprehend the dark forces that hold racism in place. These dark forces form a part of what I think of as *cultural shadow:* what each culture acts out but would find unacceptable, even evil, if examined in the light of day. I propose that if we can begin to recognise that the source of our discomfort lies in our cultural shadows and understand that, as in work on the personal shadow, staying present and engaged while doing our best to tolerate the discomfort, we will move closer to wholeness as individuals and as a nation. As Jung pointed out,

> Without a tension of the opposites no forward movement is possible. The shadow is a tight passage, a narrow door, whose painful constriction no one is spared who goes down to the deep well what comes after the door is, surprisingly enough, a boundless expanse full of unprecedented uncertainty.
>
> (1936/1954, CW 9i, para. 45)

The opposites here are what we are conscious of as white people and what we keep in our white shadows. We who identify as white need to go through the tight passage Jung describes, to the expanse awaiting us when we can incorporate our white shadows into consciousness. Then we will be able to invoke a generous temenos that welcomes culturally difficult, emotionally charged material and begin a true dialogue with the racial Other.

Jung pointed out, 'The [personal] shadow is a moral problem that challenges the whole ego-personality, for no one can become conscious of the shadow without considerable moral effort. To become conscious of it involves recognizing the dark aspects of the personality as present and real' (1959/1978, CW 9ii, para. 14). And 'This confrontation [with the shadow] is the first test of courage of the inner way, ... for the meeting with ourselves can be avoided so long as we can project everything negative into the environment' (1936/1954, CW 9i, para. 44).

Perhaps humans never get to the point where confronting their own personal shadow does not require considerable moral effort, but culture's shadow is more unconscious and is, therefore, much harder to grapple with; thus, we are even more likely to project cultural shadow into the environment, as the white man in DiAngelo's example does.

In Jung's diagram of the 'geology of the unconscious', in his analytical psychology lectures of 1925, he placed 'clans' under the waters of the unconscious, 'nations' below 'clans' and large groups such as 'European man' below 'nations' (Jung, 1989, p. 133); that is, these layers are much further from consciousness. Each layer represents groups that hold sway in the life of an individual; each group has a culture unique to itself and each culture has a characteristic psychology.

These lower levels in Jung's 'geology of the unconscious' have only recently begun to receive attention. Our current understanding of the relationships between personal, cultural and archetypal shadow in the unconscious is quite vague. Here, I am not attempting to provide answers but rather to open up discussion about and exploration of these various layers of shadow. I think we can say that every layer has an archetypal aspect, for example, the mother and father archetypes in the family layer. I propose that through cultural shadow, archetypal shadow can take hold of the ego collectively (a cultural manifestation of archetypal shadow), resulting in atrocities with which we are all familiar. The atrocities committed during the Holocaust, for example, while led by Hitler, were a cultural phenomenon; something quite powerful and transpersonal took over the German people, something in their cultural shadow (Goldhagen, 1997). The atrocities toward African Americans during and after slavery in the United States is another example. Ordinary, otherwise 'good' people collectively participated in evil acts towards those they viewed as Other.

Although Jung did not go into any detail about the influence of each stratum or layer on the development of the personality, post-Jungian writers Thomas Singer and Samuel Kimbles (2004), then Singer (2010) and Kimbles (2014), individually, continued to focus on specific aspects of these lower layers, which they call *cultural complexes*. Their contention is that in addition to our personal shadow aspects, we all have cultural shadow aspects. Kimbles's and Singer's descriptions of cultural complexes include the following:

- A cultural complex expresses itself in powerful moods and repetitive behaviours – both in a group as a whole and in its individual members.
- Cultural complexes function in an involuntary, autonomous fashion and tend to affirm a simplistic point of view that replaces more everyday ambiguity and uncertainty with fixed, often self-righteous and sometimes extreme attitudes to the world.
- A cultural complex accumulates experiences that validate its point of view and creates a storehouse of self-affirming ancestral memories.
- Cultural complexes have archetypal cores; … making them very hard to resist, reflect upon and discriminate (Singer, 2010).

A view of Jung's cultural complex

We can see the cultural complex at work in Jung in a dream he talks about in *Memories, Dreams, Reflections:*

> An American Negro. In the dream he was holding a tremendous, red-hot curling iron to my head, intending to make my hair kinky; that is,

to give me Negro hair. I could already feel the painful heat, and awoke with a sense of terror. I took this dream as a warning from the unconscious; it was saying that the primitive was a danger to me. ...

The only thing I could conclude from this was that my European personality must under all circumstances be preserved intact. ... The trip [to Africa] revealed itself as less an investigation of primitive psychology than a probing into the rather embarrassing question: What is going to happen to Jung the psychologist in the wilds of Africa? This was a question I had constantly sought to evade ... It became clear to me that this study had been not so much an objective scientific project as an intensely personal one, and that any attempt to go deeper into it touched every possible sore spot in my own psychology.

(1961, p. 272)

I believe Jung is saying that for him, the threat of losing his identity as a white European was totally intolerable to his ego and he refused to go further. His interpretation about the 'primitive' being dangerous to him was, in my view, a sign that he, as a European man, was not able to withdraw his projection of the primitiveness and inferiority in his own cultural shadow from the Black man. The fact that the man in the dream was an African American might also reflect Jung's discomfort with being around Americans, whom he belittled for taking on 'negro' characteristics. The African American man in his dream was going to give him a 'negro' characteristic as well. Jung resisted exploring what this shadow aspect might uncover in his psyche, fearing it might expose a threat to his European personality. Here we see how much stronger culture's shadow is than individual shadow – Jung simply could not face it.

If we look at the dream, the threat does not appear to be to his life, but to his hair, to give him the hair of an African. If we take hair as symbolic of power, then Jung may fear having his power taken away. The curling iron is gigantic and red hot (phallic?). The barber wants him to experience being 'negro', and Jung cannot tolerate and be curious about what that would be like because it feels far too dangerous to him. In his reaction we could postulate the presence of the archetypal Other, perceived as able to totally obliterate one's own sense of self.

A master-slave archetype

'Self and Other' or 'Belongingness and Otherness' has existed throughout human history and likely long before humans evolved. I propose that it is an archetypal pattern, and that likewise, master-slave is an archetypal pattern. The master-slave archetype is an issue of power. There is always a rationalisation for assuming that one group or person is superior to another and that the superior group therefore has the right to oppress the inferior group. After all, the colonisation of people of colour throughout Africa, Asia and the Americas was justified based on the rationalisation by Europeans seeking power through conquest that these were inferior groups that needed civilising and conversion to Christianity.

In his *Politics* of 350 BCE, Aristotle takes it up:

> Is there any one thus intended by nature to be a slave, and for whom such a condition is expedient and right, or rather is not all slavery a violation of nature? There is no difficulty in answering this question, on grounds both of reason and of fact. For that some should rule and others be ruled is a thing not only necessary, but expedient; from the hour of their birth, some are marked out for subjection, others for rule.

Despite Aristotle's conclusion, from very early times there also existed the idea of slavery as an evil – 'a violation of nature'.

By the 19th century the German philosopher Hegel, in his *Phenomenology of Spirit* (1807/1977), wrote of the dialectic of the master and slave, essentially claiming that although one needs the *recognition* of the Other for consciousness of self to exist, one must dominate the Other to avoid the threat of being annihilated by the Other. However, in that stance is the dependence of the self on the Other, which eventually evolves into a reversal of roles. Hegel also held that slavery belongs to a necessary stage of history and has to be replaced by legal relations between equal 'persons', and that the abolition of slavery is accomplished as a result of the progress of reason and the consciousness of freedom (1807/1977).

Jessica Benjamin, a white psychoanalyst, has viewed this notion of master and slave through a psychoanalytic lens in terms of the nature of relationship between the sexes in her book *Bonds of Love*, where she talks about the relational paradigm of domination/submission versus the paradigm of mutuality. Benjamin writes that 'domination and submission result from a breakdown of the necessary tension between self-assertion and mutual recognition that allows self and other to meet as sovereign equals' (1988, p. 12). The same principles can be applied to a racial or ethnic Other.

Throughout human history the dominant paradigm could be said to be domination/ submission – slavery in ancient Egypt, Greece and Rome; the caste system in India; feudal lords and serfs in Europe; and colonisation throughout Africa, Asia, the Americas and Australia, for example. The idea that some human beings were meant to serve, to be the chattel of others, was a constant. That began to change in the West in the 18th century, as revolution began to foment in Europe and the American colonies. The idea that all people had certain inalienable rights, and even the idea of equality of all men, began to take hold.

Formation of the American white cultural complex

How then, did the newly formed United States of America, founded on the principle that *all* men are created equal, justify slavery? An unconscious process of splitting and dissociating had to occur. 'The Story We Tell', the second episode of the documentary *Race: The Power of an Illusion* (Strain, 2003), demonstrates the ways in which, early in its history as a nation, those in power in the United States created a story that racial differences existed and that the white race was superior to all others, especially the Black race, which was not even quite human. The story of race was created to keep in the shadows the political and economic rationale for oppression in a country whose founding principle was equality of all men. (It is important to note that slavery did not exist only in the South: some Northerners also held slaves, and slaves were part of the 'wealth' of several Ivy League universities.) In the documentary, the case is made that wealthy Americans used the story of race to push moral implications of their enslavement of Africans into the shadows of the unconscious so they could have a ready workforce and still see themselves as good men who cherished the ideal of equality. Working-class European Americans, who were the existing 'inferior' class, gained in prestige and power and now had a scapegoat upon which to project their own feelings of inferiority. The impact on the psyches of those who perpetrated this and on those who went along with it, through psychological processes of splitting and dissociating, was to create a closed system that Singer and Kimbles (2004) have aptly called a cultural complex. Then, as in all complexes, this cultural complex proceeded to enlarge and strengthen itself against the growing objections to the institution of slavery. And the greater the evils of slavery that were perpetrated, the more the white people needed to push their own evil actions into the shadows and to project them onto those they subjugated. In her recent book, *The Origin of Others*, Toni Morrison remarks:

> The necessity of rendering the slave a foreign species appears to be a desperate attempt to confirm one's own [white] self as normal. ... The danger of sympathizing with the [other] is the possibility of becoming a[n other]. To lose one's racialized rank is to lose one's own valued and enshrined difference.
>
> (2017, p. 30)

Key here is the meaning that is made of difference – 'Race is never about how you look; it's about how people assign meaning to how you look' (Strain, 2003). From the founding of United States to the present, there has been a 'mandate' in the unconscious of European Americans as a culture,

created by the American white cultural complex, to assign meaning to African Americans and themselves: dark skin means inferiority; white skin
means superiority.

As the documentary also demonstrates, the misinformation that sup-
ported viewing African Americans as inferior, dangerous and so on only
increased with emancipation. The Jim Crow laws that came into being reinforced the idea of the inferiority and dangerousness of African Americans
and justified the horrendous acts that were perpetrated: beatings, torture,
rape, murder and the lynching of Black people all occurred in the South with
no repercussions. African Americans were still in bondage, still deprived of
equal treatment, equal opportunity and the vote by the threat of these kinds
of violence. Such conditions were the prime motivation for the tremendous
migration of African Americans out of the South and into Northern cities
from 1915 until after the civil rights movement.

Even when emancipation came at the end of the US Civil War, the relational paradigm, the cultural complexes and therefore the rationalisation
for 'slavery' now expressed as racism remained. For people who had come
to recognise themselves as superior simply because they were white and who
had treated their slaves in ways they would have to recognise as oppressive
and evil if they viewed the former slaves as equal to themselves, the shock of
the reality that they were not superior and that they had perpetrated heinous
crimes would be unbearable. Such realisations would have to be repressed
and rationalised at all costs, pushed far into the shadows. The brief glimpse
of evil would have redoubled the need to project it onto the subjugated to
dispel the knowledge of their own evil. Further, one could say that within
the archetypal paradigm of master-slave, letting go of the stance of master
evokes the primitive (archetypal) terror of the threat of annihilation by the
Other.

Culture shapes consciousness

What else holds the old relational paradigm in place? Fanny Brewster (2013)
has pointed out that 'Culture shapes consciousness ... [it] begins at an early
age from initial child-rearing practices and develops later through other
experiences, so that cultural consciousness permeates every aspect of life'
(p. 71).

I won't get into an exploration of the origins and adaptive power of identification with the group, but it seems clear that the power of the culture one
grows up in and identifies with is exponentially more powerful than that
of an individual. The need to belong to a group is an extremely potent and
primal force, ensuring survival. People are much more likely to go along
with dominating, aggressive or self-serving actions if they are 'sanctified' by

the group they belong to, especially since going against the culture's belief system would almost always lead to expulsion, shaming and possibly even violence to the person doing so. Moral conflict about going along with or perpetrating evil acts is banned to the unconscious. One grows up within a culture, and that culture, including its complexes, is essentially 'mother's milk'.

In the film version (Taylor, 2011) and in the book *The Help* (2009), written by Kathryn Stockett, one can see these forces at work and examples of how the cultural complexes are maintained: intimidation; shaming; the threat of humiliation, ostracism and even violence; along with the comfort, safety and advantages coming from staying within the white culture's complex, all operating to keep racism firmly entrenched.

In both book and film, the tremendous danger posed to the Black maids who dare to tell their stories and the complete ostracism of the white woman who orchestrates the project are chilling to witness. The maids suffer the threat of losing their jobs and being blackballed, of their husbands losing their jobs, of violence and of incarceration. The white woman is ejected from her social groups, shunned or sabotaged by those she thought were friends and rejected by her fiancé when he finds out she has spearheaded the writing of the book. The other theme in this film, however, is the courage that the maids demonstrate in telling their stories and having them published in the face of cultural complexes whose role is to keep them voiceless. And there is – vital for we who identify as white to see – the fear, ostracism and pain that the central white character must confront and tolerate in order not to be devoured by the white cultural complex herself.

The situation in the South is more extreme and, therefore, more clear-cut, making it easier to see the cultural complexes at work. But we *all* suffer from the cultural complex of white superiority. Isabel Wilkerson, author of *The Warmth of Other Suns: The Epic Story of America's Great Migration,* chronicles the exodus of almost six million African Americans over five-and-a-half decades. It is clear from her book that the problems Blacks faced in the North, although very different from the problems in the South, had their origins in the pervasive idea, which came from the weaving of the stories of race, of the inferiority of African Americans and of the superiority of white Americans, which had invaded the psyches of *everyone* in America.

Blacks were not allowed to live in most areas of the big Northern cities, and as more and more came North, they were forced to crowd into the areas designated for them.

> Blacks in the North could already vote and sit at a lunch counter or anywhere they wanted on an elevated train. Yet they were hemmed in and isolated into two overcrowded sections of Chicago – restricted in the jobs they could hold and the mortgages they could get, their children

attending segregated and inferior schools, not by edict as in the South but by circumstance in the North, with the results pretty much the same.

The unequal living conditions produced the expected unequal results: blacks working long hours for overpriced flats, their children left unsupervised and open to gangs, the resulting rise in crime and drugs, with few people able to get out and the problems so complex as to make it impossible to identify a single cause or solution.

(Wilkerson, 2010, p. 386)

Talking of Northern racism, Wilkerson says, 'The very thing that made black life hard in the North, the very nature of northern hostility – unwritten, mercurial, opaque, and eminently deniable – made it hard for [Martin Luther] King to nail down an obvious right-versus-wrong cause to protest' (2010, p. 386).

To summarise, three things that I believe have kept (and continue to keep) unconscious racial bias alive and active in our societies are as follows:

(1) The deep unconsciousness of cultural complexes formed by means of beliefs taught about the cultural Other by parents' and communities' child-rearing practices early in life
(2) Fear of the emotional impact of becoming conscious of one's own collusion in racial bias because in one's cultural shadow linger remnants of archetypal shadow
(3) Unwillingness to become conscious of and take back one's own cultural and personal shadow material that they have projected onto people of colour

Letting go of racial bias

To me, there are two imperatives supporting our doing the hard work of letting go of racial bias and thereby emerging from the white cultural complex. One is the self-evident moral imperative due to the suffering it perpetrates on people of colour; the other is that it harms white people as well. I believe it is important for white people to become more conscious of the negative impact on themselves of the trauma of slavery and the legacy of slavery. Then we can begin to comprehend the immense harm to *ourselves* that is caused by keeping institutional racial bias alive and active.

In the mid-19th century, Harriet Jacobs, in her autobiography *Incidents in the Life of a Slave Girl* (1861/2017), writes:

I can testify, from my own experience and observation, that slavery is a curse to the whites as well as to the blacks. It makes the white fathers cruel and sensual; the sons violent and licentious; it contaminates the daughters and makes the wives wretched.

Despite the strenuousness with which white culture keeps racism and oppression in place, the cost to society is enormous. In an article titled 'Justice Delayed' in the 22 August 2016 issue of *The New Yorker,* Bryan Stevenson, founder of the Equal Justice Initiative, is quoted as follows:

> I continue to believe that we're not free in this country, that we're not free at birth by a history of racial injustice. ... There are spaces that are occupied by the legacy of that history that weigh on us. We talk a lot about freedom. We talk a lot about equality. We talk a lot about justice. But we're not free. There are shadows that follow us.

All this applies to white people as well: we're not free either, and there are shadows that follow us, *phantom narratives* to use Sam Kimbles's phrase (2014), that live in white culture's shadows and that haunt us.

In Toni Morrison's novel *Beloved,* one of her characters depicts in stark relief the way white people, in denying the humanity of the 'coloured people' they subjugated and oppressed, created instead a white fantasy of a 'jungle' under their dark skin, of 'swift unnavigable waters, swinging screaming baboons, sleeping snakes, red gums ready for their sweet white blood ... It was the jungle white folks planted in them', which grew and spread, until it invaded the psyches of the white people themselves and 'made them worse than even they wanted to be, so scared were they of the jungle they had made' (Morrison 1987, p. 234).

Here is an immensely powerful depiction of the creation of cultural complexes and the projection of cultural shadow, with the consequent negative repercussions to Black people *and* white people. Singer and Kimbles, in *The Cultural Complex,* note that

> Failure to consider cultural complexes as part of the work of individuation puts a tremendous burden on both the personal and archetypal realms of the psyche ... [and] does not allow for the freeing up of the tremendous energy held in the grip of the cultural complexes ...
>
> (2004, p. 33)

Repairing

Janice Gump, an African American psychoanalyst, writes in *Psychoanalytic Psychology,* 'Institutional slavery in the United States, which lasted for centuries, has been denied to the extent that its affective and traumatic aspects remain widely undiscussed and unknown to many' (2010, p. 46). She also makes the important point that 'Trauma leaves a void that can be filled only by the revisiting of it'. If white people can begin to revisit some of that trauma as well, in the context of searching for a way to achieve some healing for whites as well as people of colour, we may come closer to filling that void.

Jessica Benjamin points out,

> The reciprocal [equal] relationship between self and other can be compared with the optical illusion in which the figure and ground are constantly changing their relation even as their outlines remain clearly distinct – as in Escher's birds, which appear to fly in both directions.
>
> (1988, p. 12)

The difficulty, she says, is that we are asked to 'look in both directions simultaneously' (p. 12). I believe it is also a matter of moral courage in facing the harm done by the master to the slave and the inevitable deflation of giving up one's sense of superiority vis-à-vis the Other. Deflation might feel like annihilation, but it is actually the blow to the supremacy of the ego that allows for the opening of consciousness necessary for psychological growth.

We who are identified as white must do what Jung could not do – to tolerate becoming conscious of the qualities we project onto people of colour that are in our own shadow and to tolerate the shame we will feel if we allow ourselves to see how we as individuals and as a society continue to support institutions of oppression, so that healing of this trauma can happen, for *everyone* concerned.

The Psychotherapy Institute, a clinical training organisation in Berkeley, California, is intensely involved in such work. In their newsletter *Viewpoint* (January/February 2018) are several responses of participants at their Fall 2017 Symposium, 'Confronting White Fragility', led by Robin DiAngelo. Responses of participants show the deflation of white entitlement and building of white resilience at work. The response of Nat Torrens, LCSW, was especially notable:

> Relief. Then warm wash of shame. Gratitude. Glint of hope? As I sit in the audience as Robin DiAngelo speaks, I am by turns excited and nauseated. The energy in the room feels crackling. Fertile. Palpable. Alive. This woman knows the shape of it – the shape of us, our diagnosis, our liberal White syndrome, our grouped patterned behavior. This is the shape of my whiteawkwardness, my whiteavoidance, my whitecollusion, my whiteunskillfulness. My whitedefense … For example, I can hold my individual whitehomepurchase as an incredible gift … but holding it in isolation spares me the discomfort – [DiAngelo] offered 'moral trauma' – of seeing it as part of a larger Whitening of my former mostly Black neighborhood. This truth is incongruent with my self-concept as a good, moral being. … This fierce White woman modeled

using her capacities at full throttle, and I left inspired; my biggest self called upon. What is the full stretch of my whitecapacity, and what is holding me back from it?

Conclusion

The intent of this chapter has been to demonstrate the role of cultural complexes, especially the white cultural complex, in keeping unconscious racial bias alive and active in our societies, even in those of us who believe we are not racist. It has also aimed to demonstrate the forces that created white cultural complexes – and those that make them so powerful and so seemingly impenetrable. Finally, I hoped to unveil the harm done to everyone, both Black and white, by the absence of recognition of our white shadows.

For those of us with, as Jung says, the moral courage to confront our white shadows, there can be an enormous payoff. It can feel like putting down a burden you didn't know you were carrying. We long for deliverance from our shadow selves, but only by going through that tight passage, that painful constriction, may we emerge transformed as individuals and as a nation. Let us as Jungians carry forward the tremendous contributions of both Jung and those who have moved his work forward; let us confront our white shadows and do the work required to begin to emerge from our white cultural complexes.

References

Aristotle. (350 BCE). *Politics*. B. Jowett (Trans.). Classics.MIT.edu. http://classics. mit.edu/Aristotle/ politics.html

Benjamin, J. (1988). *The bonds of love*. Pantheon Books/Random House.

Brewster, F. (2017). *African Americans and Jungian psychology: Leaving the shadows*. Routledge.

Brewster, F. (2013). Wheel of fire: The African American dreamer and cultural consciousness. *Jung Journal: Culture & Psyche, 7*(1), 70–87.

DiAngelo, R. (2011). White fragility. *International Journal of Critical Pedagogy, 3*(3), 54–70.

Goldhagen, D.J. (1997). *Hitler's willing executioners: Ordinary Germans and the Holocaust*. Vintage Books.

Gump, J. (2010). Reality matters: The shadow of trauma on African-American subjectivity. *Psychoanalytic Psychology, 27*(1), 42–54.

Hegel, G.F. (1807/1977). *Phenomenology of spirit*. Oxford University Press.

Jacobs, H. (1861/2017). *Incidents in the life of a slave girl*. CreateSpace Independent Publishing Platform.

Jung, C.G. (1936/1954). Archetypes of the collective unconscious. In H. Read, M. Fordham, G. Adler & W. McGuire (Eds.), *The collected works of C.G. Jung: Vol. 9i. The Archetypes and the Collective Unconscious*. (R. F. C. Hull, Trans.). Princeton University Press.

Jung, C.G. (1959/1978). The shadow. In H. Read, M. Fordham, G. Adler & W. McGuire (Eds.), *The collected works of C.G. Jung: Vol. 9ii. Aion*. (R. F. C. Hull, Trans.). Princeton University Press.

Jung, C.G. (1961). *Memories, dreams, reflections*. Pantheon Books/Random House.

Jung, C.G. (1989). *Analytical psychology: Notes of the seminar given in 1925*. Princeton University Press.

Kimbles, S. (2014). *Phantom narratives: The unseen contributions of culture to psyche*. Rowman & Littlefield.

Morrison, T. (1987). *Beloved*. Alfred A. Knopf.

Morrison, T. (2017). *The origin of others*. Harvard University Press.

Singer, T. (2010). Playing the race card: A cultural complex in action. In G. Heuer (Ed.), *Sacral revolution: Reflecting on the work of Andrew Samuels* (pp. 252–60). Routledge.

Singer, T., & Kimbles, S. 2004. *The cultural complex*. Routledge.

Stevenson, B. (2016, 22 August). Justice delayed. *The New Yorker*, 38–47.

Strain, T.H. (Director & Writer). (2003). Episode 2: the story we tell [Television series episode]. In L. Adelman (Producer), *Race, the power of an illusion*. California Newsreel.

Taylor, T. (Director & Writer). (2011). *The help*. Based on the novel by K. Stockett, *The help*. New York, NY: Press/Penguin Group, 2009. DreamWorks Pictures.

Torrens, N. (2018, January/February). Reflections on the fall symposium. *Viewpoint*, Newsletter of The Psychotherapy Institute.

Wilkerson, E. (2010). *The warmth of other suns: The epic story of America's great migration*. Random House.

Chapter 8

Sitting on the impossible bench

Reflections on the bridge between social and analytical justice

Gustavo Beck

The method: on not doing justice to justice

This text, by necessity, begins with a note on failure as psychological method. So let me be clear: the essay that follows, an essay about injustice, stands absolutely no chance of doing justice to its subject matter. Its central theme is economic inequality. More precisely, economic inequality within the context of the psychotherapeutic process and the analytical relationship. This is a vast, complex and elusive topic, and it is the first time I have delved into the matter directly. For these reasons, I will adopt what might appear to be an unorthodox approach. A few methodological clarifications are thus required: this paper is personal, evocative and intuitive at its core. By personal, I mean consciously self-referential; by evocative, I mean ultimately inconclusive; by intuitive, I mean that it is rooted in something I can perceive but cannot pin down with precision. This is, in other words, an exploratory and tentative text. It aims, at most, at opening new possibilities through articulating affectively charged questions. The inquiry is driven by strong convictions regarding the importance of social justice and the imperative necessity of studying its relationship with psychotherapeutic practice; however, it does not argue anything with too much vigour – at least not anything that is too new or too well put together. In fact, it will only touch its actual subject tangentially and indirectly.

Still it is crucial to understand that this is a methodological choice: a choice that does emerge partially from necessity (given my lack of formal training in economic, social and political theory), but a choice, nevertheless. The weakness, looseness and indirectness of the argument are forced upon me by my technical limitations, but my acceptance of such limitations is deliberate. I start from two basic premises: (1) there is an unavoidable necessity to meticulously research the role of socioeconomic inequality in-depth psychotherapeutic practice, and (2) there is a certain value in having such research be done, initially, from a psychological point of view. By 'psychological', I mean a primordially affective, relational and subjective stance. In this text, I am fundamentally interested in *how the impact of social disparity and*

DOI: 10.4324/9781003223481-11

economic inequality is experienced in the analytical encounter. This is why my ignorance regarding economics is, unwittingly and for this particular text, an asset. It provides my writing with an awareness of its blind spots and its inarticulateness, or its unconsciousness, if you will. Such unconsciousness, I believe, can be very helpful as a point of entry into this matter, provided the text remains mostly experiential and does not claim to reach any positive truth in its conclusions. The intention here is not to prove a hypothesis but rather to remain ambivalent and engage affectively with the phenomenon of economic inequality as it manifests within the analytic relationship. This text is, in plainer terms, a struggle to find the right words and images to contain economic inequality in the analytic relationship.

To my mind the topic of economic injustice in relation to analytic practice requires deeper psychological reflection, and psychological reflection requires, at least at moments, certain diffidence, the type of cautious movement that derives from awareness of being in the dark. While writing this paper, I felt a profound sense of inferiority and incompetence. I know, *a priori,* that my effort will fall short and that I will ultimately fail. In staying with this feeling I follow James Hillman, who describes the relationship of analysis and failure as follows:

> Analysis may continue as before even where it conceives itself not only as having failed historically and clinically, but as *being failure archetypally*; as being concerned with failure in the dictionary sense of failure: weakness, defectiveness, absence of victory, bankruptcy, deception, lack and incompletion.
>
> (1975, p. 102)

This provides me with a convenient way of describing this essay: it has been bankrupt from its conception, and it is in this bankruptcy where it can find the source of its potency. In other words, I wish to explore the weakness, defectiveness and absence of victory in economics through the exploration of the same phenomena in clinical psychology and analytic work. Elsewhere, James Hillman (1983) and Rafael López-Pedraza (1990) have written more extensively about failure as a fertile space for a psychologist. The ground they laid is the ground for this paper. I will remain close to their vision, embrace my inadequateness and thus stick with the psychologist in me, who is affected by economic affairs but incapable of deep scrutiny of their financial technicalities. Hopefully, more competent scholars in the field of economics will further explore the matter in order to provide a more lucid economic analysis of psychology as an economic phenomenon. Other psychologists, notably Andrew Samuels (1993, 2015), have already expounded on this topic before and have done so quite articulately. This specific essay, however, is more modest: it is aimed at articulating questions, generating emotions and fostering reflective thought. It is, if you may, an attempt to trigger dialogue –

an excuse for future conversation. Shall it be successful (that is, shall it successfully fail) perhaps more psychologists and non-psychologists will also feel inferior, incompetent and doomed to fail when facing the issue of economic inequality in psychotherapy. If Hillman and López-Pedraza are right, this will trigger further psychic movement and engagement with economics through psychology.

The myth: Hermes and fooling oneself into psycho-economic honesty

The fact that this paper takes a more personal, evocative approach does not imply that it takes the problem it addresses any less seriously. On the contrary, I posit the problem of economic inequality, and its relation to psychotherapeutic work is perhaps one of the most important problems faced by clinical practitioners today. As mentioned, one of the psychologists who has explored this with most rigor is Andrew Samuels. In his view, 'Depth psychologists rarely address the questions that arise from an inequitable distribution of wealth. Therefore we do not know very much about the depth psychological implications of seeking a more equitable distribution' (1993, p. 100). Here, I want to follow Hillman's and López-Pedraza's trust in failure and movement, but I also want to address the questions that Samuels is referring to with honesty. Therefore, I will be travelling two paths simultaneously. This text, on the one hand, is anchored in my very particular experience of inequality in analysis (an experience much closer to failure and psychic movement); on the other hand, my reflections are held by a much wider and impersonal, economic environment (which is unconcerned with personal experience). The difficult trick here is to contain the tension so that the personal *experience* and the collective *reality* of economic inequality can share the same space.

With this approach I am trying to shift what seems to be the usual tendency among psychologists with regard to money. This inclination, like my essay, takes a double path, but in this case doubleness takes the form of dissociation. With a few exceptions, such as Samuels, psychologists tend to follow one of two attitudes when speaking about economics and money: one is too personal and clinical; the other too impersonal and abstract. It is as if for analysts, money and economy are either always about the therapeutic process (as if psychotherapy was not an economic activity and therefore, money is *only* symbolic, *only* about transference) or entirely foreign to the analytic relationship (as if capitalism and its wider economic patterns were not part of the analytic relationship and thus had no emotional or relational impact in the psychotherapeutic process). Or to be more precise, clinical psychologists seem to be prone to dislodge money from economy, so they can treat money as an exclusively personal/clinical phenomenon and economy as a topic that might be of collective/psychological interest, but which has no direct or meaningful relationship with the consulting room. In that sense, money is always a phenomenon that occurs within the analytic relationship, but the economy in which such money exists happens always outside of the therapeutic bond.

Both these approaches are, in my view, dissociative. In this approximation to economy, money is an affective and relational phenomenon when it appears within the therapeutic relationship, but an economic and abstract phenomenon when it appears anywhere else. It almost seems as if psychologists, when talking about money and finances, need to forget one of two things: either that they are clinicians or that they are economic agents (that money is part of their lives and that analysis is an economic activity). This dissociation, in which a psychotherapist cannot experience himself or herself to be simultaneously a clinician *and* an economic subject, needs to be addressed.

For this we need to transform dissociation into duplicitousness. The intention is to engage this concrete problem, first as a psychological (that is, affective and relational) one, in order to then proceed to more specific down-to-earth implications. To hold this tension, I resort to the figure of Hermes. Samuels, when talking about psychology and economics, invokes this Greek god and uses his image as a container for duplicitousness: 'Hermes speaks for both the inequitable, unjust, cheating side – and the creative, transformative, compassionate side of the market' (1993, p. 102). It is this two-sided, somewhat deceitful approach that we need if we wish to transform the dissociation into ambivalence. Samuels carries on to say:

> By engaging with Hermes, we also have to engage with the warring sides of our Hermes-selves: On the one hand, our fraud, our criminality, our belief in magic, our love of economic inequality, our own depression-inducing violence. On the other hand, our capacity for exchange, integrity, relatedness, flexibility, our own love of dignity and freedom, our desire to reject coercion and bullying, our skill at making peace.
>
> (1993, p. 102)

So in addition to the duplicity of the personal and the impersonal, Samuels also points out the duplicity of the creative and the destructive. The questions that arise for clinicians are then quite straightforward: How is analysis or psychotherapy a fraud or a crime? How invested are analysts in economic inequality? How, when and where do they *love* such inequality? How are therapists economically violent? And more importantly, how does this violence, this love for inequality, this fraud and this crime relate to a clinician's quest for integrity, relatedness, flexibility or love for dignity and freedom? Responding to these questions is a complex task. It admits no easy answers or clear-cut conclusions. It is, in fact, quite possible that none of these questions have answers at all.

This is why duplicitousness and failure go hand in hand as psychological methodology: being deceitful is vital, because we have to deceive ourselves into defeat. Rafael López-Pedraza understood this pairing well, particularly in relation to psychotherapy. In his book about Hermes, he emphasized the importance of this particular god as a guide for psychotherapists. Hermes, López-Pedraza thought, fostered what he named a 'hermaphroditic consciousness' (2006, p. 65, my translation), where 'weakness is the achievement' (2006, p. 62, my translation) and which implies an archetypal attraction and repulsion that 'could be seen as the dynamism that moves the psyche and life itself' (2006, p. 65, my translation).

This essay – following Hillman, López-Pedraza and Samuels – is framed within a dubious (and devious) methodology that is aimed at precisely detonating psychological movement through failure, duplicity and an honest engagement with our psychological and economic selves. To induce such movement, the argument moves forwards through moving backwards or outwards through moving inwards. In this essay, I speak about my personal experience in analysis in order to connect with the impersonal context in which such experience occurs. This text deceives the reader in order to deceive the writer. The only way of writing this text is to trick myself into doing so.

Before moving forwards, backwards, outwards or inwards, however, it is necessary to take a step sideways. So let me push economics and psychology aside in order to step into literature and magical realism.

The story: Borges, duplicity and money as bridges to the inaccessible Other

In 1975, Jorge Luis Borges published a collection of short stories titled *The Book of Sand*. The first of those stories is titled 'The Other', and it tells the tale of a conversation between two people who could be described as intimate strangers. For reasons that will hopefully become clear as I move forwards, I will now take some time to describe this encounter, as narrated by Borges in his exquisite, dreamlike imagery.

The protagonist of the story is Borges himself. Borges, then, is writing about Borges: here we find a first duplicity in a story that is structured through duplicity. Borges describes the event that occupies most of the story as 'almost horrific' (2007, p. 3), which of course begs the question: why 'almost'? Perhaps, I surmise because the text is not only embedded in the imagery of duplicity but also in the logic of failure. There is, at the heart of the story, something that never quite connects or works. But before exploring this let me relay the tale of the encounter. Borges's description begins as follows: 'It was about ten o'clock in the morning. I was sitting comfortably on a bench beside the Charles River. ... Large chunks of ice were floating down the gray current' (p. 3).

This is old Borges talking, a man in his 70s who is already almost completely blind. He narrates the encounter in first person. While watching (with *almost* blind eyes) the chunks of ice floating past him, Borges (Borges the writer through the voice of old Borges in the story) tells us that something happens: 'Suddenly, I had the sense (which psychologists tell us is associated with states of fatigue) that I had lived this moment before. Someone had sat down on the other end of my bench' (2007, p. 3). Old Borges soon realizes that the man sitting on the other end of the bench is also Jorge Luis Borges, but a younger Borges, who lives in Geneva in the 1920s. What we have here, then, is old Borges sitting on a bench with young Borges – a second duplicity. This double duplicity can be summarized as follows: Borges writes a story about Borges's encounter with Borges.

Borges the writer tells us that old Borges is the one who recognizes young Borges and that the latter is quite sceptical about the realness of this encounter. After guessing (remembering?) young Borges's address in Geneva, old Borges initiates the following conversation:

'In that case', I resolutely said to him, 'your name is Jorge Luis Borges. I too am Jorge Luis Borges. We are in 1969, in the city of Cambridge'.

'No', he answered in my own, slightly distant, voice, 'I am here in Geneva, on a bench, a few steps from the Rhône'.

(2007, p. 4)

Let us imagine this: recognizing one's own younger, slightly distant voice speaking and rejecting us from another place and another time. When facing this, old Borges attempts to prove to young Borges that this dialogue is actually happening and proceeds to describe many private details of the young man's life, including the contents of his bookshelves. Young Borges, however, does not find this convincing and resorts to an interesting hypothesis. He replies to old Borges: 'Those "proofs" of yours prove nothing. If I'm dreaming you, it's only natural that you would know what I know' (2007, p. 5). Old Borges concedes to the objection but responds with a much more psychological (and Jungian) attitude to the hypothetical dream:

If this morning and this encounter are dreams, ... then each of us does have to think that he alone is the dreamer. Perhaps our dream will end, perhaps it won't. Meanwhile, our clear obligation is to accept the dream, as we have accepted the universe and our having been brought into it and the fact that we see with our eyes and that we breathe.

(2007, p. 5)

Old Borges, speaking almost (again: *almost*) like an analyst, maintains the distance between him and his bench companion. He respects the other's rejection and scepticism but provides a space in which such rejection and scepticism can be accepted (as a dream). They then start to speak about family, history and books. All this is in old Borges's past, but in young Borges's future. Young Borges speaks about reading Dostoyevsky, and when old Borges asks which books, he is reading, an interesting title comes up: *The Double*. Young Borges tells old Borges about his plans to write a book that was to be 'a hymn to the brotherhood of all mankind' (2007, p. 7), and this turns the tables, for now it is time for old Borges to be sceptical:

> I thought about this for a while, and then asked if he really felt that he was brother to every living person – every undertaker, for example? every letter carrier? every undersea diver, everybody that lives on the even-numbered side of the street, all the people with laryngitis? (The list could go on.) He said his book would address the great oppressed and outcast masses.
>
> 'Your oppressed and outcast masses', I replied, 'are nothing but an abstraction. Only individuals exist – if, in fact, anyone does'.
>
> (pp. 7–8)

It is interesting to note how *the topic of oppression is the one that divides Borges from Borges*. It is when they start talking about this subject that what was already a stark split between old and young Borges becomes even starker. If young Borges was sceptical about the reality of the dream, old Borges was sceptical about the reality of people. The impossibility of the encounter had not been a major obstacle for conversation; but when young Borges's idealistic enthusiasm crosses paths with old Borges's grounded scorn, the interface risks collapse. Both have a valid point, and both have a legitimate reason to be suspicious of the other. There comes a point in which old Borges seems to lose hope of connection:

> Beneath our conversation, the conversation of two men of miscellaneous readings and diverse tastes, I realized that we would not find common ground. We were too different, yet too alike. We could not deceive one another, and that makes conversation hard.
>
> (2007, p. 9)

In this juxtaposition of similarity and difference, when the sense of our incapability to find a common ground emerges and we start feeling a need for deceit, Hermes makes an appearance. Just when we think we are about to lose the connection, he slips unnoticed through the least expected crack. In Borges's story, he slides in through an abrupt remembrance in old Borges.

'Suddenly', he says, 'I recalled a fantasy by Coleridge. A man dreams that he is in paradise, and he is given a flower as proof. When he wakes up, there is the flower' (2007, p. 9). Borges the writer has already set the story within a dreamlike framework, but now the story is pushed even further. Within this impossible imagery, *the story is moved forwards by the memory of a fantasy of a dream*. Were this not a tale by Borges, it would be the epitome of Jungian clichés. But what is most curious (and convenient for this chapter's purposes) is that this hermetic appearance has a further twist. After pushing so far out into fantasy, memory and dream, the story moves abruptly into the most mundane of topics: money. Old Borges has an idea: he will switch Coleridge's flower for Swiss and American currency. In order to bridge the apparently impossible gap that now divided him from himself, he asks young Borges for money. This propitiated the following exchange:

> He took three silver pieces and several smaller coins out of his pocket. He held out one of the silver pieces to me; he didn't understand.
>
> I handed him one of those ill-advised American bills that are all of the same size though of very different denominations. He examined it avidly.
>
> 'Impossible!' he cried. 'It's dated 1964'.
>
> (p. 10)

Young Borges was finally convinced. A bridge had been built through money. The two Borges might have been incapable of connecting, but coins and banknotes deceived them both into relationship. In the very next line, old Borges provides us with a parenthetical clarification: 'Months later', he tells us, 'Someone told me that banknotes are not dated' (2007, p. 10). Some dreamlike fantasy lingers within the very real, almost vulgar money: young Borges was thus convinced by an illusory date in a banknote, an illusion that also convinced old Borges initially. The unreal marking printed in the very real money had deceived both and thus allowed for connection. The gap had been somehow bridged in that 'bench that existed in two times and two places' (p. 10). After this moment, which young Borges considers to be miraculous, they part ways 'without having touched one another' (p. 10). Borges the writer then closes his short story with the conclusion that old Borges has of the encounter:

> The encounter was real, but the other man spoke to me in a dream, which was why he could forget me; I spoke to him while I was awake, and so I am still tormented by the memory.
>
> The other man dreamed me, but did not dream me *rigorously* – he dreamed, I now realize, the impossible date on that dollar bill.
>
> (p. 11)

The tale about duplicity was embedded in a much wider duplicity the entire time. The encounter was occurring, simultaneously, in the dream world and the waking world. The dialogue was, in fact, a bridge between these two worlds – and what sealed the bridge was the appearance of money, real money with dreamlike attributes.

Having the imagery of this tale in mind, I now wish to enter the duplicitous phenomenon that interests us today: money in the context of the therapeutic relationship.

The numbers: images of inequality and the 65-dollar coin

Much like old Borges, I think that it is through money that I might find the key to work through the dissociation that operates within psychology when speaking about economics. Much like young Borges, however, I will not write about money *rigorously*. Therefore, I will not speak exclusively about real money or about the fantasy of money. I will use current financial data, official information provided by governments and NGOs, real information about costs of analysis, tuition and so on. I will be doing literal (although not at all sophisticated) math. My intention, however, remains not exclusively literalistic. These numbers are meant to ground our experience of economic inequality. The intention is to use the numbers as an anchor for reflection and affective engagement with the topic of economic injustice within the therapeutic relationship.

Samuels has addressed the neglect that psychotherapists have for economic inequality, suggesting that 'without a change in awareness and the backing of many groups – including analysts – for a new approach to economics, it will be hard to achieve change' (2015, p. 39). In much blunter wording, he states:

> Shameful economic fantasy tells us how even people of progressive views are deeply invested in a system of economic injustice. If we want to change this system, we need to recognize what we are up against. It's about owning our own bit of the system, a piece of shadow from which we can all too glibly detach ourselves. The lesson is that economic sadism is not something you can escape just because you want to leap out of the pit.
>
> (p. 39)

I include the numbers that follow with this precise intention: owning my bit of the system and shadow, locating my own economic sadism and the way in which it is placed within the wider sadistic shadow of psychotherapy and analysis, which are, as Samuels points out, also a part of the system. Or putting it in his plainer terms, 'It's not just the hubris of the bankers. It's ours, too' (2015, p. 39). Clients, clinicians and the consulting room partic-ipate in economic inequality just as Wall Street does. Through these num-bers, I wish to create a Borges-like illusion and slightly distance myself from my voice in order to listen to it and feel rejected by it.

Being an archetypal psychologist, however, the first number I will intro-duce is (partially) imagined. Here I present a fantasized piece of currency, which was minted for the first time in my analyst's office about five years ago. This particular coin, which was coined exclusively for one specific re-lationship (the one between my analyst and myself), will be the centre of my numerical imaginings, and it is worth 65 dollars.

First, however, some context is required: in June 2013 I contacted a com-plete stranger, who lived in a different country and did not speak my native language, to ask if he wished to be my analyst. He graciously replied and after an informal conversation we decided to start analysis.

It did not take long for me to feel quite comfortable with my new analyst. The therapeutic alliance coagulated rather nicely and soon I felt content with my process. But we ran into an obstacle: one of the first things my analyst and I had to settle was the fee I would pay for our sessions. My analyst (who lives in the United States) charges 150 US dollars per hour. This was not realistic for me to pay, partly because I live in Mexico City and earn my living in Mexican pesos. After some negotiation, I proposed that I pay the equivalent in dollars of my hourly fee as a psychotherapist in Mexico City. Back then I charged 800 Mexican pesos, which with the currency rate at the time translated approxi-mately into 65 US dollars. This is how the 65-dollar coin was born.

My interest here is to follow Borges and emulate his image. I wish to illus-trate the ways in which money can serve as a bridge: between people, places and countries, or between psychological and economic dimensions. More importantly, however, I wish to illustrate how money, like in Borges's tale, unites and separates at the same time. Or to be more radical – how *money bridges and unites through separation.* Economic systems connect people with people, yes, but they also divide people – they divide people from other peo-ple and divide individual persons internally. More crucially, money links the material with the immaterial, the real with the unreal and the visible with the invisible. Through money, the subtlest and most refined psychological states can connect with the most tangible and mundane events of everyday living. Like the impossible dollar bill that crossed through time and space, bridging the dream world with waking consciousness in order to connect Borges with Borges, I want to perform here a psycho-economic trick that might connect the personal conflicts of a patient and an analyst with the in-tangible network that simultaneously contains them and eludes their grasp.

The psychic processes that take place within the analytic hour, I propose, are at least partially economically conditioned. I assume that most (if not all) analytic relationships in the 21st century occur within a capitalistic structure that is regulated fundamentally by macroeconomic variables and the rules of the free market, which in turn means that analysis has an inevitable component of inherent inequality and injustice. This is why I wish to use my 65-dollar fee: it is an interpersonal arrangement meant to negotiate personal conflicts, all embedded in an impersonal network. It holds my inner troubles, within a relationship with my analyst, within a larger economic context. The 65-dollar coins that I pay weekly, then, are the bricks of a bridge that could connect these three dimensions of the analytic encounter, even if I am currently behind in my payments.

Finally, one last clarification regarding the data I share here and the story it tells: this is fundamentally a psychological exercise and a numerical fantasy. It is not, by any means, a statistical analysis. In strictly economic or mathematical terms, my sources are reliable but insufficient; my procedures are correct but very loose. I will use graphs and numbers, but such use is not the one of a statistician or an actuary; I use these graphs as an archetypal psychotherapist, which is what I am at the core. Graphs, in this context, are as much images that move the psyche as they are representations of literal data. Again, I need to find a strange middle ground: the implausible bench that stretches from Cambridge to Geneva and the bill with the impossible date printed on it. These graphs are not graphs, but they *are* graphs. The data that follows, which is not actual data, *is* actual data.

With this said, let us move to the figures. The first thing to know about the 65-dollar coin is that it moves. Its value is not static; it varies on multiple levels throughout space and time. It fluctuates; it rises and descends like the water on the Charles or the Rhône. Figure 8.1 illustrates such movement with a simple variable: the exchange rate between the US dollar and the Mexican peso.

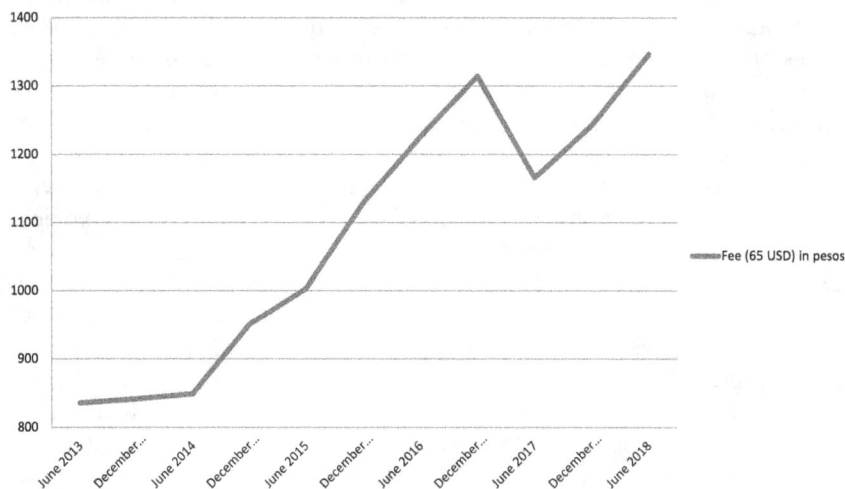

Figure 8.1 65 US dollars in pesos

As I said before, my analyst lives in the United States and I live in Mexico. This means that his fee is charged in US dollars, whereas I earn my living in Mexican pesos. What I pay is contingent on macroeconomic variables, among them the value of my currency with respect to his. When my analyst and I originally settled our analytical fee, 1 US dollar cost 12.86 pesos, which meant that 65 dollars were roughly equivalent to 800 pesos. I paid for an hour of analysis with an hour of my own work. But since my analysis started, the exchange rate has fluctuated significantly, mostly in favour of the dollar. This means that my psychotherapy has become increasingly more expensive. The movement does not always play against me; there are moments when the peso recovers, and the analysis becomes less expensive. In any case, neither my analyst nor I can rely on a fixed value of the fee.

So my fee, even if it has not changed numerically in the five years that I have spent in analysis, has fluctuated constantly in terms of how much it impacts my bank account in Mexican pesos. I must note that my analyst is not making more money with these fluctuations; not to mention his expenses are also subject to other macroeconomic variables. He conceded to charge me almost one-third of his usual fee; he has not adjusted the fee in accordance with inflation and is thus earning much less than he would usually. For reasons entirely outside of our control, the cost and value of my analysis varies: today (when the dollar costs 19.92 pesos), I pay approximately 1300 pesos for an hour of analysis – roughly a 50 per cent increase from the original fee. This does not translate, I insist, in a profit for my analyst. To put it in plainer words, as the analysis has advanced, in real terms, my analyst earns less and I pay more.

In addition to these fluctuations (the way the money moves through time), there is also the issue of space. The space I want to address now concerns wage gaps and their implications. Given that my analyst is a member of the C. G. Jung Institute of Chicago and that I am currently enrolled in the analytic training program in that same institution, in Figure 8.2, I contrast the hourly wages of psychologists in Mexico and in Chicago, comparing them to the corresponding local minimum wage and to my own hourly rate[1] – which, as the graph shows, is less than 65 US dollars now, even though I have increased my rate to 900 pesos.

The numbers speak for themselves, so I will simply point out certain aspects of the graph that seem particularly important. First, an average Chicago psychologist makes 22 times what an average Mexican psychologist makes. This makes economic sense, since the minimum wage in Chicago is 20 times higher than the minimum wage in Mexico. Now to complicate things further: I am a Mexican psychologist who trains in Chicago. I earn two-thirds of what a Chicago psychologist does (roughly four times the Chicago minimum wage). This puts me in a slight disadvantage with my peers in Chicago. However, my hourly fee is more than 15 times the income of the average psychologist in my country. And it gets worse: a Chicago psychologist

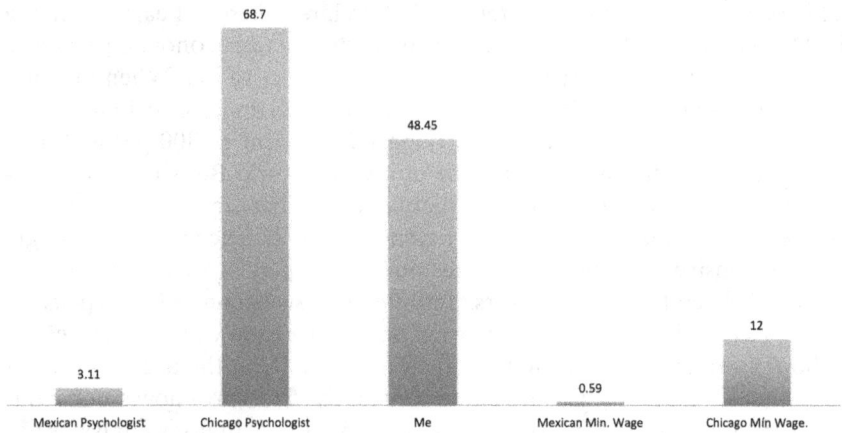

Figure 8.2 Hourly income in US dollars

makes roughly five times more than a worker who earns the minimum wage in Chicago, but I make 82 times more than someone who earns the Mexican minimum wage. This means that someone who earns the minimum wage in my country would need to work for more than ten regular workdays in order to make what I charge for one hour.

These numbers start to draw the very grim picture of economic injustice, and how psychologists, as workers, are inserted in it. However, as stark as the figures are when I consider minimum wages, I wish to stay with psychologists here. In Figures 8.3 and 8.4, therefore, I compare the costs of psychotherapeutic or analytic training in terms of work hours. Figure 8.3, for instance, shows the number of hours that a Chicago psychologist, a Mexican psychologist, my analyst and myself would have to work in order to pay for one hour of supervision or analysis. The costs that I include here are the ones I am charged.

The most noticeable feature of the graph is the enormous difference that exists between an average Mexican psychologist and the rest. If we consider the 65-dollar coin, for instance, a Mexican psychologist would need to work for 2.5 days in order to pay for one hour of analysis at the reduced fee; with the regular fee, it would take them more than a week's work to pay for one hour of analysis and four days of work to pay for an hour of supervision. Regarding my analyst, his reduced fee is almost equal to the average hourly rate of a Chicago psychologist – he is charging 43 per cent of his usual fee. As for me, the graph shows with clarity that I am much closer to the economic reality of a Chicago psychologist than to the economic world of a

■ Mexican Psychologiest ■ Chicago Psychologist ▢ Me ▨ My analyst

48.23

31.14

20.90

0.95   1.34   0.43

2.18   3.10   1.00

1.41   2.00   0.65

Analysis (Reduced Fee)   Analysis (Regular Fee)   Supervision

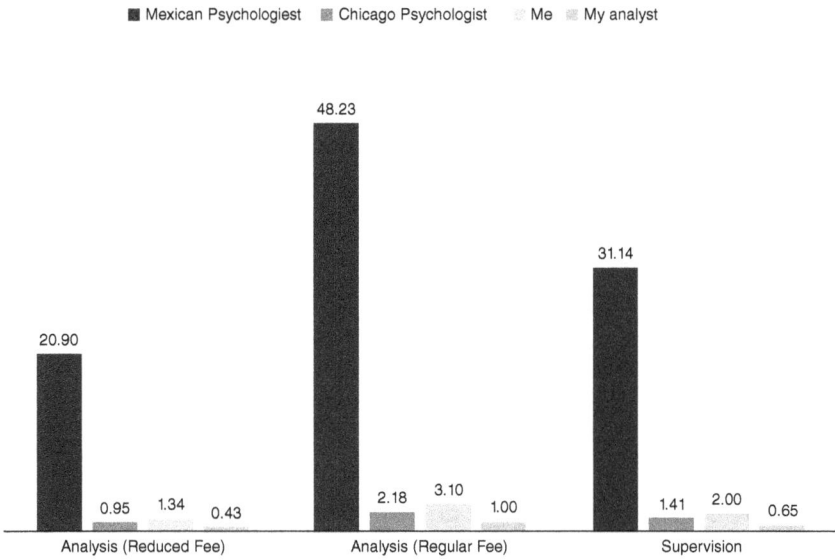

Figure 8.3 Amount of work hours required to pay for analysis and supervision

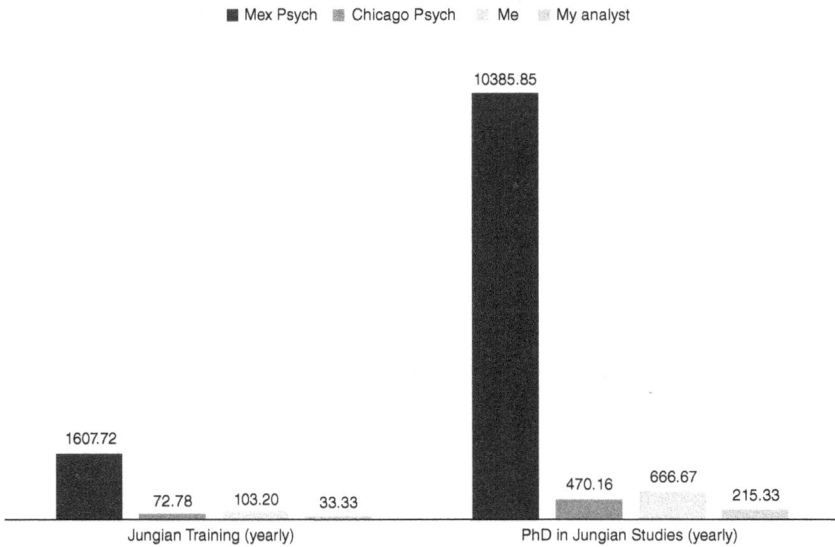

■ Mex Psych ■ Chicago Psych ▢ Me ▨ My analyst

10385.85

1607.72

72.78   103.20   33.33

470.16   666.67   215.33

Jungian Training (yearly)   PhD in Jungian Studies (yearly)

Figure 8.4 Amount of work hours required to pay tuition for analytical training
and a graduate degree in Jungian studies

Mexican psychologist. In this sense, I am being an economic sadist and am quite invested (even if unwittingly) in such injustice.

Finally, Figure 8.4 is concerned with the accessibility of formal Jungian training. I want to focus here on what it would mean for a Mexican psychologist to pay for analytic training or for a PhD in Jungian Studies. Assuming they work 40 hours per week, do not take any vacation and devote *the entirety* of their earnings to pay for tuition, the average Mexican psychologist would need to use 75 per cent of their yearly income to pay for analytic training and would have to work for more than four years to pay for one year of PhD tuition. This, of course, assumes there are no other expenses, neither in life nor in the training. There may be many reasons for the scarcity of Jungian psychotherapists and analysts in Mexico, but this is very likely one of them. And here I should emphasize that this economic disparity has psychological consequences. To illustrate, let me return to my personal analysis.

The impossible bench: on connecting through 'being screwed'

Here we face what seems to be an impossible equation. The coldness and cruelty of the numbers is difficult, if not impossible, to navigate. As predicted, the text will fail. However, if James Hillman is right and analysis is failure archetypally, my own experience in psychotherapy might open a small possibility for connection.

For this I wish to return to the first time my 65-dollar fee peaked, which coincided with the inauguration of Donald Trump. His hateful rhetoric against Mexicans as well as his pronouncements regarding the border wall and NAFTA significantly weakened the Mexican peso. This made my analysis 50 per cent more expensive, and the volatility continued through the four years of the Trump Administration. Every time Trump gave a speech, signed a new executive order or even hinted at future policy, Mexican economic structures trembled. Although the fluctuations were not exclusively a result of Trump's actions (the responses of Mexican officials were equally important), I was initially mostly angry with the Americans – my analyst among them – for choosing this individual as president. Trump, and his economic and political effects, became a crucial part of my analysis. The impact was so profound that I even contemplated abandoning the treatment; paying in dollars to an American felt like a betrayal of my own country.

As I processed this in analysis, I was moved to recall a moment early in my therapeutic process, which I now identify as the precise instant when I began to trust and connect with my analyst. A few sessions after minting our 65-dollar coin I had fallen behind in my payments. First for two sessions, then for another two, until there came a point when I was two months behind. At this point, my analyst started one of our sessions with one of the most beautiful interventions I have ever experienced: 'Before we begin, I need us to talk about something – money. I am confused. I cannot figure out whether you are having trouble paying me what we agreed, or you are trying to screw me'.

I do not remember how I reacted, but something clicked within me in that moment. I did not realize it at the time, but the reason this was so important, of course, was that both were true: I was having trouble paying him, and I did want to screw him. Here, the sardonic old Borges began a true conversation with the young idealistic Borges. With this intervention, my analyst addressed the three levels of the conflict that I have been trying to elucidate in this text: first, he integrated my own pain and aggression; second, he anchored them in our relationship; and third, he gave them simultaneously a psychic and an economical dimension. Although this might seem, in certain ways, like a standard move, my analyst's openness to discussing the nonpersonal socioeconomic aspects of the conflict was quite powerful and paradoxically allowed me to enter more deeply into my own inner conflict: mainly that in this relationship I was, simultaneously, the privileged and the underprivileged. Through his cold and somewhat harsh comment, he made me feel both ashamed and understood. I felt further from him (the American analyst) than ever, and with the recognition of such distance, I felt a much more intimate connection. He was the American, living in the rich country with a mighty currency; I was at the mercy of his president and his policies. But in relative terms, I had more power. I was the rich young man who could afford (even if with reduced fee) analysis with an American Jungian, and I was holding back my payments.

I was, in Freirean terms, simultaneously the oppressor and the oppressed in this relationship, and so was my analyst – our relationship was perfectly balanced in what might be called a mutual asymmetry: our relationship was based in equality because it was unequal in both directions.

As foreseen and warned, this is a rather anticlimactic way to conclude such an ambitious essay. Still, in closing, I simply suggest two inconclusive conclusions:

(1) It is crucial to allow economic inequality and its implications to enter the analytic relationship – and the best place to start this is with the acknowledgement that any analytic relationship is, almost by definition, embedded in economic inequality.

(2) In these times of rampant capitalism, Jungians must think of themselves as economic beings and acknowledge the shadow that this entails. This is particularly important at the institutional level, where Jungian education – or even conversation – remains mostly unattainable unless people come from privileged backgrounds. Let us keep in mind, as Jungians, that most of the available Jungian communities, trainings, events and literature have their home in the United States and in Europe. This,

by itself, makes it much more difficult for someone from an economically weaker country (in Africa or Latin America, for instance) to have access to the Jungian world.

Andrew Samuels, in his clever examination of market economy through the story of Hermes stealing Apollo's cattle, wrote about the importance of bargaining. 'The bargaining process supports and fosters compassion for the other, without whom there would be no bargaining possible. ... The image of bargaining is, therefore, not an unrealistic basis for a rectification of economic injustice'. That is how I got to the 65-dollar coin, through bargaining. That number, 65, allows me to relate to my analyst as a human and as an economic being, as someone who is very generous towards me while he also profits from my suffering. It also allows me to experience myself as a suffering patient who has his own economic privilege and shadow. In short, this fake, but real currency enables the constantly moving, forever unjust, economic system that holds the unique experience called analysis. Perhaps it is this relational quality of money that facilitates my bridging with people and with the invisible forces that move us – this hermetic quality of economics that separates and unites at the same time – that makes those 65 dollars so important to me. The 65-dollar coin is my impossible dollar bill, my implausible bench in front of the Charles or the Rhône River. From this bench I can contemplate injustice; while sitting on it, I can experience the shadow of my own economic being as well as of analysis as an economic phenomenon and of the capitalistic system as a whole. And this contemplation and this experience, because they will fail, will eventually move me to engage increasingly more fairly with others, even if the system that holds us together will never be truly fair.

Note

1 In these figures I draw several inferences and extrapolations in order to make comparisons (in Mexico the minimum wage is standardized per day, not per hour, as in the United States, for instance). I also make three basic assumptions: (1) the work week is constituted of 40 hours (eight hours a day, five days a week – I am not counting for extra hours or second or third jobs); (2) those of us who charge an hourly fee have a flat rate that does not vary (this is hardly the actual case, because most therapists, like my analyst, use sliding scales to adjust their fees) and (3) the exchange rate of 17 June 2021.

References

Borges, J.L. (2007). *Book of sand and Shakespeare's memory.* Penguin.
Hillman, J. (1975). *Loose ends: Primary papers in archetypal psychology.* Spring Publications.
Hillman, J. (1983). *Healing fiction.* Spring Publications.

López Pedraza, R. (2006). *Hermes y sus hijos: imágenes y vivencias de la locura a la curación.* Fata Morgana.

López-Pedraza, R. (1990). *Cultural anxiety.* Daimon Verlag.

Samuels, A. (1993). *The political psyche.* Routledge.

Samuels, A. (2015). *A new therapy for politics?* Karnac Books.

Chapter 9

Jung's Others

Society, nationalism and crowds

Johann Graaff

In this chapter I am concerned with furthering the process of constructing a Jungian sociology. Jung is not very helpful here because he sets a bad example in three different ways. In 1936, and ten years later in 1946, he produced a series of articles in which he analysed German society, German nationalism and crowds (Jung, 1946/1970c, CW 10). In addressing himself to bounded social phenomena, he laid down an exemplar of what a possible Jungian sociology might look like. By so doing, however, he put himself deep down on one end of three long-running debates in recent sociology.

The first of these debates concerns the relationship between individual and structure. Although he is not consistent, Jung seems at times to take a strong individualist line, thereby blocking out the option of seeing 'society' as an autonomous entity. But without such a notion of society, no real sociology is possible. It implies problematically that the nature of a society can be deduced only from the size of its population and that social change can happen only through individual change. It is important therefore to review the ways in which sociology establishes the viability of this 'something else' called society.

The second debate concerns the nature of nationalism. In addressing Germany as a national cultural entity in the grip of an archetype, Jung puts himself within what could be termed a primordialist and essentialist framework. And there is much social science that is deeply critical of these positions.

The third and final debate arises in relation to Jung's analysis of the 'mass psychosis' that the German people fell into and the key role that Hitler played in this. There are strong echoes of Gustave le Bon's 1895 work on crowds and leaders in Jung's writing (1946/1970b, CW 10). Contrary to his earlier individualist position and much like le Bon, Jung gives considerable power to the collective unconscious in possessing individuals. Individuals are to be regarded, he says, not as authors of their own actions but as victims. Here too the debate in contemporary sociology has moved far from both le Bon and Jung to emphasize contexts, rationality and bounded action rather than frenzied, blind mob-like behaviour.

In the following sections I explain in more detail Jung's views on the relationship between the individual and society, on nationalism and on crowds/

DOI: 10.4324/9781003223481-12

mobs. Subsequent to that I consider each of these three views in the context of recent social science research.

Jung on the individual in society

Frequently in Jung's writing he insists that all social change is nothing more than individual change. So, for example, he claims, 'the psychopathology of the masses is rooted in the psychology of the individual' (1946/1970a, CW 10, para. 445), and 'The psychologist believes firmly in the individual as the sole carrier of mind and life. Society and the state derive their quality from the individual's mental condition, for they are made up of individuals and the way they are organized' (para. 457). Of course, Jung is technically correct. Nothing in society can happen without it happening to, or through, individuals. But this does not mean that one ignores the deeply influential ways in which society in its regularized routines, rituals, habits, customs or institutions resists and shapes individual choice and freedom.

There are a number of significant consequences that flow from Jung's position. First, Jung indulges in a curious mathematical individualism to determine levels of morality in different countries. This is individualist in the sense that society is seen simply as a multiplication of individuals rather than a bonded entity. So, in comparing the morality of Switzerland and Germany he can say,

> We have only to multiply the population of Switzerland by twenty to become a nation of eighty millions, and our public intelligence and morality would then be automatically divided by twenty in consequence of the devastating moral and psychic effects of living together in huge masses.
> (Jung, 1946/1970a, CW 10, para. 412)

Another offshoot of this individualism is apparent in Jung's use of terms like 'mass psychosis' or 'psychic epidemic'. An *epidemic* is a medical term indicating, again, a multiplication of individual cases. But saying there is a 'culture of psychosis', or, like Christopher Lasch, that there is a 'culture of narcissism' is quite different (Lasch, 1980).

A final consequence of Jung's individualism is his proposal that social change can only happen by changing individuals. 'But in reality only a change in the attitude of the individual can bring about a renewal in the spirit of nations. Everything begins with the individual' (1946/1970b, CW 10, para. 459).

Jung on nations and nationalism

Jung's views on Germany in this period must be seen against the background of two key factors. First, these articles were written at a time when Jung was being accused of being anti-Semitic and pro-Nazi, so they are quite fraught, not to say combative, pieces. As a result, there are sharp differences between the 1936 'Wotan' essay, before the controversy had set in, and those written ten years later in 1946 when the controversy was in full swing. It seems prudent then to take his more excessive views 'with a pinch of salt'. Second, Jung's views on national entities follow from his strong views on the problems of modernity. National culture and nationalism therefore are, for Jung, products of 'man's (sic) loss of soul'. Hence, nationalism is not a problem that is restricted to Germany but is, says Jung, found in many European countries.

In Jung's view, in 'modernity' the processes of secularization have deprived individuals of access to the old religious archetypes through which they could express their souls. The resulting abyss of existential meaninglessness has been filled with the various '-isms' of modernity – capitalism, communism and then nationalism. In 'After the Catastrophe' he writes,

> It is an immutable psychological law that when a projection has come to an end it always returns to its origin. So when somebody hits on the singular idea that God is dead ... the psychic God-image ... finds its way back into the subject and produces a condition of 'God-Almightiness' ... [which] does not make man divine, it merely fills him with arrogance and arouses everything evil in him.

> (1946/1970a, CW 10, para. 437)

In this view, then, nationalism, in general, and German fascism, in particular, are phenomena of modernity, not just of Germany. Within this modern condition of mass alienation there is, for Jung, a significantly greater likelihood of possession by various archetypes.

The 'Wotan' essay, however, creates a different impression (Jung, 1936/1970, CW 10). Instead of being a modern phenomenon, in this essay the German people have been possessed by a very ancient archetype, that of the Norse god of war, Wotan: '[Wotan] ... remained invisible for more than a thousand years, working anonymously and indirectly' (para. 395). And, finally, Wotan is 'a Germanic datum of first importance, the truest expression and unsurpassed personification of a fundamental quality of the Germans' (para. 389). Overall, the Wotan article is a powerfully lyrical piece. Jung's writing is filled with energy; he quotes extensively from poetic sources and he is full of admiration for this magnificent god.

Jung on crowds and mobs

Jung's view on crowds, as set out most explicitly in his essay 'Epilogue to "Essays on Contemporary Events"' (1946/1970b), follows closely on his analysis of nationalism, since the same collapse of religious symbols and the resultant existential crisis that produces nationalism also produce the propensity for crowds to become mindless mobs. In this essay Jung is sharply sceptical of the impact of society in general. In line with his previous writing, his view here is that 'the morality of society is in inverse ratio to its size ... Hence every man is, in a certain sense, unconsciously a worse man when he is in society than when acting alone'. This cynicism is summed up in the Roman adage: *Senatus bestia, senatores boni viri* [The Senate is a beast, the senators are good men] (Jung, 1946/1970b, CW 10, para. 460).

But then the object of analysis changes from 'society' to '*the mass*'. He quotes from a 1933 article: 'The mass as such is always anonymous and always irresponsible' (1946/1970b, CW 10, para. 462). And in 1937 he refers to a '*mob*': 'But if people crowd together and form a mob, then the dynamisms of the collective man are let loose – beasts or demons that lie dormant in every person until he is part of a mob' (para. 463). Jung continues with descriptive terms like 'mass psychoses' and 'an epidemic of madness' (para. 467). Now all of this is reminiscent of Gustave le Bon's view as set out in his 1895 work, *The Crowd: A Study of the Psychology of the Popular Mind*, and Jung specifically and approvingly references le Bon – a problematic move, as we shall see.

Again, Jung's views on nationalism and mobs are sharply at odds with his views on the individual and society; the latter is individualist, as I have indicated, whereas the former is structuralist in the sense that society has a dominant effect on individuals. Let us now put Jung's views within the broader perspective of more recent sociological writing.

Recent sociology on the individual in society

Let us start by noting the contrast between the certainty of sociologists (like Émile Durkheim) that there is a clear distinction between the individual and society and the certainty of psychologists (like Freud also following le Bon) that there is not. Jerome Bernstein quotes Marie-Louise von Franz: 'Jung never tired of emphasizing ... that any healing transformation can occur only in the individual' (Bernstein, 1992). And Freud said, 'For sociology, too, dealing as it does with the behaviour of people in society, cannot be anything but applied psychology. Strictly speaking there are only two sciences: psychology, pure and applied, and natural science' (quoted in Bocock, 1976, p. 19).

Why would psychologists say that there is nothing new to say about society? For the very simple reason that the individual is never separate from society. From the moment of birth (and some might say, even before that) the human infant is in interaction with her mother. Her most basic consciousness of self is formed on the basis of the mother's responses to her. So, in order to gain traction in this debate, sociologists need to qualify their statements about 'society'. And they do. Sociologists acknowledge that society is inescapably present from the beginning. But they say that society-as-family is significantly different from society-as-group or society-as-tribe or society-as-nation.

If both Jung and Freud denied the autonomy of society, what is it that makes sociologists so convinced of the opposite? And convinced they are. Founding father of sociology, Émile Durkheim, states it firmly:

> Society is not a mere sum of individuals. Rather, the system formed by their association represents a specific reality which has its own characteristics ... The group thinks, feels, and acts quite differently from the way in which its members would were they isolated. If, then, we begin with the individual, we shall be able to understand nothing of what takes place in the group.
>
> (1895/1964, pp. 103–4)

If we are looking for someone to help us distinguish psychology from sociology or the individual from society, Durkheim is a good place to start. At the time he was writing, in the late 19th and early 20th centuries, the status of sociology was still quite shaky. He gave himself, therefore, the task of putting it on a firm footing by clearly pegging out his territory. And he did this from the perspective of a structuralist sociologist, that is, by understanding individuals as secondary to society.

It is, however, possible to consider this problem from a very different angle, that is from the angle of the individual. In 1971 Peter Berger and Thomas Luckmann's hugely influential book, *The Social Construction of Reality,* asked the key question: what is the individual experience in meeting the very real facticity and structural rigidity of this thing called society? Berger and Luckmann (hereafter B&L), as microsociologists, could not have approached the problem of society in a way more radically opposed to that of Durkheim. And yet what is remarkable is that they came to conclusions that are entirely compatible with those of Durkheim.

Durkheim: individual and society

In his work *The Rules of Sociological Method* (1895/1964), Durkheim sketched out three key characteristics of society: externality, constraint and emergence. By the notion of *externality*, Durkheim meant the way in which society is independent of the individual; things happen in ways that individuals might not intend. Society is like an already flowing river into which the individual is born, gets swept along by the current for a while and then exits the stream when he or she dies. Society then exists before the individual's birth and continues to exist after death.

For Durkheim *constraint* is most easily seen by the resistance that people feel when they try to break the rules and conventions by which society governs itself. For example, a father might never feel the presence of his obligations as a father until the moment he contravenes convention. At that moment he will experience pressures ranging from quite mild expressions of disapproval from family and friends to the intervention of officers of the law or child welfare authorities (Giddens, 1971). A second form of constraint can be seen in the way that society stretches away in time and space around an individual. The laws of a country stretch across the whole country, and it becomes more and more difficult for an individual to change them the further they stretch.

Durkheim's principle of *emergence*, well known today in systems or *gestalt* theory, is that the whole is greater than the sum of the parts. This is the 'something else' that appears when, for example, a number of people milling around the town square join together into a sports crowd or a political rally, or when individuals, previously unknown to each other, find themselves in a therapeutic group. In these situations, we might say that reactions are infectious: a ripple of laughter can induce more people to laugh; a roar of excitement from a sports crowd is itself exciting.

The social construction of reality

Let us now return to Berger and Luckmann (B&L). One might, they say, consider the phenomenon of society through the notion of *facticity*, that is, how society gradually gains a hard reality over and against the individual. B&L (1971) elaborate on this process of 'objectivation' in great detail, but for the sake of brevity, I will extract three key moments from this process for the purposes of illuminating the issue I am pursuing.

For B&L, this 'hardening' process starts in newly initiated spheres of action through the two processes of habituation and typification. *Habituation*, doing things by habit, has the considerable advantage of removing the anxiety of decision-making from a chain of activities. A man who has never skinned an animal before will experiment until he discovers an efficient method of doing it and will then keep repeating that method. He will say to himself, 'There I go again'. *Typification* is the differentiation of one set of actions from another. Our young hunter will say, 'This is a part of hunting'. These two steps also occur when two or more people are interacting. They can say through habituation, 'There we go again', and by typification, 'There we go hunting again'. Already these two steps form a degree of 'hardness' because it will take an effort to break out of the routine. The longer that routines persist, the more difficult it is to try out alternatives (Berger & Luckmann, 1971, pp. 70–5).

A key step in the objectivation process is the moment when individuals get born into these already existing routines. These individuals were not present when the existing practices and institutions were initiated so they need to be legitimated for young individuals. The practices must be explained and justified. B&L echo Durkheim: 'For children the social world becomes the world, it is opaque in its origins, it was there before he was born, and it will be there after his death' (1971, p. 77). People now say, 'This is how these things are done'. Breaking established routines is then not only difficult to conceive but also may be seen as wrong, sinful and punishable.

A final key moment is the *reification* of social practices and institutions. This occurs when social phenomena are seen as nonhuman products caused by nature or by divine intervention or by cosmic laws. In this case, say B&L, following Marx, 'the real relationship between man and his world is reversed in consciousness. Man, the producer of a world, is apprehended as its product ...' (1971, p. 107). In this situation it is extremely difficult for humans to even conceive of changing society.

This brief exploration of the facticity of society and of the extent to which 'society' constitutes a very particular reality reveals the 'something else' that is qualitatively different from a mere collection of individuals thrown randomly together and also different from a mathematical multiplication of discrete entities, as Jung would have it. Even though individuals, and individuals alone, construct society, it is society that acts back on them, constitutes them and resists them in extremely powerful ways.

Recent sociology on nationalism

Anthony Smith's helpful 1998 work *Nationalism and Modernism* provides a clear idea of the range of theories and conceptions around nationalism. This categorization places Jung quite precisely within a particular spectrum and allows us to understand the strengths and weaknesses of his approach. The spectrum of theories of nationalism stretches from what are called political messianist, primordialist and perennialist theories, at the more Romantic end, to instrumentalist, postmodern and ethno-symbolist theories, at the other more rationalist and sceptical end.

Messianism, primordialism and perennialism

Political *messianism* sees nationalism as a political religion that has arisen to compensate for the collapse of family, community and religion in modernity. But this new political religion is the active product of alienated intellectuals who, for various reasons, feel excluded from modern life. They draw on popular religion and culture to mobilize the population to support them.

Key examples here are the Romantic intellectuals of 18th- and 19th-century Germany, like Johann Herder, Friedrich Schleiermacher and Johann Fichte (A. Smith, 1998, Chap. 5).

Primordialist theories, by contrast, propose that nations are just that, primordial, deeply embedded in the biological and cultural roots of a people (A. Smith, 1998, Chap. 7). In Clifford Geertz's definition,

> One is bound to one's kinsman, one's neighbour, one's fellow believer, ipso facto; as the result not merely of personal affection, practical necessity, common interest, or incurred obligation, but at least in great part by virtue of some *unaccountable absolute import* attributed to the very tie itself.
>
> (1973, p. 152, emphasis added)

For Geertz there is a deep ethnic essence that lies below the variety of political and cultural forms.

Finally, *perennialist* theories, says Anthony Smith, deny that nationalism is a modern phenomenon as many would say today (1998, Chap. 7). Rather it is a quite ancient one that can be shown to stretch back to medieval times and beyond. To be sure, there were in that earlier time no recognizable nations as they are known today, but their ethnic and religious roots were already present. A key example is the 'nation' of Israel, which from as far back as the 7th century BCE held the powerful belief in a single people in a single land under a single god.

There are perennialists who acknowledge that there is a distinct form of modern nationalism based as it is on a nation state with recognized boundaries, expanded administrative systems, a monopoly of the means of violence, universal education and notions of citizenship and the franchise. Nevertheless, they do insist on a firm mystical link between such modern nationalisms and ancient ethnicity.

Now Jung fits comfortably into all three of these categories, especially given that they all draw on so much material from the unconscious. So, like the *messianists*, Jung sees nationalism arising out of the fact that modern 'man' has lost 'his' soul, making people vulnerable to the seductive call of the nation. Like *primordialists*, Jung sees nationalism driven by ineffable archetypes whose depth cannot be fathomed. Often this is a single archetype, like that of Wotan, which lays down what the unchangeable essence of the movement is. And, like *perennialists*, he considers these archetypes to be ancient, going back 'more than a thousand years'.

Clearly, here, Jung contradicts his own principle of individualism to a great degree. In Jung's view, the nation mediated by the archetype exerts huge influence on the individual, to the extent that the individual becomes a victim of the social structure. 'We who stand outside judge the Germans far too much as if they were responsible agents, but perhaps it would be nearer the truth to regard them also as *victims'* (Jung, 1936/1970, para. 398). For Jung the nation is a powerful 'something else'. It is worth emphasizing that, contrary to his previously quoted mathematical calculations of morality, this has very little to do with the numerical size of the population. By his own telling, it is the level to which religious belief has risen or fallen, the degree to which society holds or abandons its central archetypal symbols, which is the key to nationalism, not the numbers.

Instrumentalism and ethno-symbolism

I now consider the theories of nationalism at the other end of the spectrum to understand where much of the critique has come from against the first group and, therefore of course, also against Jung. *Instrumentalist* writers like Paul Brass argue that cultural and religious identities are often the new products of shifting processes like syncretism, mergers, migration and diaspora or cross-cultural marriages (A. Smith, 1998, p. 153). There is no unchanging primordial essence. In addition, nationalist movements often pursue clear material and political advantages like political independence from colonialism or the economic exclusion of minority groups. It is the skill of political elites that they can weave and blend different ethnic and political elements to catch temporary contexts. Much of this is far from unconscious emotional appeal.

In addition, there are a range of different kinds of nationalism, some arising in older political settings like Europe, others in anti-colonial movements in Africa and Asia and yet others according to the bureaucratic needs of empires, as in China. A whole range of writers emphasize the key differences that arise in ethnic movements compared to the rise of the modern state. Ethnic identity might in itself be ancient, but the nationalism that is built on it is a very different animal.

Ethno-symbolism, as set out by Anthony Smith and John Armstrong, combines the notions of (recent) nationalism and (more ancient) ethnicity by drawing historical threads between them, backwards from nationalism to ethnicity and forwards from ethnicity to nationalism. In this way ethno-symbolism also seems (at first) to bring together the outer poles of nationalism theory, primordialism and perennialism, on the one hand, and instrumentalism, on the other. The keys to these moves lie in the ideas of symbols or myths and group borders. For Smith and Armstrong, symbols and their associated myths exercise an extremely powerful hold over people, far more powerful than is possible from supranational identities like Christian universalism, pan-European union or global humanity.

In addition, ethnic identity is as much about what people believe they are *not* as what they think they *are*. It is at this point that the fluidity of symbols and myths comes into play because they are so powerfully influenced by the time- and place-bound contexts of intergroup conflict. So, for example, the specific parameters of Christianity in medieval times were powerfully shaped by the Crusades against Islam. Also the more recent notion of intersectionality proposes that identities are composed of multiple and shifting elements – religion, language, class, race, gender – depending on circumstance (S. Smith, 2014). This helps us to understand how *some* ethnic identities can be very ancient and *others* much more recent.

How does all this mesh with Jungian sociology? Symbol and myth are, of course, the bread and butter of Jungian theory, but borders and intersectionality are, in Jung's writing on Germany, quite foreign.

Recent sociology on crowds

I now turn to the third aspect of my discussion, that of crowds and mobs. Let us consider the particular energy that emerges from crowds, what Durkheim called 'collective effervescence'. We see this most clearly when an audience applauds a moving performance, or a sports crowd roars their approval, or a congregation is respectfully silent or, famously, a protest march turns into a destructive mob. The mob is significant because in 1896 Gustave le Bon wrote a book entitled *The Crowd: A Study of the Popular Mind*, which became at the time a publishing phenomenon and more than a 100 years later was still fascinating readers (Le Bon, 1896/2001; Reicher, 1996).

Le Bon's main theme can be expressed quite briefly. When individuals join a crowd, their consciousness gets taken over by, and they regress to, an atavistic and primitive racial unconscious that is extremely emotional and volatile. They lose their conscious personality and their control over themselves; they are submerged into a group mind that is irrational, destructive and fickle. And modernity feeds this outcome with its creation of rootless and alienated masses shorn of their religious and community anchors. Le Bon was much influenced by Darwinism, on the one hand, and hypnotism, on the other: Darwinism in the sense that human beings were seen to be descended from primitive animals and this historic past was still lodged not far below the surface in their unconscious; and hypnotism because this therapeutic practice was very much in vogue at this time in European psychology, and thinking about the unconscious was understood by analogy with hypnotism (Ellenberger, 1970, p. 110ff).

In crowd situations, said le Bon, leaders, themselves already hypnotized, can have a profound impact by using quite elementary strategies like the simplification of complex issues, the repetition of stock themes and the affirmation of identity. It is not surprising that both Hitler and Mussolini had read le Bon (Le Bon, 1896/2001; McClelland, 1989; Reicher, 1996).

Problems with le Bon

A first key shortcoming of le Bon's framework is that it removes crowds from their social and ideological context; it casts crowds as having a dynamic quite independent of where individuals come from. So, for example, le Bon seldom asks how crowds get formed in the first place; why people gather at a particular point of time and place; what they bring with them into the gathering; what their concerns, angers and anxieties are that bring them to constitute a crowd – this is before any leader makes his or her appearance (Scott, 1977).

This decontextualizing move follows often from the distance that earlier writers sometimes maintained from the actual experience of crowd action. Coming as they did from the wealthier classes, these writers would not themselves have participated in the flow of crowd action. Consequently, they very often projected their own fears on to crowds; crowds easily became stigmatized as 'mobs' with all the insinuations that go with that label (McClelland, 1989; Chabani Manganyi, 1990).

It is notable with le Bon, first, how rapidly the unconscious can take over and then, how devastating this takeover can be. His first argument arises from the shallow understanding among writers at the time of both the unconscious and 'collective mind'. For le Bon, anything that was not rational and purposeful in human action was automatically unconscious. But sociology has now shown that much social activity is 'unthinking' – habitual and unaware – rather than governed by the unconscious. People in conversation do not consciously rehearse the skills of polite and appropriate dialogue – but that does not mean they are out of control.

The second argument, the devastating consequences of control by the unconscious, is part Darwin and part hypnosis. In evolutionary terms there was, as I have indicated, a belief in an atavistic and barbaric past still lurking in the minds of modern individuals. Crowds were, in this sense, not just a threat to particular political regimes, but also a threat to civilization in general. The dramatic change in behaviour among those under hypnosis was taken at the time to be a predictable model of what happened to crowds, with the hypnotist's role now performed by the crowd leader. Under these circumstances, it was easy to talk of 'possession' (Ellenberger, 1970, see Chap. 3; McClelland, 1989).

But recent research on crowds has not indicated a total loss of control as indicated by le Bon, but rather a taking up of a different set of values and beliefs. Reicher, for example, argues that in modern urban riots participants do not lose control but rather shift the guiding values of their behaviour from a personal to a social identity like class or race. From here it is possible to understand crowd behaviour as quite consciously targeted and shaped. In the 1980 St Paul's riot in Bristol, England, which he analyses in some detail, the quite specific target of crowd displeasure was the police and their vehicles. Other people, vehicles and property were not touched (Reicher, 1984).

Symbolism and crowds

Seen within the framework of the theories of nationalism that I discussed earlier, one might say that le Bon erred in the direction of a primordialist view of crowds, that is, crowds have an inherent tendency to resort to atavistic behaviour and there is one fundamental pattern of behaviour common to all of them – they will turn into mindless mobs. The critique against this form of crowd writing has followed a path similar to that set out in the literature on nationalism, namely, that crowds are much more variable in their behaviour than previously thought, that they act in much more purposeful and rational ways and that there are a great variety of different kinds of crowds.

The social psychology of collective action, under which the topic of crowds has mostly resided, starting in the 1960s with writers like Leon Festinger, Stanley Milgram and P.G. Zimbardo, went through a quite sterile positivist and laboratory-based phase. There were endless experiments to test the linkages of cause and effect, but very little investigation of symbols and meaning or of real-world situations.

More recently in the literature on crowd sociology something quite similar to the ethno-symbolic theory of nationalism has arisen. This is the current of symbolic anthropological theories by authors like Robert Darnton (1984), Clifford Geertz (1973) and Mona Ozouf (1988). In an article entitled, *Reading a Riot*, Darnton argues that understanding a riot is a hermeneutic exercise. It must be interpreted like a piece of text, unravelling the metaphors and images, showing their historical context and tracking cultural associations (Darnton, 1992). In one of his own historical pieces, *The Great Cat Massacre*, he shows how the unruly behaviour of a group of printing shop apprentices in 18th-century Paris revolved around the various meanings attached to cats, the multiple sexual and religious allusions and rituals that came into play. He calls this a case of 'ritual punning', when conventional judicial and church rituals were taken out of context and used for assorted ribald purposes. Far from being manic frenzy, this was an uproarious joke (Darnton, 1984). Darnton is not a Jungian, but this is very close to what good Jungian sociology might be.

Conclusion

The central theme of this chapter has been to elucidate Jung's views on sociology via his written pieces in 1936 and 1946 on the topics of society, German nationalism and the crowd. By placing them within the framework of recent sociological and social psychological writing outside of 'pure' psychology, writing of which Jung was mostly unaware, I have attempted to show where, within the context of this later writing, Jung's views make sense, where they are one-sided and where they are just wrong. Within this context, Jung's views are not so much wrong as just significantly one-sided. Let us reconsider briefly then the three areas I have explored.

On the relationship between individual and society, Jung is not only a strong individualist but, at the same time, contradictorily, also a structuralist. He makes no attempt to reconcile these views. For my purposes, Anthony Giddens's (1984) view that individual and society (or, in other terms, agent and structure) are mutually constitutive is one very fruitful way to achieve this reconciliation.

On the issue of German nationalism, Jung's romantic and archetypal stance led him to an excessively primordialist, messianist and perennialist view. However, these perspectives could be combined with a more pragmatic, contextualized and ethno-symbolist view to achieve a rounded and viable theory. The ethno-symbolist views proposed by John Armstrong and Anthony Smith have already in many ways forged something on the way to a feasible Jungian theory.

Jung's views on the crowd and the mob are perhaps his most extreme sociological writings. They appear at times combined with a quite elitist cynicism about the prospects for humanity. Seemingly, Jung was much influenced by le Bon, but both theoretical and social attitudes to crowds have changed since then. Late 20th-century constitutionalism has, for example, recognized the right of ordinary citizens to public protest. And research from the 1970s onwards has taken a more optimistic view of the actions and rationality of collective action. The work by Robert Darnton and Clifford Geertz are examples of writing that makes fruitful use of images and symbols without falling into notions of 'mass psychosis' (Geertz, 1973; Darnton, 1984).

Acknowledgements

I am grateful for comments and suggestions by Johann Muller and Stephen Bloch.

References

Berger, P.L., & Luckmann, T. (1971). *The social construction of reality: A treatise on the sociology of knowledge.* Penguin.

Bernstein, J. (1992). Beyond the personal: Analytical psychology applied to groups and nations. In R. Papadopoulos (Ed.), *Carl Gustav Jung: Critical assessments (Critical assessments of leading psychologists)*: Vol. IV (pp. 22–37). Routledge.

Bocock, R. (1976). *Freud and modern society: An outline and analysis of Freud's sociology*. Nelson.

Chabani Manganyi, N. (1990). Crowds and their vicissitudes: Psychology and law in a South African court-room. In N. Chabani Manganyi & A. Du Toit (Eds.), *Political violence and the struggle in South Africa* (pp. 287–303). Palgrave Macmillan.

Darnton, R. (1984). *The great cat massacre and other episodes in French cultural history*. Penguin Books.

Darnton, R. (1992, October 22). Reading a riot [Review of the book *The vanishing children of Paris: Rumor and politics before the French Revolution*, by A. Farge & J. Revel]. *New York Review of Books* (44–46). Retrieved from https://www.nybooks.com/articles/1992/10/22/reading-a-riot/

Durkheim, E. (1895/1964). *The rules of sociological method* (8th Ed.). (S. Solovay & J. Mueller, Trans.). Free Press.

Ellenberger, H.F. (1970). *The discovery of the unconscious: The history and evolution of dynamic psychiatry*. Basic Books.

Frisby, D. (2011). *Simmel and since: Essays on Georg Simmel's social theory*. Routledge. Kindle Edition.

Geertz, C. (1973). Notes on the Balinese cockfight. In C. Geertz (Ed.), *The interpretation of cultures: Selected essays by Clifford Geertz* (pp. 412–55). Basic Books.

Giddens, A. (1971). *Capitalism and modern social theory: An analysis of the writings of Marx, Durkheim and Weber*. Cambridge University Press.

Giddens, A. (1984). *The constitution of society*. Polity Press.

Jung, C.G. (1936/1970). Wotan. In H. Read, M. Fordham, G. Adler & W. McGuire (Eds.), *The collected works of C. G. Jung: Vol. 10. Civilization in transition* (pp. 179–93). (R. F. C. Hull, Trans.). Princeton University Press.

Jung, C.G. (1946/1970a). After the catastrophe. In H. Read, M. Fordham, G. Adler & W. McGuire, Eds., *The collected works of C. G. Jung: Vol. 10. Civilization in transition* (pp. 194–217). (R. F. C. Hull, Trans.). Princeton University Press.

Jung, C.G. (1946/1970b). Epilogue to 'Essays on Contemporary Events'. In H. Read, M. Fordham, G. Adler & W. McGuire (Eds.), *The collected works of C. G. Jung: Vol. 10. Civilization in transition* (pp. 227–43). (R. F. C. Hull, Trans.). Princeton University Press.

Jung, C.G. (1946/1970c). The fight with the shadow. In H. Read, M. Fordham, G. Adler & W. McGuire (Eds.), *The collected works of C. G. Jung: Vol. 10. Civilization in transition* (pp. 218–26). (R. F. C. Hull, Trans.). Princeton University Press.

Lasch, C. (1980). *The culture of narcissism: American life in an age of diminishing expectations*. W.W. Norton & Company.

Le Bon, G. (1896/2001). *The crowd: A study of the popular mind*. Batoche Books.

McClelland, J.S. (1989). *The crowd and the mob: From Plato to Canetti*. Unwin Hyman.

Ozouf, M. (1988). *Revolutionary pomp and circumstance: Festivals and the French Revolution*. Harvard University Press.

Reicher, S.D. (1984). The St. Pauls' riot: An explanation of the limits of crowd action in terms of a social identity model? *European Journal of Social Psychology, 14*(1), 1–21.

Reicher, S.D. (1996). 'The Crowd' century: Reconciling practical success with theoretical failure. *British Journal of Social Psychology, 35*(4), 535–53.

Scott, J.C. (1977). *The moral economy of the peasant: Rebellion and subsistence in Southeast Asia.* Yale University Press.

Smith, A. (1998). *Nationalism and modernism: A critical survey of recent theories of nations and nationalism.* Routledge.

Smith, S. (2014). Black feminism and intersectionality. *International Socialist Review, 91.* Retrieved from http://isreview.org/issue/91/black-feminism-and-intersectionality

Chapter 10

Picturing the Sámi and *participation mystique*

Barbara Helen Miller

The Sámi are, for Scandinavia, *Other*, even though they are the long-established population of this region. Experiencing a people as Other implies a certain non-participation, observable in that the Sámi are still viewed by their neighbours with social evolutionary concepts. In particular, the Sámi healer is seen as primitive. How did that happen and how can we rid ourselves of this surely tainted picture? In an attempt to answer this question, I reverse the order of primogenitor on some of our favourite psychoanalytic notions. I observe that the myth in the culture of origin is employed by the local traditional healer in a similar fashion to how Freud and Jung have claimed to use myth *for the first time in the history* in psychoanalysis. My research among Sámi healers attests to the similarity between analytical psychology and their healing practice and to a high level of awareness of what they are doing. To rid psychoanalysis of the tainted picture, I suggest a change in primogeniture for *participation mystique.*

In analytical psychology, we still have Jung's unadjusted use of *participation mystique* that continues to categorise a so-called primitive people while effectively silencing the people for whom this concept carries meaning. We can trace the steps that silence a people as follows: Jung reversed Mauss's original work. For Marcel Mauss, a society did not receive its institutional characters from the individual modalities of its members' personalities; rather the individual psychical structure and psychological formulation was a translation of a sociological structure (see Lévi-Strauss, 1963, pp. 161–3). To see how the culture itself is then silenced, consider Jung's commentary for Paul Radin's *The Trickster: A Study in American Indian Mythology.* The trickster figure reminded Jung of the motifs found in the alchemical figure of Mercurius and carnival clowns in the medieval Church; he, therefore, concluded: 'In his [trickster's] clearest manifestation he is a faithful reflection of an absolutely undifferentiated human consciousness, corresponding to a psyche that has hardly left the animal level' (Jung, 1954/1969b, CW 9i, para. 465). My critique is not massive; I continue to learn and gain psychological insight from Jung's use of *participation mystique* to interpret alchemical

DOI: 10.4324/9781003223481-13

imagery, which speaks of stages of union and disintegration. Jung employs *participation mystique* for the first stage: before any differentiation of oneself from the world, and for the third stage: the discovery of divinity in the world and in oneself. However, as Tatsuhiro Nakajima (2017) has explained, in Jung's theories around the trickster we learn less about the Native American cultural application of trickster and more about the Western intellectual perspectives that inform the theories.

I see the threads of Social Darwinism (used in the late 19th and early 20th centuries to justify political conservatism, imperialism and racism, discouraging intervention and reform) when Jung writes: 'is only a shade more characteristic of the primitive than of the civilized mind', and 'primitive man' demonstrates 'archaic identity'. Even when he additionally acknowledges that 'archaic identity' is fully present in civilised man's development, there is still a clear evolutionary perspective. 'Archaic identity' would be sufficient to express Jung's notion, if he meant that primitive thinking is the initial psychological state of *all* human beings, but he consistently adds 'primitive man' in connection with an existing group, such as his Elgonyi porters in his visit to Africa.

The reflexive turn in anthropology (see Clifford & Marcus, 1986; Geertz, 1990) has tried to address the tendency for ethnocentrisms in ethnographic writing. For example, today, an ethnographer will not write: 'I expected to find xyz, and that is exactly what I found, xyz'. In such writing, the local people being studied are silent; the theory the ethnographer posits is his or her own but applied to a people having a different (their own) theory. How does this problem play out when Jung uses 'primitive man' in his essay 'Archaic Man'? He employs the seeming similarity in the lack of understanding for religious ritual of his Elgonyi porter's greeting of the sun and his Zürich neighbour hiding Easter eggs (Jung, 1931/1968, CW 10, paras. 143–6). In gist, he is saying my Elgonyi porter is living in unreflective archaic identity, just as I expected he would before I made this visit. That Jung finds his neighbour labouring under a similar archaic identity is not poor ethnographically. To assure the sighting of the problem, I offer an example, and for this I stay with the Sámi.

The following story was told to me by an adult named Karen (Miller, 2007, p. 81). As a child, Karen listened to her father repeat a story known in the family. Her father's younger brother was walking home; he had been walking probably for a few days. Coming down one hill he saw in the distance a village. When he arrived, he saw the people were beautiful, friendly and rich. They invited him to sit at the dinner table and to join them in a meal. But he felt that something was not right, and he continued on his way. At some farther distance he turned to check for the village and there was no village. Karen asked her father, 'What would have happened had he eaten the offered food?' Father said, 'Well, he would have been one of them'. Certainly, this is a soft way to say, 'He would have frozen to death'; but Father also provides a lesson in participation: 'in eating together, becoming one of them'.

For Karen and her father there was no doubt. The younger brother, after walking for several days without sleep, was hallucinating. Keep in mind that in this far north region during the summer the sun neither sets nor does it rise during the winter months. I could report even more stories. Even at 12 years old, boys on a fishing trip (without sleep for several days) knew to help one of their comrades home when he became convinced that he needed to herd the (invisible) cows. How did the father's brother *know* to even consider 'it felt not right' during his hallucination and to decide to continue to walk? My hunch is that he had heard similar stories – myths. Hence, even in his 'unconsciousness' he had a guide. What most alerted him, it has been suggested to me, was that the villagers were all so beautiful and rich, a characteristic often mentioned in the myths. These stories are important 'knowledge' for survival in these climes.

Unfortunately, in today's health narratives of the Sámi a common response from local psychiatrists is 'You Sámi people still believe in that kind of shit in these enlightened times?' (Miller, 2015, p. 93). Even if the psychiatrist had read and even appreciated Jung's essay 'Archaic Man' such a reproach might still be made. Jung lived and wrote before the reflexive turn in anthropology. Anthropology's battle to defeat Social Darwinism was available to Jung; however, he did not engage with Franz Boas.

To address Jung's approach, I set out the problems around *participation mystique*. Then I examine the scholarship leading up to Lucien Lévy-Bruhl's evolutionism, which was corrected in anthropology with the work of Franz Boas in the early 20th century. Third, I look at the picturing of the Sami that followed on these early research agendas. Finally, a Sámi healer shares his understanding of *participation mystique*.

C.G. Jung and participation mystique

I take as my starting point a note in Jung's introduction to W.Y. Evans-Wentz's *The Tibetan Book of the Great Liberation* (1954/1969a, CW 11). I wanted a quote that represented Jung's later thinking and a commentary that reflected his discussion of 'Mind' to show fully his position on *participation mystique*:

> Wherever there is a lowering of the conscious level we come across instances of unconscious identity, or what Lévy-Bruhl calls 'participation mystique'.
>
> (para. 817)

Then in the following footnote Jung asks the reader to compare Lévy-Bruhl's *How Natives Think*.

Recently this concept as well as that of the *état prélogigue* have been severely criticized by ethnologists, and moreover Lévy-Bruhl himself began to doubt their validity in the last years of his life. First he cancelled the adjective 'mystique', growing afraid of the term's bad reputation in intellectual circles. It is rather to be regretted that he made such a concession to rationalistic superstition, since 'mystique' is just the right word to characterize the peculiar quality of 'unconscious identity'. There is always something numinous about it. Unconscious identity is a well-known psychological and psychopathological phenomenon (identity with persons, things, functions, roles, positions, creeds, etc.), which is only a shade more characteristic of the primitive than of the civilized mind. Lévy-Bruhl unfortunately having no psychological knowledge was not aware of this fact, and his opponents ignore it.

(note 28)

Has Jung correctly sketched the response of ethnologists to Lévy-Bruhl? No. Certainly *participation mystique* is anthropologist Lévy-Bruhl's brilliant term, brilliant because it so well evokes the experience. Jung's offer 'There is always something numinous about it' is also exemplary. The term is problematic when we try to determine who has the experience. Modern anthropology and ethnology severely criticised Lévy-Bruhl for the implicit evolutionism in his concept of a prelogical mentality of primitive peoples and later has attempted to rescue the notion of psychic unity contained in *participation mystique*. Lévy-Bruhl's error was in characterising this mode of thought as (1) prelogical and (2) associated with only one sort of human being. Current anthropology, taking out these 'errors' in the definition, credits Lévy-Bruhl's characterisation, saying '*participation mystique* is a key aspect of meaning-construction for all people that is also called "embodiment"' (Shore, 1996, p. 183).

In his essay 'Archaic Man' Jung indicates that projection and identification are the primary psychological processes by which *participation mystique* is activated:

These identifications, brought about by projection, create a world in which man is completely contained psychically as well as physically.... For archaic man this distinction does not exist, because psychic happenings are projected so completely that they cannot be distinguished from objective, physical events.

(1931/1968, CW 10, paras. 134–35)

Hence, Robert Segal (2007) points out that for Jung, primitive thinking is the initial psychological state of all human beings, and primitive people think as they do because they live in a state of unconsciousness. Jung continued to use *participation mystique* in Lévy-Bruhl's original sense as a stage of development, a prelogical stage of unity prior to differentiation, that is, a mode that characterises primitive man – even though he had the opportunity to adjust his *participation mystique* notion to align with Segal (2007): (1) *participation mystique* is not prelogical and has nothing to do with primitive thinking in particular; (2) projection has nothing to do with prelogical thinking or even with *participation mystique*.

For psychoanalytic practice, Eric Neumann made the adjustment to *participation mystique* that is in line with current anthropology. By doing so, he successfully resurrected the idea of *participation mystique,* creating distance from the characterisation of primitive forms of thinking toward the idea of *participation mystique* offering a greater availability for a specific type of knowledge (see Winborn, 2014, p. 17). Along this line, Mark Winborn sees an example of *participation mystique* in reverie (as coined by Bion). Reveries are states encountered in the analytic setting that lead to effective communication (pp. 75, 91). These adjustments to the definition are widely available. Still the patterns of projection and identification are seen as the primary psychological processes contributing to *participation mystique*, and *participation mystique* is compared with Melanie Klein's term *projective identification*, where there is unconscious identity between subject and object prior to differentiation (see West, 2014, p. 51). Klein introduced projective identification in 1946 with 'Notes on some schizoid mechanisms':

> [Projection] helps the ego to overcome anxiety by ridding it of danger and badness. Introjections of the good object is also used by the ego as a defense against anxiety … The processes of splitting off parts of the self and projecting them into objects are thus of vital importance for normal development as well as for abnormal object-relations. The effect of introjections on object relations is equally important. The introjections of the good object, first of all the mother's breast, is a precondition for normal development … It comes to form a focal point in the ego and makes for cohesiveness of the ego … I suggest for these processes the term 'projective identification'.
>
> (Klein, 1946, pp. 100, 102)

Jung's use of *participation mystique* and Klein's use of *projective identification* are apparently seen as describing similar phenomena. However, in the adjustments made by Neumann and Winborn (among others), the myth *projective identification* does not fit the myth *participation mystique* as well as that of another myth. That myth explores the primacy of 'being in contact with' rather than the central story of 'getting inside' (see Mitrani, 2001, p. 20). James Grotstein (2000) may have been speaking of something similar when he commented that children are ideally born with a background holding object. That background holding object would likely feel like God. This myth of 'being with' can be seen in the work of Esther Bick (1968) and Joan

Symington (1985). Bick proposes the notion of a psychic skin, which serves to bind together experiences to help an increasingly coherent sense of self. Symington (1985) notes defensive manoeuvres for failures in secure holding experiences and that with early unheld precariousness the baby tightens or constricts muscles (see Mitrani, 2001, p. 23). Hence, the category I propose for *participation mystique* is not 'identifications brought about by projection' but rather a helpful 'being with'.

In my final remarks, I return to 'being with' and to the muscular tightening when there is early unheld precariousness for the baby.

Developments in the field of anthropology

Anthropology is the study of humankind, and ethnology is the study of peoples and nations: in the early formative years of these fields, in Germany of the late 1600s and early 1700s, there was an endeavour to formulate the object of study. The thought was that together with the history of humankind and nations, the object of study was the search for origins. Ethnology also addressed the question of what could qualify to group together a people. The biblical genealogy table in Genesis traces all known peoples back to Noah's three sons. For the Greeks a people (*ethnos*) was primarily defined by its origin and descent, including cultural traditions. The Romans adopted this meaning as *origo* and had concepts *gens*, *populous* and *natio* (Vermeulen, 2015, p. 328).

Gottfried Wilhelm Leibniz (1646–1716), in his linguistic studies pursued between 1679 and 1716, proposed 'that the historic-comparative study of language is the only reliable method of determining ethnic origins and affinities' (Waterman, 1963, p. 28) and that 'a careful study of language was the surest way of reconstructing the prehistorical record of the human race' (as quoted in Vermeulen, 2015, p. 77). His approach of arranging people through language differed from the age-old study of manners and customs and was an alternative to the other often employed method for grouping together a people according to levels or stages of their civilisation (see Vermeulen, 2015, pp. 80, 85). Leibniz was also responding to a mythopoetic conjecture by Swedish historians who argued that the origins of the Germanic nations were in Sweden: Olof Rudbeck, a physician and antiquarian in Uppsala, published his study on 'Scytho-Scandicae' in a three-volume work *Atlantica* (1675–98), trying to prove that Sweden was Atlantis, that Swedish was Adam's original language and that all major nations of Europe had migrated from Sweden. Leibniz refuted what he called this 'Gothic doctrine' as lacking in solid foundation (see Vermeulen, 2015, p. 69).

At this time ethnology was not a field of study, but Leibniz's historical linguistics served as a major incentive for its formation. And 'nations' were not seen as political entities, as is the nation-state that developed after 1800.

Rather nations were groups of people bound by a history and a territory and characterised, for Leibniz, predominantly by their languages.

Gerhard Friedrich Müller, employed by the newly established Imperial Academy of Sciences in St. Petersburg and given numerous assignments by the Tsar and Tsarina for expeditions to map the peoples of their extensive empire, founded ethnography as an academic study in the 1730s and 1740s. Müller agreed with Leibniz: for a nation we look not to 'mores and customs, not food and economic pursuits, and not religion, for all these may be the same in peoples of different tribes and different in peoples of the same tribe. The only foolproof standard is language' (as quoted in Vermeulen, 2015, p. 209). Ethnography was a way of arranging historical material by focusing on peoples rather than on periods (p. 299).

Parallel but related studies combining ethnology and anthropology did not see language as the focus but instead focused on periods (Vermeulen, 2015, p. 445). An example is the Swiss pedagogue Chavanne (writing 1766–87) who built on the 'conjectural' research tradition and the Late Enlightenment theory of stage-like progress. Societies seen as 'savage' and 'civilised' were juxtaposed, he stated, in order to find 'a living image of our ancestors', by studying 'the history of wild peoples' (p. 320). The conjectural tradition and its theory of three or four stages of progress remained influential until the 19th century and stood as the basis of social evolutionism (p. 321). The literature from this 'conjectural' tradition is substantial; most everyone is familiar with Jean-Jacques Rousseau. The Scottish Enlightenment scholar Adam Ferguson gave the following explanation of the principle in 1767:

> It is in their present condition [of Arabic clans and American tribes] that we are to behold, as in a mirror, the features of our own progenitors; and from thence we are to draw our conclusions with respect to the influence of situations, in which, we have reason to believe, our fathers were placed.
>
> (as quoted in Vermeulen, 2015, p. 320)

A third perspective on ethnology was developed by the theologian, philosopher and historian Johann Gottfried Herder (1744–1803) who became influential in Northern and Eastern Europe (Vermeulen, 2015, p. 321). He added to ethnology the subjects 'organic growth', 'national identity' and 'national spirit', revealing the originality of 'folk-life'. Herder understood *folk* to be a natural and organic entity in which humanity expressed itself. For him, people are unfolding towards humanness and should not be judged by classification in a 'stage' (p. 323). Through collecting folk songs and his emphasis on the German language, Herder inspired the Grimm brothers to collect folktales. Franz Boas used Herder's view of people unfolding towards humanity when founding modern anthropology in the United States in the early 1900s (p. 322). Ironically, Herder inadvertently contributed to the rise of nationalism in Europe. He saw the excess that national sentiment could acquire, although his concept of *Humanitat* was meant to transcend the national aspirations of peoples. He also gave a valid warning: 'National glory is a deceiving seducer. When it reaches a certain height, it clasps the head with an iron band. The enclosed sees nothing in the mist but his own picture; he is susceptible to no foreign impressions' (as quoted in Adler, 1994, p. 68).

The three perspectives create pictures

The focus on language did not distort a picture of the Sámi. Leibniz paid attention to Finno-Ugric languages. This language group was fascinating for comparative linguists and Siberianists alike because these languages were geographically so far apart and included Sámi, Finnish, Estonian and Hungarian in Europe and languages in Siberia. Leibniz pointed to the connection between these languages in his 1710 article (see Vermeulen, 2015, p. 66).

The botanist and physician Carl von Linnaeus (1707–78) travelled in 1732 to the Sámi area and gathered flora as well as the Sámi's medicinal use of their flora. The folklorist Stein Mathisen (2015), himself Sámi, while reading Linnaeus's diary of his travel, noted the narrative being constructed. Weaving in the new Linnaean understanding of nature as a system, the Sámi take on the role of nature people in which their life in nature, their diet and their medicine form an ideal that could function as a model for people too used to life in the cities, having been destroyed by so-called civilisation (Mathisen, 2015, pp. 5–8). Essentially Linnaeus tells a version of the myth of the Noble Savage. Back in Europe he occasionally donned Sámi clothes and said he had mastered an unknown medicine originating from a nature people (see Mathisen, 2015, p. 7).

The Norwegian folklorist and philologist Just Knud Qvigstad (1853–1957) was considered one of the most prominent and respected collectors in the 1900s of Sámi folklore. The term used for this field was *lappology*. The lappology of his day owed much to Social Darwinist attitudes. There are still today many Sámi cranial specimens in the major Scandinavian University archives. Employing theories around dissemination that saw cultural borrowing or appropriation radiating out from the locus of origin, Qvigstad scathingly concluded that the Sámi borrowed most of their culture (superstitions, heathen religion and language) from neighbouring people (the neighbouring people being Qvigstad's own group) that, according to Qvigstad, are superior in culture to the Sámi (1932, p. 227).

We can see this in the search for origins. Each nation did not want to be a derivative of its neighbour. However, the claiming of a derivative culture would be possible when studying a people who were not members of the European nation undertaking the study. The Others voice in the studies by

Linnaeus and Qvigstad is not included. The result is an inaccurate telling of the Sámi creation myths; instead, they take the Sámi peoples' material into, in the case of Linnaeus, his own personal creation myth and, in the case of Qvigstad, his own national creation myth.

Sámi perspective

I am, for better or worse, an anthropologist in the line of Boas and Mauss and here present my findings for picturing the Sámi. Note that in the early 20th century, Boasian anthropology drew a clear distinction between the cultural and the biological approaches to the study of humankind, separating the then conflated notions of race and nation. Recent developments in anthropology include, for ethnology, the distinction between emic and etic, which is used for two kinds of field research: *emic*, the view from within the social group, and *etic*, the view from observations of the researched people. When picturing a people there is now clarity about whose view is being presented. For the purpose of this chapter, I limit 'picturing the Sámi' to the Sámi healers' discussion of *participation mystique*.

Two Sámi healers, Nanna and Sigvald, tell me they use *bundle* and *release* and *participation* –what they consider to be effective during healing. Framed in practices they call *naming* (Miller, 2015, pp. 71–82), they speak about the working of projection and identification; so when they say 'participation', we can appreciate that they are aware of the mechanisms of projection and identification. For their practice of naming, the powerful healer knows to correctly diagnose (in analytical psychology this might be interpreted as knowing how to correctly name the archetypal situation). The following is a case I witnessed that employed bundling and participation: a Sami reindeer herder consulted Sigvald, telling him that his herd was not manageable; the deer were running all over the place. Sigvald said, 'Let us bundle our thoughts and see what happens'. The next day the herder phoned Sigvald to report that the herd became manageable overnight.

Among Sámi healers who employ the concept of *participation mystique*, the term does not suggest unconscious identification as in Jung's definition of *participation mystique*. To arrive at such a definition as 'unconscious identification' there would be an impoverishment or factoring out of essential elements that these Sámi healers practice. *Participation mystique* for these Sámi healers includes the activities of play, imagination, aesthetic intuition, semblance and determining, much as I note in Friedrich Schiller's concept for Aesthetic Education (for an exploration of Jung's interpretation on Aesthetic Education, see Bishop [2008, p. 135]).

The Sámi healing activity I consistently have observed is *meeting* and *response*. What is building that I cannot observe (as Sigvald explained, unless I am a part of it) is the path on which one's *values* enter the meeting. Here is Sigvald's experiential understanding of *participation mystique*:

Building up to the moment of truth, is *participation mystique*. With two individual thoughts there comes agreement on 'this is what we want'; 'this is how we understand'. It is a magical moment, it is a building, and it is creative, with the recognition: 'Oh, this is the direction!' [Then touching his head, his chest, his thigh]: Thought is the whole you.

With close attention to Sigvald's sharing, I hope you can sense the profound experience of 'being with' (as mentioned previously, ala Bick, Symington, Grotstein and Mitrani). In addition, you might recognise the 'Something More' than interpretation with 'moments of meeting', as described by Daniel Stern (BCPSG, 2010), that build from dialogue. Sigvald's practice of participation involves the sharing of his own group's stories and myths, which can build cohesion among people and among the various motivational systems in an individual.

Final remarks

Why is all of this so important to me? When, where and how *was* Jung cured of his Social Darwinism? In my story/myth, Jung was cured when he received the correct diagnosis for Westerners' ills from Ochwiay Biano: 'See, how cruel the whites look. Their lips are thin, faces furrowed' (Jung, 1963, p. 247). Jung (in my myth) experienced at that moment the archetype of 'participation', having somatically understood the archetypal pathology (constricted musculature) that is connected to 'participation' or 'being with'. This is my sense for how Ochwiay Biano's diagnosis (could have) hit the mark for Jung, because it tells of the muscular tension that is the result of too little 'being with'. 'Being with' serves to bind together experiences that help form an increasingly coherent sense of self. As Symington (1985) noted, if there is a precarious lack of holding in an infant's environment, defensive manoeuvres will be formed due to the failure in experiencing a secure holding. These defensive manoeuvres will trigger the baby to tighten and constrict their muscles. In a parallel fashion, if this is our experience, how do any of us get unstuck from an outdated defensive reaction, such as Social Darwinism? We remain stuck when we do not tell our own creation myth. And how do we heal? Jung and traditional healers seem to know how to get us to experience our roots, out of which we can grow and thrive.

References

Adler, H. (1994). Johann Gottfried Herders concept of humanity. *Studies in Eighteenth-Century Culture, 23*, 55–74.

Bick, E. (1968). The experience of the skin in early object-relations. *International Journal of Psycho-Analysis, 49*(2–3), 484–486.

Bishop, P. (2008). *Analytical psychology and German classical aesthetics: Goethe, Schiller, and Jung: Vol. I. The development of the personality.* Routledge.

Boston Change Process Study Group (BCPSG). (2010). *Change in psychotherapy: A unifying paradigm.* W.W. Norton & Company.

Clifford, J., & Marcus, G. (1986). *Writing culture: The poetics and politics of ethnography.* University of California Press.

Jung, C.G. (1931/1968). Archaic man. In H. Read, M. Fordham, G. Adler & W. McGuire (Eds.), *The collected works of C.G. Jung: Vol. 10. Civilization in transition* (pp. 50–73). (R. F. C. Hull, Trans.). Princeton University Press.

Jung, C.G. (1954/1969a). Psychological commentary on The Tibetan Book of the Great Liberation. In H. Read, M. Fordham, G. Adler & W. McGuire (Eds.), *The collected works of C. G. Jung: Vol 11. Psychology and religion: East and West* (pp. 475–508). (R. F. C. Hull, Trans.). Princeton University Press.

Jung, C.G. (1954/1969b). On the psychology of the trickster-figure. In H. Read, M. Fordham, G. Adler & W. McGuire (Eds.), *The collected works of C.G. Jung: Vol. 9i. The archetypes and the collective unconscious* (pp. 255–72). (R. F. C. Hull, Trans.). Princeton University Press.

Jung, C.G. (1963). *Memories dreams and reflections.* Fontana.

Geertz, C. (1990). *Works and lives: The anthropologist as author.* Stanford University Press.

Grotstein, J.S. (2000). *Who is the dreamer who dreams the dream? A study of psychic presences.* The Analytic Press.

Klein, M. (1975). Notes on some schizoid mechanisms. *International Journal of Psychoanalysis, 27,* 99–110.

Lévi-Strauss, C. (1963). *Structural anthropology.* (C. Jacobson & B.G. Shoepf, Trans.). Basic Books.

Mathisen, S. (2015). Constituting scholarly versions of a 'Sámi Folk Medicine'. In B.H. Miller (Ed.), *Idioms of Sámi health and healing* (pp. 1–23). The University of Alberta Press.

Miller, B.H. (2007). *Connecting and correcting: A case study of Sámi Healers in Porsanger.* CNWS Publications.

Miller, B.H. (2015). *Idioms of Sámi health and healing.* University of Alberta Press.

Mitrani, J.L. (2001). *Ordinary people and extra-ordinary protections. A post-Kleinian approach to the treatment of primitive mental states.* Taylor & Francis.

Nakajima, T. (2017). Jung and Lévi-Strauss. Unpublished paper presented to 'The Spectre of the Other', Cape Town, South Africa, July 27–30, 2017.

Qvigstad, J. (1932). *Lappische Heilkunde.* Instituttet for Sammenlignende Kulturforskning, Aschehoug & Co.

Schiller, F. (1795/1954). *On the aesthetic education of man.* Yale University Press.

Segal, R. (2007). Jung and Lévy-Bruhl. *Journal of Analytical Psychology, 52*(5), 635–58.

Shore, B. (1996). *Culture in mind: Cognition, culture, and the problem of meaning.* Oxford University Press.

Symington, J. (1985). The survival function of primitive omnipotence. *International Journal of Psycho-Analysis, 66,* 481–488.

Vermeulen, H. (2015). *Before Boas: The genesis of ethnography and ethnology in the German Enlightenment.* University of Nebraska Press.

Waterman, J.T. (1963). The languages of the world: A classification by G.W. Leibniz. In E. Hofacker & L. Dieckmann (Eds.), *Studies in Germanic languages and literatures* (pp. 27–34). Washington University Press.

West, M. (2014). Trauma, *participation mystique*, projective identification and analytic attitude. In M. Winborn (Ed.), *Shared realities, participation mystique and beyond* (pp. 51–69). Fisher King Press.

Winborn, M. (2014). *Shared realities, participation mystique and beyond*. Fisher King Press.

Part III

The mythopoetic Other through film, art and literature

Chapter 11

On being an Other

John Beebe

The philosopher Bernard Williams (1981) introduced the term *moral luck* into philosophy to get his colleagues to consider the unusual opportunities that some people are given to recognize a moral responsibility for their impact on the fate of others even when they cannot discover in themselves any intent either to benefit or to harm them. As an analytical psychologist, I see such opportunities as fortunate in the way that they help us to realize an attitude towards otherness that might otherwise be kept in shadow by the self. I invoke the concept of moral luck here to pay homage to the agency of my mother who, separated from my father by both war and native temperament (she was strongly intuitive, and he was not), used to take me to movies that most parents, including my father, would have deemed me too young to see. These were often dramas of the mystery variety in which the unexpected consequences of innocently intended actions were a frequent subject. In 1945, when my memories of moviegoing begin, the films I saw with my mother were often rather dark and mirrored her own peculiar moral fate. She was an unusually beautiful young woman who frequently became the object of the desire and envy of others, with all the complications that ensued not only for herself but also for those around her. My mother chose the movies we saw, I think, at least in part because of her own narcissistic interest in the opportunities women as interesting to look at as she was could have to grow wiser – if not practically then at least spiritually when given the kinds of life stories Hollywood could provide. In 1945, which also brought the death of Franklin Roosevelt and the dropping of the first atomic bombs over Japan, beautiful people in the movies my mother took me to see were at unusual risk from others they had allowed to get too close.

This was the takeaway of many of the films we saw that year, which happened to be the year I turned six. I consider myself lucky, from the standpoint of my own moral development, to have had this chance to be initiated so young into my potential impact on people whom my upbringing had taught me to consider Other from me. Coming from parents who were quick-minded and good looking, this could have been a blind spot. The movies

DOI: 10.4324/9781003223481-15

I saw with my mother, who looked good enough to have starred in some of them, helped me to realize that grace and beauty do not always protect one from setting evil consequences in motion.

By far the most frightening movie we saw in 1945 was *The Picture of Dorian Gray* directed by Albert Lewin. It featured, as readers of the Oscar Wilde novel from which its scenario was taken will know, a painting of the title character that changed its features, which gave me nightmares for weeks afterwards. The moment that, for me, was most consciously upsetting, however, was not the final shot of the fully metamorphosed portrait rendered through worm-shaped brushstrokes delivered in hideous colours by the surrealist painter Ivan Albright to reveal the actual look of moral decay. That horror may have inspired the nightmares in colour that followed, but to my waking self the indelible memory that gave me such a shock in the theatre the night my mother and I saw the film, was the very black and white first change in the portrait of Dorian, which turned just a few lines in his face in a downward direction, so as to reverse its innocent handsomeness and replace it with an ugly, self-doubting frown. I was instantly horrified that anything like this could await a nice-looking person. My mother's way of helping me recover from the shock was to adopt an unusually handsome young male kitten that we named 'Dorian Gray'. This Dorian never aged during the relatively short time we had him before we had to leave Baltimore in 1946 to join my father in China, where he had been posted after taking part in the US military's occupation of Japan.

But before then, my mother had also taken me to see Otto Preminger's film *Laura*, which had come out in 1944 but was still an attraction through much of 1945. The movie enchanted me with its surprise of seeing Laura herself walk in on the detective investigating her supposed murder. When she unlocks the door to her apartment, she is intruding on what the film historian David Thomson, in his wonderful book *Moments that Made the Movies* (2014, p. 73), calls the 'gloomy rapture' of the detective she rouses from sleep. He has fallen in love with the portrait of Laura that hangs in the apartment. He has even just put a bid on it for the planned auction of Laura's belongings. It was this moment that opened my eyes both to the perils and the possibilities of things that are other than we think they are supposed to be, and to the realization that we are going to have to take responsibility for this aspect of their otherness, no matter how different that makes them from what we imagine we know about ourselves. Seeing the film again recently, I realized that the misery for Laura herself of having been thought dead is that it has initiated her, for the first time, into being an Other. She even has to endure the unspoken disappointment of the sleeping detective, smitten by the portrait of a woman he imagines he will never know, that she isn't only a dream. He is forced to awaken to her curiosity as to what he is doing in her apartment at all. Fortunately, he says, with just a hint of joy in his voice, 'You're alive'. This is the first indication that he can accept that the real Laura could be of any value. Although he will soon suspect her of being the murderer of the misidentified corpse that was found with her face blown off, this part of the story was fortunately lost on me as a child. I was simply delighted by the real Laura. I felt her innocence. I can also see now, with a lifetime of filmgoing behind me, that the real Laura, played by Gene Tierney dressed in a white raincoat, is far more like a 1940's American man's 'girl' than the alluring 'dame' the detective, Mark McPherson, played by Dana Andrews, goes to sleep believing he has fallen for. Tierney's otherness will be familiar to veteran filmgoers: it stems from Gene Tierney's having been cast in a role usually assigned to a socially discredited, dangerous, dark lady in *film noir* and then turning out to not be that kind of person at all. It also seems that her not being that is what instinctively attracts Mark the moment he wakes up and sees her. His liking her not being dark makes him an Other, too, disappointing the standard expectation that a film noir detective always remains cynical. That was, in fact, how he played the early scenes of the film spent with the acid-tongued, effeminate, older newspaper columnist Waldo Lydecker.

Otherness in a variety of senses, from being other than what we expect to being other than what social convention has taught us to disrespect, is the leitmotif of *Laura*. Clifton Webb, who plays Lydecker, asserts a manner that makes viewers think of his character as gay. His stint in the role begins with him taking a bath in front of the obviously contemptuous McPherson. I can still recall my mother in 1945 murmuring in my ear that the character was a 'homosexual', and if memory serves that was probably the first time I heard that particular signifier of my own otherness from her. Later, when Laura walks into her own apartment and finds Mark there uninvited, we realize that, in her eyes, Mark is just as Other to her as Lydecker. Remarkably, her well-developed extraverted feeling has allowed her to accept Others that someone like Mark would rather have seen her shun. For instance, the main supporting players in the film are all played by actors who read easily as what we now call LGBTQ, in accord with their offscreen reputations: Vincent Price as Laura's effete fiancé, Shelby, and Judith Anderson as Laura's deep-voiced wealthy aunt who reasonably enough thinks that Shelby belongs with herself and not Laura, who is too good for him. It is against the backdrop of these three variations on the homosexual theme that Mark and Laura are forced to come to terms with their own otherness as heterosexual people in this particular cinematic world. Their tension with each other is around the different ways they hold awareness of this way of being Other: Mark too much, Laura not enough. The ambivalence on the part of the film as to which is better is part of its moral ambiguity. The director, Otto Preminger, gives us the lucky chance to sort this out decades before this problematic of sexual orientation became something everyone in American society had to contend with. In the first serious effort by an American film critic to consider American film directors from the standpoint of French *auteur* criticism, Andrew Sarris (1963) commented on Preminger's style in a film he made the year after *Laura*:

> There is one unforgettable moment in *Fallen Angel* when all the murder suspects are grouped together in the same shot with a woman who might possibly identify the possible murderer. The meaning of that shot is not apparent at that point in the plot, and thus Preminger cannot be charged with milking the screen for suspense. It is only toward the end of the film that the spectator comes to realize that innocence and guilt are quite relative in Preminger's conception of characters. Only one of the suspects is technically guilty, but no one is entirely innocent. By placing them in the same frame, Preminger places them on the same moral plane. Preminger's camera never takes sides even when the plot does.

(p. 15)

There are many such scenes in *Laura*, in which we realize that both Mark and Laura are forced to confront the shadow side of her idealism and of his cynicism about relationships, both attitudes being dependent upon making and receiving projections that either ignore or overemphasize the difference between self and Other. What is actually Other for Laura and Mark in the movie, as they stare at one another with mutual suspicion, is the possibility of a human relationship that does not depend on that antagonism. That possibility, however, emerges right at the beginning in the confidence one can see in Gene Tierney's face when she insists that Mark McPherson needs to leave her apartment. This Laura is adept at staying serene in the face of the unexpected, and in person she is far less needing of admiration than the pre-murder Laura who must have hung the idealized painting of herself over the mantel of her expensive apartment. That Laura, if we can trust the portrait, seemed to be yearning to be looked at while entertaining the possibility of an even more beautiful future with whomever was admiring her idealized image. She was a little like my own mother, who too frequently arrived in new life adventures simply by steering what people saw in her at some particular moment when she turned on her immense personal charm. My mother was able to count on the fact that people would make room for whatever she brought with her, including of course me, just to get a closer look at her. But to me, my mother brought *Laura*, and with her a cast of characters who were Others. Because they were Laura's friends, it was absolutely okay to get close to them too. Most viewers today enjoy what Eddie Muller, the great aficionado of film noir has called the 'affluent avarice' (2001, p. 46) of Waldo, Ann and Shelby, who seem to have no awareness that the world beyond their charmed circle in Manhattan is at war. What I think

I enjoyed, as a little boy who had been taught to worry about the war all through my infancy, since my father was in the military, was to see Vincent Price and Judith Anderson so enmeshed in a mother-child relationship, and Clifton Webb so narcissistically in love with what he supposed his own face looked like, that they simply couldn't be bothered with the fate of the rest of the world. These were people who, being sophisticated, could live alternative lives permanently innocent of guilt. It was a perverse but satisfying way to learn that one could be Other from most of society and get away with it.

Today I see the way Waldo, Ann and Shelby display the otherness of social indifference in the culture McPherson polices for respectability, more psychoanalytically, as expressions of the character neurosis that threatens the heroine, Laura. As she is presented in Preminger's film, Laura is a perfect candidate for analysis with the most culturally sensitive and feminist psychoanalyst of the 1940s, Karen Horney, whose book *Our Inner Conflicts* was published in 1945 when Horney herself was still in practice in New York City. There we can read about the series of overlapping conflicts Horney uncovered in evolving her understanding of neurotic self-organization beyond the concepts that the first generation of analysts trained by Freud had to offer. Karl Abraham, who was the founder of the Berlin Psychoanalytic Institute, had been her personal analyst, but by 1945, Horney had decided that the key to the treatment of a neurosis was the understanding of the neurotic character structure, or what we nowadays call *neurotic self-organization*, that kept it alive. A neurotic character, she postulated, was constructed as a compromise between a series of conflicts between different ways of defending against being human by 'moving toward people' and 'moving away from people' with equal alacrity, in the attempt to maintain 'an idealized image' through an extreme 'externalization' of the way one lives one's life as an object for the attention and projections of others. One could not describe better the character of Laura as played by Gene Tierney under Preminger's direction.

The central icon of the film is the 'idealized image' of the heroine that we see in the portrait of Laura, which shows exactly what Horney is talking about when she speaks of the 'static quality' of such self-idealization. The tenderness the Laura of the portrait promises is nothing more than an eternal promissory note, exactly the problem of the woman whose own development stands still so that she can receive the projection of the anima from others. This unites the three people closest to her when Mark comes on the scene to interrogate the woman he too has identified, briefly, with this image. Waldo Lydecker, Shelby Carpenter and Ann Treadwell all have different reasons for wanting to appropriate Laura's idealized image for their own uses. For Waldo, she is a work of art to add to his own collection, and for that reason he cannot stand the thought of her living a 'biological' life of her own. For Shelby she is a mimetic rival of the kind that René Girard

(2001) has described. Shelby, handsome in a feminine way, is used to being the beauty that others fall for and support. He hopes to experience this vicariously through Laura's ability to attract clients and benefactors through her success in the advertising business, which has made her both sought after and wealthy while only in her 20s. Ann can argue, in the powder room at the party given for Laura's return from the dead, that Laura is too good for Shelby and that Shelby belongs with her, Ann, because 'I'm not a nice person', which she proves by admitting that she has even thought of killing Laura to get Shelby for herself.

Waldo, Ann and Shelby have together contrived an insidious system of governing the social aspect of Laura's life that is reminiscent of how C.G. Jung saw complexes acting upon the neurotic patient, which is to take possession and set up 'a shadow-government of the ego' of the person (Jung, 1966, CW 16, para. 196). His first-generation Jungian analyst follower Esther Harding, a contemporary of Karen Horney who was also practising in New York in 1945, would have had no difficulty in recognizing Laura as an 'anima woman', one who lives to attract the anima projections of others. Only later would it become clear to Jungian analysts of my own generation, who started their training reading Marie Louise von Franz's book on the *puer aeternus* (1970/1981), the archetype of the eternal boy, that what Harding had called the anima woman is nothing other than a female version of the puer, the *puella aeterna*, a woman who like an eternal girl needs to receive idealizing projections onto herself to feel loved and lovable. To this archetypal vision can be added how the typology of consciousness is constructed through a series of positions of consciousness, starting with a heroic first function, a parental auxiliary function and a third function of consciousness that is structured as a child by the archetype of the puer aeternus or puella aeterna (Beebe, 2017, pp. 19–50). From this perspective, it is possible to say that the anima woman is someone who is able to deploy the puella aeterna in herself manipulatively, inducing others, whether envious women or desirous men, to project the anima onto that part of the way she presents herself.

In Laura's case, this is not entirely easy to see, unless we consider the way the portrait, as in *The Picture of Dorian Gray*, reveals how the seemingly simple and direct Laura is unconsciously succeeding in doing something so shadowy. If we look at the evidence of the character of Laura that Otto Preminger presents in the film, we immediately notice only that the real Laura is mainly someone who steers by extraverted feeling – that she is very good indeed at disarming others through her ability to accept their feeling for her. The only thing that is upsetting about her is that she seems to have no introverted function at all that she can draw upon for reflection. So we have to look a little deeper to see where the mystery of her attraction of projections arises and why she is so important to others. Since *Laura* is a mystery in which this aspect of the central character is at the heart of the intrigue of why someone might wish to kill her, we can follow Ann Ulanov's lead (2009, p. 17) by quoting something Jung said in his *Zarathustra* lectures: 'The mystery always begins in the inferior function, that is the place where new life, regeneration is to be found' (Jung, 1988, p. 954). But as Ulanov also knows, renewal is not the only possibility when the inferior function is accessed. The inferior function is a place where many figures, including shadow figures, can find a foothold, because it is like the psyche's open door (von Franz, 1971/1998). Our lack of development in this area, our tendency to avoid the function of consciousness that is proper to it, because it is too Other from our dominant function, is what leaves that door open to invasions from outside, from those who see an opportunity in what we have left untended.

One of the best scenes in *Laura* is when Waldo Lydecker visits the office Laura has been working in when she first meets him. He simply slips in through a door someone has just walked through and is still therefore open. This is a cinematic way of saying that, in fact, it is through the open door of her inferior function that Waldo Lydecker can steal into Laura's life and direct her career in New York, which is obviously on shaky ground. Seeing that all she has is her well-developed extraverted feeling and a puella extraverted intuitive courage with which to venture forward, it is extremely easy for him to use his native introverted thinking to take over and define her. The scenes in which Lydecker seizes control of Laura's education in New York sophistication were deemed too entirely focused on Laura's personal gentrification for an American audience to want to watch while the war was going on, so they were cut before the film's first release in the fall of 1944 (Eyquem, 2014). These scenes, which are now available as part of the film on DVD, can be off-putting today for an entirely different reason: they show a Laura who is not psychologically alert enough to satisfy contemporary tastes. She seems oblivious to how narcissistic Lydecker is, and how sadistic, even though he had shown this side of himself in their first encounter. Karen Horney would have recognized immediately the fears, the impoverishment of personality, the hopelessness and the sadistic trends in the unconscious of a patient who presented herself as Laura does, but Otto Preminger wisely lets Lydecker, Ann Treadwell and Shelby carry these traits as Laura's significant others. They would not surface as parts of her in most analyses, even today, until many months of uncovering work had been done, but they belong to her shadow. They are part of what is in the dark background of the idealized image of her portrait with its extraverted intuitive promise of a life that has no actual future. Though Mark McPherson puts a bid on it in the movie, the portrait that the movie features is not really even a painting. It was created by studio photographer Frank Polony who took a picture of Gene Tierney that was then lightly airbrushed with paint to make it look like oil on canvas.

Ulanov (2009) has written brilliantly about 'The danger and treasure of the inferior function' in a way that explains the kind of Other that Waldo Lydecker turns out to be for Laura, if we recall that the inferior function is where the animus needs to be able to function in a woman, however difficult that may be for her. In the case of the anima woman, which Laura certainly is, Harding (1952) made clear that being an anima woman is a form of animus possession – what she calls the 'passive' form of it, which depends not (as with obvious 'active' animus possession) on being opinionated and controlling in a pseudo-masculine way, but the opposite, presenting oneself as utterly accepting, indeed inviting the projections of others. Jung had said something like this by suggesting that 'emptiness' could be a woman's great secret (1954/1959, CW 9i, para. 183). In the way Gene Tierney plays Laura, we can see exactly what both Harding and Jung before her were getting at. Without an introverted life that belongs to her, her animus, projected onto Lydecker, can define her entirely in terms of what other people want to do with her. An extraverted feeling type woman like Laura has an introverted thinking animus, but since she is still in her 20s and located in a time of rather strictly divided gender roles, Laura has little consciousness of this part of her personality. Lydecker is thus free to take over and to construct the layers of lies that clothe Laura's neurotic character. Wisely, Preminger decided not to make this explicit in the final version of the script, although earlier versions had Laura allowing Lydecker even to create a fictional personal history for her. In the finished script, Lydecker is only concentrating on the 'weekend Laura died', which suggests that the film is really about the end of a false self, and the healthy beginning, in a woman still young enough to fully realize it, of a true self, someone who as Horney puts it is 'able to love and is not afraid to fight' (1945, p. 239). Laura, by the end of the film, has defined her own desire and knows, in a crucial moment, how to fight for her life with 'spontaneity of feeling' against Lydecker's appropriation of her (pp. 241–42). By allying herself with Mark, an introverted sensation type, she also begins to integrate another kind of introverted consciousness, that of her natural auxiliary function.

At the end of the film, she has learned to leave behind the empty promise depicted in her portrait and return to her naturally superior extraverted feeling self now adequately grounded by an introverted thinking animus of her own that can define who she is and what she wants (the 'spine' of a true self that indicates its 'integrity in depth'). This transformation is synchronistically echoed, after the monothematic haunting score described in the film as 'Laura's favourite song', by the way this developed into an actual song, with a lyric by Johnny Mercer that became a jazz standard (see Furia & Lasser, 2006, pp. 233–34), once the composer, David Raksin, figured out how to adjust the melody into something a human could actually sing. As Raksin later explained:

As I used it in the score, the second half of the melody modulated to become a fifth (five tones) higher than when it began. I did this so that the theme would end in the same key as it started which was G. But this extended the range beyond that of most pop singers, so I altered the two measures that led to the return of the initial phrase so that the melody was reprised in its original position. This produced the result – unprecedented in popular tones, I think, that the song, which began in the key of G ended in C. I had prepared a copy of the theme in this version, which I gave to Mercer.

(Raksin, 2012, Kindle location 924 of 7492)

Something like this musical key change occurs psychologically in the shift from the archetype of *puella aeterna* carrying limitless, but unreal, extraverted intuitive promise to the more humanly heroic extraverted feeling that we see in Laura at the end of the film – and that Gene Tierney seems to have achieved as a hero in a personal sense, creating a life for herself despite the mental illness that emerged 13 years after *Laura* was filmed. As her sympathetic biographer Michelle Vogel has observed, Otto Preminger was interested in the story about a 'girl presumed dead who was actually alive', but 'in some ways Gene was quite the opposite' (2005, p. 94). One sees in her Laura a character who can live beyond her own self-idealization and become real.

What I have learned in the years since first seeing *Laura* about the use of the inferior function to achieve self-identification and release the healthy animus or anima from the spell of projections is a different way of 'being an Other'. This is to realize one's otherness within, a process through which we can discover how to deal with every other Other that we encounter in the course of life in a much more humanly appropriate way. This way is not the same as an uncritical, if admirable, extraverted feeling of the kind Gene Tierney's Laura seems to command. Rather, led by the introverted thinking ability to define herself and her wish to live her own life that has come alive in Laura at the end of the film, it is an ability to discriminate what is true for herself and how she needs to relate to others to understand them in a life-sustaining way.

This was Horney's goal for her patients, as expressed in the final chapter of *Our Neurotic Conflicts*, but it can be fleshed out in Jungian terms, if we accept what Jung's typology can teach about animus development in a woman and anima development in a man. Being an Other to the ego of the patient (Hill, 1998), the healthy anima or animus associated with the inferior function, when made conscious, becomes not an empty slot for someone else to take command of, but a bridge to the self that knows what is good for itself. Getting a glimpse of this was the gift my mother gave me by letting me see this film with her, which both mirrored her own neurosis and what my anima had to do to free itself from identification with her. Seeing it so soon after *The Picture of Dorian Gray* gave my still very unconscious anima hope that it could realize itself in a way other than what the heterosexism of 1945 would have imagined was in store for it. I was not doomed to become what Dana Andrews's Mark encountering Clifton Webb's Waldo at the beginning of the film could only have scorned. The way Gene Tierney's Laura redeemed them both showed me a way to live my own otherness without cynicism or despair. Seeing her do that has served me as a lucky charm.

References

Beebe, J. (2017). *Energies and patterns in psychological type: The reservoir of consciousness*. Routledge.

Eyquem, O. (2014). Laura's cut scenes [Blog post]. *Preminger Films Noir*. Retrieved from http://premingernoir.co/2014/01/23/lauras-cut-scenes/

Furia, P., & Lasser, M. (2006). *America's songs: The stories behind the songs of Broadway, Hollywood, and Tin Pan Alley*. Routledge.

Girard, R. (2001). *I see Satan fall like lightning*. Orbis Books.

Harding, M.E. (1952). Anima and animus: A curtain lecture. *Spring Journal* (annual), 25–43.

Hill, G. (1998). Men, the anima, and the feminine. *San Francisco Jung Institute Library Journal*, *17*(3), 49–62.

Horney, K. (1945). *Our inner conflicts: A constructive theory of neurosis*. W. W. Norton & Co.

Jung, C.G. (1954/1959). Psychological aspects of the mother archetype. In H. Read, M. Fordham, G. Adler & W. McGuire (Eds.), *The collected works of C.G. Jung: Vol. 9i. The archetypes and the collective unconscious.* (R. F. C. Hull, Trans.). Princeton University Press.

Jung, C.G. (1966). Medicine and psychotherapy. In H. Read, M. Fordham, G. Adler & W. McGuire (Eds.), *The collected works of C.G. Jung: Vol. 16. The Practice of Psychotherapy.* (R. F. C. Hull, Trans.). Princeton University Press.

Jung, C.G. (1988) *Nietzsche's Zarathustra: Notes of the seminar given in 1934–1939*. J.J. Jarrett (Ed.). Princeton University Press.

Muller, E. (2001). *Dark city dames: The wicked women of film noir*. Harper Collins.

Raksin, D. (2012). *The bad and the beautiful: My life in a golden age of film music*. Kindle.

Sarris, A. (1963). The American cinema. *Film Culture, 28*, 1–51.

Thomson, D. (2014). *Moments that made the movies*. Thames & Hudson Inc.

Ulanov, A. (2009). The danger and the treasure of the inferior function. *Psychological Perspectives, 52*(1), 9–23.

Vogel, M. (2005). *Gene Tierney: A biography*. McFarland & Co.

von Franz, M-L. (1970/1981). *Puer aeternus*. Sigo Press.

von Franz, M.-L. (1971/1998). The inferior function. In M.-L. von Franz & J. Hillman (Eds.), *Lectures on Jung's typology* (pp. 3–88). Spring Publications.

Williams, B. (1981). *Moral luck*. Cambridge University Press.

Chapter 12

The Freak

In search of Jung's second personality

Stephen Anthony Farah

In this chapter I explore the *Freak*, a term I coined a few years ago, in 2015 to be precise, for an archetypal structure and its location in the Jungian model of the psyche. I am interested in and frame the Freak as the North Star and telos of the individuation process and as the subject's authentic identity. Within the context of the current anthology on the topic of the Other, the Freak, both in the technical sense I employ here and in its common usage, is an obvious and explicit instance of otherness.

I find this framing and coinage of the Self archetype, or second personality, as 'the Freak' to be both valuable and true. *Freak* is a term commonly used to denote a form of otherness and identity at odds with mainstream culture. A freak is an instance of otherness that is typically the target for vilification or, more rarely, idealisation, but in both instances as that which is not me. Unless of course, I understand myself to be a freak, in which case such identification is usually one of self-alienation. In my view it is this freakish dimension of the personality that is most in need of inclusion and integration into the subject's identity. Such potential for inclusion offers a significant opportunity for healing and individuation, if, by *healing*, I mean a remedy to self-alienation and a return to a more integrated, whole and authentic self-identity. Furthermore, building on Jung's aspirational notion of individuation as a more honest and complete form of self-realisation or expression, the Freak is an ideal de-idealised candidate for the trajectory of the individuation process, as I claim and elaborate on in this chapter, prior to the veil of self-illusion cast by inculturation into society.

Individuation as a process of authentic identification

My own engagement with Jungian studies is unusual, an outlier in the broader field – an application of Jungian theory outside of the academy or analysis, at least in the traditional sense. I am, if I may say so, albeit at the

DOI: 10.4324/9781003223481-16

risk of hubris, something of a freak myself within the field. My research and professional focus have been on the application of Jungian studies as a cultural and psychological education or 'psychoeducation'.[1] As a consequence of this educational focus, the orientation of my teaching has been less on pathology and more on individuation or the 'individuation project'. During my research and reflection on the nature of individuation, I have come to conclude that it is concerned with and centres on identity. Therefore, individuation, in my reading of Jungian theory and in my own teaching, is a search for an alternate identity.

To individuate, as Jung characterises it, is to constellate a new identity – in other words, an alternate identity to that of the provisional ego identity of the subject. This new identity is an intrapsychic other that Jung refers to as the 'Self' and regards as the ego's superior. The individuation process then, following Jung, appears to be a 'centring', a movement from a provisional identity closer to the margin or circumference towards the 'Self' that is at the centre of the subject's psyche.[2]

> Struggling against that dangerous trend towards disintegration, there arises out of this same collective unconscious a counteraction, characterized by symbols which point unmistakably to a process of centering. This process creates nothing less than a new center of personality, which the symbols show from the first to be superordinate to the ego and which later proves its superiority empirically. The center cannot therefore be classed with the ego, but must be accorded a higher value. Nor can we continue to give it the name of 'ego', for which reason I have called it the Self ... I have called the process that leads to this experience the 'process of individuation'.
>
> (Jung, 1966b, CW 16, para. 219)

This process of individuation – or let me here introduce an alternate phrasing to help convey my focus on individuation as a search for an identity, the process of *authentic identification* – is not simply a relationship of binaries. It has at a certain level of analysis and modelling a binary character: we speak of the relationship of the conscious and unconscious psyche, of the manifest to the latent and of the ego to the Self;[3] however, in neither the classical Freudian model, nor the Jungian model of the psyche, is it simply a binary structure. Freud offers us a *psychic triptych*, with id, ego and super-ego (*'das Es', 'das Ich'* and *'das Über-Ich'*) (Freud, 1978, p. 19). Jung's model or cartography of the psyche, which is more complex and plural in character than Freud's, focuses on the archetypes or centres of the personality, the persona, ego, shadow, anima-animus and Self (Jung, 1921/1971, CW 6, pp. 165, 412, 425, 460). Other archetypes may be and sometimes are added into this mix, such as the puer-senex and mana, among others (Jung, 1956, CW 5, pp. 392, 127), but the aforementioned – persona, ego, shadow, anima-animus and

Self – are the primary and axial centres of the personality upon which Jungian theory and analysis tends to focus.

Each of these archetypes in the universal subject or complexes in the individual subject (Jung, 1966a, CW 7, pp. 84, 116, 187, 196) constitute, at least in my own view, a distinct identity. The psyche then has this plural character with a multiplicity of potential identities with which the subject may identify, adopt or constellate (Samuels, 1989). As such, the search for authentic, or at least alternate, identification to the default provisional identity has multiple options and potential coordinates. Each of these identities has an important functional role in the totality of the subject's psychological economy. The universality of this archetypal structure speaks to its evolutionary character and value.

Psychological identity or subjective identification then is not typically static within the framework of these structural archetypes or centres of the personality. The subject will move between and adopt these alternate identities, or elements of them, within the dynamics of their social interactions and environmental demands.[4] Psychological maturation or analysis will also facilitate a gradual movement, and arguably a progression, of the subject's identity from one of these centres or archetypes to another. A hypothetical subject or analysand may arrive at analysis heavily identified with her persona, for example, and, during the analysis, on becoming aware of elements of her shadow, the coordinates and character of her identity may shift. I suggest that such a shift in identification is central to the project of Jungian analysis to the degree it retains fidelity to the ethical imperative of individuation.[5]

This individuation process then follows a *telos* that entails a subjective reorientation of identity. Such reorientation involves a realisation that I, the subject, am not exclusively or even essentially who I have come to believe myself to be. Such acknowledgement creates the possibility of opening to and ultimately creating a fusion of hermeneutic horizons[6] with other alternate intrapsychic and interpersonal perspectives. It is a loosening of single-minded fidelity to entrenched perspectives and prejudices.

The symbolisation of the Self archetype or the second personality as the 'Freak'

I return now to the earlier framing of the individuation process as being the opening of a discourse between the ego and the Self archetype (Jung, 1966a, CW 7, pp. 173–87). Bearing in mind that the Self archetype holds within its ambit the totality of the psyche, hence being simultaneously single and multiple,[7] I have found it useful in my own work to adopt the term the *Freak* as a useful alternate symbolisation and signification for the 'Self archetype'. I do not intend by the adoption of this technical neologism to replace the original and existing terminology, which is essential for keeping in mind

Jung's theory and psychological cartography. This alternate signification, and the psychic modelling I have developed based on and in tandem with this idea, should be seen and regarded as arising from and resting on the existing classical Jungian framework. I would be surprised if this alternate signifying strategy gains much traction in a field that tends towards theoretical conservatism, classicism and, somewhat counterintuitively, normativism. Nevertheless, the idea has remained valuable to me and in my teaching since its coining in 2015, and so the publication of this idea and model in this chapter at this time seems appropriate.

The inspiration for this alternate formulation of Jung's second personality (Jung, 1961/1989, pp. 88–89)[8] or the Self archetype came to me, in part at least, from a remark made by Johann Mynhardt, a student of mine at the time and son of the South African actor and raconteur Patrick Mynhardt, during a lecture I gave in Cape Town, South Africa, in 2015. The remark referred to the subject's personality 'pre-wound'; by this term *wound* I understood Mynhardt to be referring to the *primal wound*. The idea of the primal wound is best articulated in psychoanalytic theory by Freud's depiction of the subject's castration at the hands of the primal father (Freud, 1909, vol. IX, pp. 215–17; vol. X, pp. 5–149). This remark and idea led me to meditate on the nature or essence of the personality in this pre-wounded or pre-fallen state – in other words, the idea of an immaculate or archetypal identity that exists within the totality of the subject's psyche.

In my reflections on the idea, I have come to believe that this personality is 'immaculate'. It exists in the Platonic realm of ideas or in the Kantian *noumenal*, outside of space and time. In a certain sense it is the archetype of the personality. Archetype, not in the sense of a universal, but rather in the sense of the unmanifest, immaculate and ideational rather than empirical. It is the possibility of the subject's existence, juxtaposed against the actuality of their existence. This idea is prefigured by Fordham's 'original' or 'primary self':

> I take [the primary self] to represent a state in which there is no past and no future, though it is present like a point which has position but no magnitude. It had no desires, no memory, no images but out of it by transformation all of these can deintegrate. There is no consciousness and no unconsciousness – it is a pregnant absence.
>
> (Fordham, 1985, p. 33)

The relationship of this primary, archetypal or immaculate self to the empirical self is analogous in the Jungian conceptual framework to the relationship of the archetype to the complex. In comparing this to existing Jungian theory, besides Fordham's 'primary self', I would say the closest idea to my idea of the Freak is the idea of Jung's 'second personality'. I like Mark Saban's elaboration on this, which is closer to my own model than the Self archetype as elaborated by Jung. Jung's model seems more like a characterisation of the totality of the psyche than a second personality. That said, I think the lines blur in distinguishing the second personality and the Self archetype, in part due to Jung's failure to elaborate this second personality directly and explicitly in his later psychological writing. Rather, Jung might be seen as being inspired by the idea of the second personality in the development of many of his key ideas, including his characterisation of the unconscious, individuation and confrontation of opposites, among others (Saban, 2019).

A distinction I want to highlight, among others I will deal with in turn, between my idea of the Freak and the Self archetype, is that I see the Freak as constituting a definite and distinct point within the model of the psyche, rather than being characterisable as the psyche in toto. This distinction is significant in that I don't conceive of the Freak as the archetype of psychic wholeness, in line with Jung's characterisation of the Self archetype, 'as an empirical concept, the self designates the whole range of psychic phenomena in man. It expresses the unity of the personality as a whole' (Jung, 1921/1971, CW 6, p. 460). Rather, and in contrast, the Freak, a single member or coordinate within the whole psyche, needs to necessarily work in tandem with other elements of the psyche. In this sense, the Freak is closer to Jung's idea of the second personality (Jung, 1961/1989; Saban, 2019) and Fordham's original or primary self.

Who or what is the Freak?

The Freak, or more precisely the *Real Freak*, as opposed to the *False Freak*,[9] is the subject's personality as it exists in *potentia*, prior to the subject being born. It is the identity of the subject *a priori* to its existence in the world. In other words, it is a non-empirical and conceptual abstraction of the subject's identity that we can infer from the subject's empirical identity. At least this is how we are obliged to view it from a conscious phenomenological perceptive. The Freak shares this empirically idiosyncratic character with the foundational idea of the unconscious in psychoanalysis. The existence of these phenomena – the Freak and the 'psychoanalytic unconscious' – although conceptually a priori to empirical consciousness, are only arrived at *a posteriori*. This obvious similarity between the Freak and the psychoanalytic unconscious acknowledged, the issue of precedence and primacy is a deeper one with respect to the Freak. Although in the model I present here it appears primary, this primacy is best and most accurately viewed as a modelling and pedological technique. Whether ontologically its existence precedes or is independent of the empirical ego is a more complex question. Possibly an alternate space-time perspective might see the Real Freak as having empirical and substantive existence, but that is beyond the scope of my theory and this chapter. Another way of putting this would be to say the Freak is an idea or an archetype rather than *a-thing-in-the-world*. The Freak is the archetype of the subject.

The Freak exists beyond the phenomenological experience of space and time. It is the a priori possibility of the subject's personality prior to her entry into the coordinates and developmental influences of her empirical life. The Freak has not been subjected to the alchemical process of being alive and of living in this world, conditioned by Freud's reality principle, at least not the 'Real Freak'. The 'False Freak', which I will come to in due course, has indeed lived in the world and been conditioned by it. The Freak then is the subject's idiosyncratic and individual personality. It is what is most individual, personal and authentic about the subject. Because the Freak is not of this world, it is a 'Freak'; it is uneducated, uncivilised, uncultured and unmodernised. The Freak could not exist in the world without the ego. As Freud tells us, the ego is conditioned by the reality principle (Freud, 1914–16/1975, vol. XIV, pp. 117–40), which, as George Bernard Shaw puts it, is 'able to choose the line of greatest advantage' (1903, p. 134).

The Freak is intrinsically and essentially idiosyncratic, existing, as it were, prior to and beyond the conditioning coordinates and milieu of the normative. This is an important and defining characteristic of the concept, as signified by the name I have adopted – the Freak. This speaks in tandem with and echoes Jung's idea of individuation as an antidote to totalitarianism. The Freaks in society would, I believe, be less amenable and influenced by prevailing collective ideology.

This relationship of the Freak – or, more broadly in psychoanalysis, the unconscious – and the ego is a cornerstone of Jungian theory and thinking. It is a relationship of interdependence, wherein, although challenging, each requires and benefits from the other. To put this another way, Freaks mediated and guided by ego consciousness are the 'geniuses' we so admire, and Freaks unmediated by ego consciousness are effectively insane and typically casualties of a social structure they cannot navigate – navigating the world being the province of the ego-persona axis.

The developmental role and location of the Freak in the personality

The diagram in Figure 12.1 illustrates the following:
  I. The distinction between and location of the Real and False Freak(s).
 II. The Real Freak is necessarily mediated for the subject through the False Freak.
III. The ego is always necessarily in discourse with the False Freak.
 IV. The Real Freak exists in the realm of the noumenal, and its existence and character can only be inferred, never known directly.
  V. The Real Freak is a conceptualisation of an idealised or immaculate spirit or archetype of the individual's identity prior to it being ensouled in the body and in the world.
 VI. The False Freak comes into existence at the location of the Primary (or Primal) Wound.

MODEL AND LOCATION OF THE FREAK IN THE INDIVIDUAL'S PSYCHIC STRUCTURE

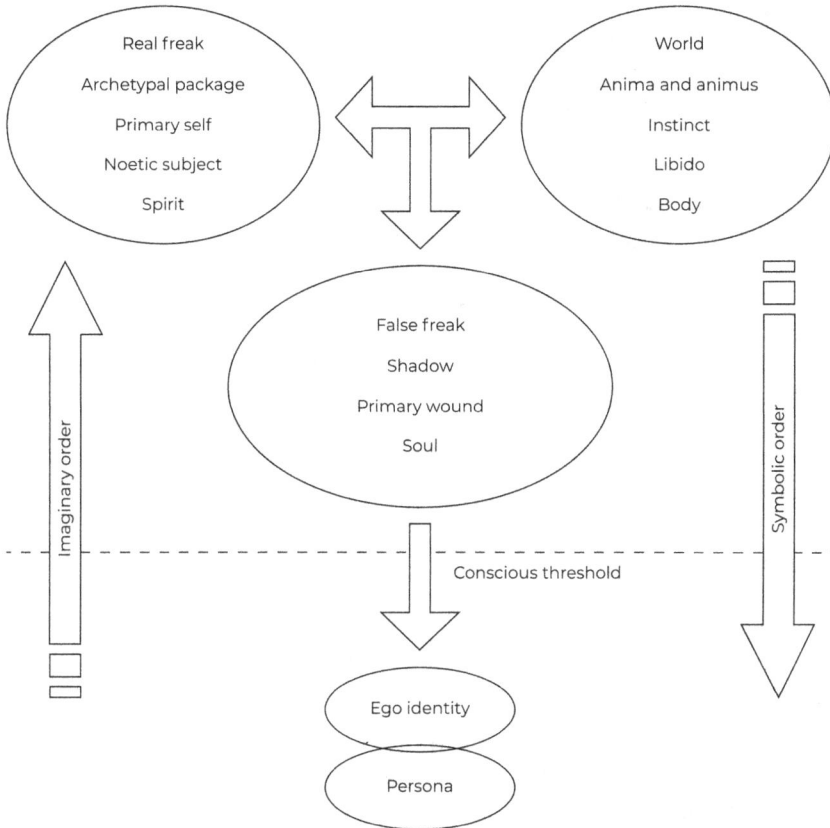

Figure 12.1 Model and location of the Freak in the individual's psychic structure (© Centre of Applied Jungian Studies, 2015).

The *Real Freak* is an abstraction, an idea of the immaculate identity of the subject. Although possibly an imperfect characterisation, the Real Freak is, in effect, the archetype of the individual subject. Practically, this stands as a type of transcendent North Star towards which individuation aims – always beyond herself – or around which it circumambulates, depending on one's perspective of individuation.

The *False Freak* or Jungian *shadow* is what emerges when the Real Freak enters the empirical world. The Real Freak exists only in the realm of the archetypal or Kantian noumenal. As such, it must, of necessity, suffer a type of distortion that the particular always displays when seen through the lens of the universal. To this distortion of the archetypal by the empirical is added the inevitable fall and developmental wounding of the subject, so well documented in psychoanalytic literature. This incarnation of the archetypal

Real Freak into the empirical world, with its intrinsic limitations and the developmental suffering of the subject, gives rise to the False Freak. In the spirit of integrative thinking, I could compare the Real and False Freaks, in esoteric terms, to the guardians of the upper and lower thresholds, respectively (Steiner, 1973). There is also a conceptual comparison between the Real Freak and the Lacanian noetic subject (Fink, 1996).

The empirical subject or ego can only enter direct dialogue with the False Freak or shadow, and this is the psychoanalytic discourse proper. This discourse, notwithstanding the signifier I have adopted of 'False Freak', is, as is well known in Jungian practice, fertile. It is the classical gateway to individuation. In this sense then the False Freak is not so much false as provisional; it acts as a symbolisation of the Real Freak in the world. Having acknowledged this idiosyncratic and arguably problematic signifier of 'false', for now, at least, I choose to continue its adoption. I find the contrast between 'real' and 'false' useful in alerting the subject to the fact that the Real Freak must remain forever behind the veil of the actual, and any identity arrived at in the individuation process should be regarded as not only provisional but also suspect.

The Freak in myth, film and psyche

Mythologically, the exemplar of the Freak can be seen in the defining myth for Western culture, the myth of Christ and the 'Mystery of Golgotha' (Steiner, 2006). We can view the person Jesus of Nazareth and the Christ as distinct psychic centres and, even, identities.[10] The Christ was Jesus of Nazareth's Freak. We can view Jesus's life and ministry as a gradual movement toward and incarnation of his Freak. The 'Mystery of Golgotha', the crucifixion and then resurrection of and incarnation of the Christ, is the moment of the incarnation of Christ (the Freak) into the body of Jesus and into this world. The crucifixion metaphor is also not without value in characterising the sacrifice of the subject's ego identity on the cross of individuation and in service to the Self.

In film, my one of my favourite examples of the Freak is from *Being There*, the 1970 classic starring Peter Sellers in his final role as the inimitable 'Chauncy Gardiner'.[11] Chauncy or Chance embodies the holy fool and navigates the world in a state of grace. He makes a profound impact on those he encounters, ultimately influencing national policy at the highest level. He does this through sharing observations about gardening that are treated as allegories by the businessmen and politicians he encounters on his journey. His miraculous status is confirmed in the final scene of the film where he literally walks on water, a rather obvious allusion to his Christ-like status.

Being There is such an illustrative example of the Freak because this is so obviously and unambiguously what Chance is. The film has an overtly mythological character where chance, guided by the screenplay writer Jerzy

Kosiński's hand, stands in for the normal ego function and allows Chance to function in the world in an egoless state of grace. Chance's world is seen and mediated as though it were a TV show, to the extent that when encountering an unpleasant scene, he attempts to change the channel. His grip on the reality of the world is tenuous at best. Despite these challenges to normal existence and function, Chance embodies the charisma of innocence and zen-like simplicity where the garden is his reference for the cosmos. He exists in an immaculate and uncompromised form. These characteristics make him fascinating and persuasive to the people he encounters throughout the story, who have been castrated and corrupted by the world, and this allows him to introduce a redemptive motif into their lives and, by extension, into the world.

One of the archetypal motifs in dreams and dream analysis is of free flight, in which the dream subject can defy the laws of gravity and fly as though she were a bird or possessed some supernatural power of flight.[12] It is, I claim, the Freak that is flying in the subject's dream. In the dream space the subject's Freak exists in the *unus mundus* (Jung, 1963/1970, CW 14, p. 537), where there is no barrier to the realisation of her desires. Whereas, as we all know only too well, in the empirical space-time world of the daytime, gratification is obstructed, delayed and necessarily mediated, and any impulse from the Freak must be negotiated by the ego.

The Freak as other

A 'freak' signifies a marginalised and rejected personality.[13] Freaks exists in tension with, and arguably compensate, the normative centre. The freak has a set of values, motivation, qualities or circumstances that, viewed from the outside, make her appear alien, frightening and often repulsive. In adopting this term, I am attempting to radically challenge the prevailing normative ethos of the subject's ego identity and orient the subject towards an alternate self and unconscious centre of identity in a fashion facilitating and preparing the subject for radical change. The Freak is precisely that which the subject cannot conceive of being or only imagines she might be in her nightmares and or morbid fantasies. The freak and the Freak, as I employ the terms here, constitute a type of apophatic centre of identity that allows individuation to be oriented towards an ever-moving reference point.

In my role teaching Jungian studies as a school of psychoeducation, I have become aware of a certain reactionary normative and conservatist ideology in many of my students.[14] More specifically and relevantly, I have noted that this reactionist ideology is projected onto the aspirations of individuation, consciousness and the Self archetype. Individuation, seen through this ideological lens, is then framed as a movement to ever greater heights of normative realisation. To the extent the subject falls prey to this ideological orientation, she has failed to grasp the essence of individuation.

Naturally, the Jungian myth of C.G. Jung as, himself, somewhat of an icon of the normative adds to the unhelpful perception. The idea then of naming and regarding the second personality as a Freak is an attempt, in part, to rehabilitate this reactionary stance that is, at least as I understand it, antithetical to what individuation is or may be as an aspirational ethic. And to liberate the individuating subject from the tyranny of normativity.

A final thought by way of conclusion. Names change their cultural meaning and value over time. It would not have been appropriate for Jung to have adopted such a naming protocol, or its historical equivalent, in the development of analytical psychology. Neither would a naming protocol, such as I am suggesting here, work outside of the existing Jungian model and lexicon. It is only as seen in tandem, contrast and, possibly, complementarity, with the prevailing naming and conceptual framework that this name for the second personality becomes meaningful and has, or at least so I am arguing, some virtue.

Notes

1 This specific term *psychoeducation* was first used in reference to the work I am involved in at the Centre for Applied Jungian Studies by Professor Andrew Samuels, at the first public presentation of this paper in 2017 at the International Association of Jungian Studies conference 'The Spectre of the Other in Jungian Studies' in Cape Town, South Africa.
2 Or, somewhat paradoxically, it might be thought of as both the centre and the whole.
3 'Two souls, alas, dwell in my breast', from Goethe's *Faust,* was the inspiration for Mark Saban's *'Two Souls Alas': Jung's Two Personalities and the Making of Analytical Psychology* (2019).
4 I am indebted to and my thinking has been influenced by the work of Carol Rovane and personal communications from her while a visiting lecturer in the philosophy department at the University of the Witwatersrand in 2012.
5 In this respect I am persuaded by and share the belief expressed by Mark Saban in his Jungian and post-Jungian Clinical Concepts lecture given in 2020 that individuation is the central tenant of Jungian theory and analysis, which underpins and synthesises the body of Jung's work.
6 *'Horizontverschmelzung',* in Hans-Georg Gadamer (2013).
7 The psychoanalytic model of the plurality of the psyche or soul finds precedent in Plato's views of the soul in *Phaedo* and *The Republic.*
8 The idea of the two personalities is extensively explored in *'Two Souls Alas': Jung's Two Personalities and the Making of Analytical Psychology,* by Mark Saban (2019).
9 I elaborate this distinction in the next section. Throughout this paper I use the terms *Freak* and *Real Freak* interchangeably. Whenever I am referring to the *False Freak,* I will denote it accordingly.
10 'Martha answered, "Yes, Lord. I believe that you are the Messiah, the Son of God. You are the one who was coming to the world"' (John 11:27).
11 Actually 'Chance … the gardener', but heard and adapted by those he encounters on his journey to 'Chauncy Gardiner'.

12 In my own dream life and mythology this occurs as though the air were like water, and I am able to take giant leaps and tread the water-air for extended periods of time and cover great distances in this fashion.
13 See Merriam-Webster, s.v. 'Freak', https://www.merriam-webster.com/dictionary/freak, where the definition ranges from 'a sudden and odd or seemingly pointless idea or turn of the mind', to 'a seemingly capricious action or event', to 'a whimsical quality', to 'one that is markedly unusual or abnormal', whether animal or person with a 'physical oddity ... sexual deviate ...' or 'who uses an illicit drug', to a hippie or 'ardent enthusiast', a person obsessed, to 'an atypical postage stamp ... or unique event in the manufacturing process...'
14 A remark along these lines was made several years ago on the International Association of Jungian Studies listserv by the Australian Jungian scholar and author David Tacey, specifically with reference to his encounters with 'Jungians' on his visit to South Africa. He found them to be politically conservative. I am South African and prior to moving in 2020 to online education, much of my teaching was in South Africa, so one might speculate that my observation and analysis is somewhat localised. Nevertheless, my impression is that this type of reactionary ideology is, although not ubiquitous in the Jungian world – as the current anthology speaks to – certainly present.

References

Ashbey, H. (Director). (1979). *Being There* [Film]. Warner Bros.

Colman, A. (2008). *A dictionary of psychology.* Oxford University Press.

Fink, B. (1996). *The Lacanian subject: Between language and jouissance.* Princeton University Press.

Fordham, M. (1958). Individuation and ego development. *Journal of Analytical Psychology, 3,* 115–30.

Fordham, M. (1985). *Explorations into the Self.* Routledge.

Freud, S. (1961). *The standard edition of the complete psychological works of Sigmund Freud: Vol. XIX (1923–26). The ego and the id and other works.* James Strachey (trans.). Hogarth Press.

Freud, S. (1959). On the sexual theories of children. *The standard edition of the complete psychological works of Sigmund Freud: Vol. IX. Jensen's 'Gradiva' and other works (1906–1909).* (James Strachey, trans.). Hogarth Press.

Freud, S. (1964). Analysis of a phobia in a five-year-old boy. *The standard edition of the complete psychological works of Sigmund Freud: Vol. X. The cases of 'Little Hans' and the 'rat man' (1909).* (James Strachey, trans.). Hogarth Press. (Original published in 1909.)

Freud, S. (1957). Instincts and their vicissitudes. *The standard edition of the complete psychological works of Sigmund Freud: Vol. XIV. On the history of the psycho-analytic movement, papers on meta-psychology and other works (1914–1916).* (James Strachey, trans.). Hogarth Press.

Gadamer, H.-G. (2013). *Truth and method* (2nd edition). (J. Weinsheimer & D.G. Marshall, trans.). Bloomsbury Academic.

Jung, C.G. (1921/1971). *The collected works of C. G. Jung: Vol. 6. Psychological types.* (H. Read, M. Fordham, G. Adler & W. McGuire, Eds.) (R. F. C. Hull, trans.). Routledge.

Jung, C.G. (1956). *The collected works of C. G. Jung: Vol. 5. Symbols of transformation.* (H. Read, M. Fordham, G. Adler & W. McGuire, Eds.) (R. F. C. Hull, trans.). Routledge.

Jung, C.G. (1961/1989). *Memories, dreams, reflections.* (A. Jaffe, Ed.). (R. Winston & C. Winston, Trans.). Random House.

Jung, C.G. (1963/1970). *The collected works of C. G. Jung: Vol. 14. Mysterium Coniunctionis.* (H. Read, M. Fordham, G. Adler & W. McGuire, Eds.) (R. F. C. Hull, trans.). Princeton University Press.

Jung, C.G. (1966a). *The collected works of C. G. Jung: Vol. 7. Two essays on analytical psychology.* (H. Read, M. Fordham, G. Adler & W. McGuire, Eds.) (R. F. C. Hull, trans.). Routledge.

Jung, C.G. (1966b). *The collected works of C. G. Jung: Vol. 16. The practice of psychotherapy.* (H. Read, M. Fordham, G. Adler & W. McGuire, Eds.) (R. F. C. Hull, trans.). Routledge.

Lorenz, H. (2009). Ancient theories of soul. In Edward N. Zalta (Ed.), *The Stanford encyclopaedia of philosophy* (Summer Edition). https://plato.stanford.edu/archives/sum2009/entries/ancient-soul/

Rovane, C. (1998). *The bounds of agency: An essay in revisionary metaphysics.* Princeton University Press.

Saban, M. (2019). *The Zurich Lecture Series: Vol 2. 'Two Souls Alas': Jung's two personalities and the making of analytical psychology.* Chiron Publications.

Samuels, A. (2015). *The plural psyche: Personality, morality and the father.* Routledge.

Shaw, G.B. (1903). *Man and superman: A comedy and a philosophy.* Brentano.

Steiner, R. (1973). *The guardian of the threshold – soul events in dramatic scenes.* Steiner Book Center.

Steiner, R. (2006). *Approaching the mystery of Golgotha.* Steiner Books.

The Holy Bible, New King James Version. 1982. HarperCollins.

Urban, E. 2015. A study of Michael Fordham's model of development: An integration of observation, research and clinical work. (Doctoral Dissertation, University of East London). Tavistock and Portman NHS Foundation Trust. https://doi.org/10.15123/PUB.5370

Chapter 13

ONE PIECE

Diversity and borderlessness

Konoyu Nakamura

Japanese anime and Jungian psychology

According to Frederik Schodt, who introduced Japanese *manga* into the United States, 'Japanese people have had a long love affair with art (especially monochrome line drawing) that is fantastic, humorous, erotic, and sometimes violent' (1996, pp. 21–22). Japanese *anime* appear in a variety of genres, including *manga* (Japanese comic books and graphic novels), films, TV series, computer games and music. Since the 1970s, they have become extraordinarily popular. Initially accepted by young, enthusiastic fans called *otaku* as part of a cool subculture (see Macias & Mochiyama, 2006), anime spread rapidly throughout Asia and Europe in the 1980s (I. Nakamura, 2006, p. 31). By 2002, as Ikumi Nakamura points out, 60 per cent of TV anime around the world were made in Japan, and in Europe the figure was 80 per cent (p. 30). Clearly, Japanese anime has become mainstream in the West, leading to innumerable studies in the fields of art, media theory, sociology, history, anthropology, psychoanalysis and psychology. As Susan Napier attests, *anime* are 'worthy of being taken seriously, both sociologically and aesthetically' (2001/2005, p. 4).

Jung, of course, was not exposed to anime; however, I believe it constitutes prime material to be analysed and interpreted in a Jungian manner.

> The essential thing, psychologically, is that in dreams, fantasies and other exceptional states of mind the most far-fetched mythological motifs and symbols can appear autochthonously at any time, often, apparently, as the result of particular influences, traditions, and excitations working on the individual, but more often without any sign of them. These 'primordial images', or 'archetypes', as I have called them, belong to the basic stock of the unconscious psyche and cannot be explained as personal acquisitions. Together they make up that psychic stratum which I have called the collective unconscious.
>
> (Jung, 1929/1969, CW 8, para. 229)

DOI: 10.4324/9781003223481-17

As Schodt has said of *anime*, 'Viewed in their totality, the phenomenal number of stories produced is like the constant chatter of the collective unconscious, an articulation of the dream world' (Schodt, 1996, p. 31). Accordingly, I have been exploring archetypal images in popular Japanese *anime* and relating them to social issues, focusing on *Star Blazers* (K. Nakamura, 2017a) and *Sailor Moon* (K. Nakamura, 2015, 2016).

In 2017, I took up another popular Japanese anime, *ONE PIECE,* in my presentation at the International Association of Jungian Studies (IAJS) conference in South Africa. *ONE PIECE*, by Eiichiro Oda (2009, 2010a, 2010b, 2010c), is a series that includes comics, films and TV programmes. It debuted in 1997, written mainly for boys, and is now up to volume 86. It is one of the best-selling comics in the world (Hayami, 2013). The story is a fantastic sea adventure. The protagonist is a 17-year-old named *Luffy* who journeys with his friends, called 'the team of straw', in search of a legendary treasure, the titular *ONE PIECE*. Luffy aims to be the king of pirates by overcoming many difficulties. Many critiques and papers have been written about it in Japan (Hirai, 2010; Suzuki, 2011; Hayashi & Takada, 2015). In the presentation, I explored Japanese traditions that reflected the collective consciousness, in particular, a code of chivalry called *Ninkyodo*. Also, I discussed the protagonist, Luffy, in terms of a child archetype, the *puer aeternus,* and why pirates, who are clearly Others, outside of social and cultural norms, are so attractive to young people (Nakamura, 2017b).

In this chapter, I focus on a feature of 'the team of straw' as an individual. Members of the team are *Roronoa Zolo* (a swordsman), *Usopp* (an expert with a slingshot), *Nami* (a navigator), *Sanji* (a cook), *Tony Tony Chopper* (a ship's doctor), *Nico Robin* (a female archaeologist), *Franky* (a ship's carpenter) and *Brook* (a musician). Here, I discuss the 'variety and differences' (Samuels, 1989/2016) that these characters represent not only in terms of the differentiation of an individual but also in relation to the diversity represented by the cultural and national borderlessness that our societies face today.

Diversity

Diversity is originally a technical term from biology. Later it was introduced in the labour market in the United States and other countries that included various races and ethnicities, where employment is often connected to immigration and human rights. Marilyn Loden and Judy Rosener define the 'primary dimensions of diversity as those immutable human differences that are inborn and/or that exert an important impact on our early socialization and an ongoing impact throughout our lives' (1991, pp. 18–19). They discuss these in relation to five parameters: (1) age, (2) gender, (3) ethnicity, (4) physical ability/qualities and (5) race and sexual orientation (pp. 18–19).

James Jones, John Dovidio and Deborah Vietze study diversity psycho-logically and maintain that human beings are 'Social Animals' (Jones et al., 2014, p. 118). 'Diversity usually refers to differences that are group based: gender, age, sexual orientation, race, ethnicity and so on' (p. 119). These differences are often accompanied by prejudice and discrimination, and thus diversity has become a serious social problem in the United States, for example, which is composed of so many racial, ethnic, religious and cultural groups (p. 32). To overcome complicated conflicts among different groups, people must undergo long struggles that require a great deal of patience. Jones, Dovidio and Vietze call this situation a 'challenge for a diverse soci-ety' (p.180). This challenge has spread to other countries around the world, even in Japan, which is, apparently, racially homogenous and which severely restricts immigration.

The first analyst to have dealt with the problem of differences from a post-Jungian viewpoint is Andrew Samuels. Pluralism, he notes, is an ap-proach to conflict that tries to reconcile differences without imposing a false synthesis on them – above all, without losing sight of the particular value and truth of each element in the conflict (Samuels, 1989/2016, p. xii). The problem is a social and political one, and at the same time it is a psychic one, because, as Jung noted, 'Complexes are *characteristic expressions* of the psy-che' (1948/1969, CW 8, para. 209). Let us look at *ONE PIECE* in such a light.

The story

As this series is ongoing and impossible to summarise completely, I will only introduce thematic concepts from Chapter 1, 'The Dawn of Adven-ture', up to Chapter 117, 'Dorry and Broggy'. The historical background is apparently the Age of Exploration (15th to 18th century), but the setting and period of this anime are completely fictional.

The head pirate, *Gold Roger*, reveals, just before his execution, that he has hidden a treasure in a dangerous location. The world then enters a great era of piracy, with all the pirates looking for this treasure called *ONE PIECE* (Oda, 2009, p. 5). Monkey D. Luffy, age seven, lives in a small harbour vil-lage and longs to be a pirate. He admires one pirate in particular, named *Red-Haired Shanks*, and asks if he can join his band of pirates, but Shanks laughs this off. After eating *Gomu no Mi* (devil's gum fruit), Luffy gains the ability to stretch like rubber, and he fights with a bandit who defames Shanks and almost loses his life. Being touched by Luffy's bravery and re-spect, Shanks helps Luffy, sacrificing his left arm in the process and giving his straw hat to Luffy as proof of their bond. Ten years later, Luffy sets out on a small boat by himself to find *ONE PIECE* and become the greatest pi-rate. He befriends Roronoa Zolo, a master of the three-sword fighting style; Nami, a thief and navigator; and Usopp, a master of the slingshot. Kaya, a rich girl, gives him a ship. They neither attack nor steal from ordinary people (see Oda, 2009, 2010a–c). On their flag is a skull with a straw hat, representing the symbol of their bond, so they are called 'the team of straw'. Later, Sanji, a skilful cook; Tony Tony Chopper, an excellent naval doctor; Nico Robin, an able female archaeologist; Franky, a ship's carpenter; and Brook, a musician, join the team. They fight with other pirates to protect their friends or ordinary people in the name of freedom, teamwork and justice (Suzuki, 2011).

Luffy as *puer aeternus*

Before discussing the team of straw, however, let us examine the character of the protagonist, Luffy, from the Jungian viewpoint of the *puer aeternus*. Jung himself mentions little regarding the *puer aeternus*. Robert Hopcke, however, explains this archetypal image in more detail:

> Hercules' youthful feats of strength are illustrations of this connection between the *puer* and the figure of the heroic demigod. Frivolity, pleasure, and play also characterize this Eternal Child, whose archetypal character means that he will never grow up'. ... These manifold qualities of the *puer,* centred on the futurity of human life and on the enlivening, charming, and refreshing elements of human experience, ensure for him a place of high regard in the pantheon of archetypal figures.
>
> (1989, pp. 107–108)

On the other hand, despite his attractive character, 'a *puer* identification may lead to a superficially entrancing but basically immature child-man who is incapable of commitment or generativity' (p. 108).

Those contradictory expressions regarding the *puer aeternus* completely suit the figure of Luffy. Although he wants to become the greatest pirate, he does not have concrete plan for achieving his goal. Somewhat like Peter Pan, cheerful, carefree and immature, psychologically Luffy does not integrate others into his psyche and does not learn anything from his painful experiences. A romantic relationship like the one between Susumu and Yuki in *Space Battleship Yamato* (Nakamura, 2017a, p. 214) could never happen between Luffy and Nami, because Luffy's vestigial erotic attention is solely homoerotic, directed toward Red-Haired Shanks. Nevertheless, like all archetypes with their positive and negative aspects, Luffy as the *puer aeternus* allows people to see their innocence, courage, strength, hope and potentiality – one of the most important reasons that the story has drawn people in for such a long time.

'The team of straw' as an individual psyche

Because the protagonist Luffy is a *puer aeternus*, his growth is not quick and clear, and he does not integrate with others. Even so, I see 'the team of straw' itself as an individual, including many complexes, Others and diversity. The number of members increases as the story progresses. The individual members of 'the team of straw' range over borders of gender, race and age, even over borders between animals and human beings, humans and cyborgs, live and dead people. Tony Tony Chopper is a reindeer; Nico Robin is a woman; Franky is a cyborg; and Brook is a dead person, a skeleton, age 90. Unfortunately, all the female characters still follow gender stereotypes – young, pretty, big-breasted and slender. However, in *Star Blazers,* from the 1970s, the crews are all Japanese (Nakamura, 2017a), and in *Sailor Moon,* from the 1990s, the characters are Japanese girls (Nakamura, 2015, 2016b); in *ONE PIECE* the characters come from broader and more diverse backgrounds. Their various talents and skills serve to keep them safe on the sea, provide them with enough to eat, keep them healthy, ensure that their ship stays in good trim and allow them to enjoy music and cultural activities. So the focus is not just on their fighting prowess, although they are *pirates.*

Also, women have intelligent roles in *ONE PIECE,* Nami as a navigator and Nico Robin *as* an archaeologist who is always cool, rational and academic, and who can read mysterious characters called *Poneglyphs* that are absolutely necessary to find the mysterious treasure they seek. Whereas the heroines in *Star Blazers* and *Sailor Moon* devote themselves to erotic relationships with men, those in *ONE PIECE* have specific talents and functions that were dominated by men in the past. They are independent, and they behave according to their own purposes, keeping on equal footing with Luffy. This reflects an important change in women's social status in actuality, and the anime provides a new gender model for girls.

Jung said, 'Complexes are in truth the living unit of the unconscious psyche, and it is only through them that we are able to deduce its existence and its constitution' (1948/1969, CW 8, para. 210). In *ONE PIECE,* the unconscious realm manifests itself through the vivid characters, each of whom has weak points. In addition, they act just as they like, since they have each joined the team for their own purposes. As Andrew Samuels has noted, however:

> Freedom does not guarantee diversity, for freedom can lead to a part of a system expanding to wield a tyrannical hold over the whole. If I am free to do or be what I like, this can produce an unequal state of affairs between you and me.
>
> (2001, p. 182)

Accordingly, misunderstandings and double-crosses often occur in *ONE PIECE,* leading to many troubles and crises for the team. Such problems reflect both our social outer conflicts and our psychic inner conflicts. On the other hand, the complex variety and diversity of the characters in the story may suggest that the individual or society has more future psychological potential.

ONE PIECE as a process of compromise

Let's consider how the characters in *ONE PIECE* compromise to resolve their conflicts. Most of them have suffered from some form of trauma in their early life. For example, Zolo lost his best female friend, Nami's family was killed by pirates and Usopp was ostracised by his community. Sanji, Tony Tony Chopper, Nico Robin, Franky and Brook also have painful and complicated pasts.

Nami first appears as a very strange figure in front of Luffy. She is pretty and very smart, but she lies without any shame. Moreover, she often betrays the team and steals treasure from them. Nevertheless, Luffy never abandons her, and readers have to wait patiently to find out the real reasons for Nami's behaviour. Luffy and Nami at last build up a true psychological bond in Volume 9, when, full of tears, she sincerely asks Luffy for his help, and he responds, 'Okay!' (Oda, 2010b, pp. 578–79), without any question. He allows her to keep the straw hat on her head as proof of his trust to her, something he has never allowed anyone else to do.

In a similar way, each member's painful background is disclosed, including Luffy's, indicating a healing process. Readers have to be patient and generous in order to grasp the enigmas of the characters, much like the process of psychoanalysis. I think that this is why *ONE PIECE* appeals not only to young people but also to adults. Similarly, overcoming differences in society is a long process, requiring generosity, patience, understanding and forgiveness. Jones, Dovidio and Vietze call this 'our challenge'. We may be able to see complexes in the psyche of an individual, but it always involves a long process to compromise and accept them. As Andrew Samuels has said,

> Each archetypal state of mind is *some* way connected to, or involved with others. … What usually happens is that the struggle between archetypal states of mind is resolved in favour of the state that provides the most complete experience, that is the closest approximation to experience as-a-whole.
>
> (1989/2016, p. 33)

Here it is important to consider the meaning of *straw*, the name of the team. When there is only one piece of straw, it is weak. 'They are as stubble before the wind, and a chaff that the storm carrieth away' (Vries, 1974/2009, p. 541). A 'man of straw' means a 'mortal man' and 'a straw man is without possession' (p. 541). However, a straw hat has a different meaning. 'Meeting the first straw-hatted man is always lucky' (p. 541). A single straw may be weak and fragile, but when straws are bundled together, as in the form of hat, they form a bond of strength. In the story, 'the straw hat' has a specific, symbolic, mystical power that brings members not only luck and happiness, but also healing. As Jesus Christ wears a crown of thorns, not of gold, to indicate that he is in the Kingdom of God, so Luffy wears the straw hat. And the team of straw flies a flag decorated with a skull wearing a straw hat (Oda, 2010a–c, p. 322). This symbolises their friendship and strong bond; it subsumes many elements, each without losing individuality.

Is Luffy a pluralistic or tyrannical leader?

Jung writes of Wotan in his 1936 essay of the same name:

> We are always convinced that the modern world is a reasonable world, basing our opinion on economic, political, and psychological factors. But if we may forget for a moment that we are living in the year of Our Lord 1936, and, laying aside our well-meaning, all-too-human reasonableness, may burden God or the gods with responsibility for contemporary events instead of man, we would find Wotan quite suitable as a causal hypothesis ... There is no doubt that each of these factors explains an important aspect of what is going on in Germany, but Wotan explains yet more.
>
> (Jung, 1936/1968, CW 10, para. 385)

Wotan has many faces, but he is a god of war and death and a wanderer like Luffy. Clearly, we live in a chaotic world in which many young people are annoyed at their situations. *ONE PIECE* was first published in 1997. With the recession that has continued largely unabated since the 1990s in Japan, the employment situation has, of course, worsened. The Japanese Ministry of Health, Labour and Welfare reported that the rate of irregular employment reached 37.5 per cent in 2015 (2016). This means that Japanese young people can't expect the security given to the previous generation, protected as it was by the lifetime employment system. Their lifelong wages will be low, and many of them will give up on marriage. Approximately one in four young men in Tokyo expect to remain single all their lives. Yet they are largely passive, both socially and politically. The voting rate among those in their 20s is exceptionally low. Since they can't realise their dreams in real life, they tend to sublimate, finding comfort in *anime*, video games and social media. The same situation can be seen among young people around the world, especially in places with high unemployment.

Loden and Rosender provide a new leadership model in relation to adapting diversity into organisations:

> Participative leadership has been the model used to guide the behavior of leaders and mangers in most successful U.S. organizations. ... Pluralistic leadership goes beyond participative leadership. While it also emphasizes empowerment and employee involvement, it assumes that the organization culture needs to change if diversity is to become a true asset.
>
> (1991, p. 181)

In Japan, *ONE PIECE* is often taken up as a representation of ideal leadership and of model teamwork in the workplace (Hirai, 2010). As mentioned, Luffy and his team are betrayed by Nami many times, but when she sincerely asks Luffy for his help, he accepts without any qualms. Luffy accepts and respects his mates' wishes and desires. When they address Luffy as captain, he responds, 'We're a team, aren't we?' (Oda, 2010a–c, p. 311). In this context, Luffy is a generous and patient leader.

However, one of the most compelling elements of the story is Luffy's superhuman fighting ability. There are many descriptions of his strong emotions, usually rage or sadness. Robert Bly has said, 'We are living at an important and fruitful moment now, for it is clear to men that the images of adult manhood given by popular culture are worn out' (1990/2004, p. ix). In *Iron John*, Bly stresses the strength of men: 'In *The Odyssey*, Hermes instructs Odysseus that when he approaches Circe, who stands for a certain kind of matriarchal energy, he is to lift or show his sword' (p. 4). This best seller from the 1990s seems to speak for men who are annoyed with 'softened men' who must live in a time when women have become much stronger politically, economically and psychologically than ever before.

All the troubles in *ONE PIECE* are finally resolved by Luffy's violent superhuman power, though this is softened by his being a gum man. Young men feel relieved by these scenes, which compensate for their anger and frustration as men. Young women who are still suffering from more severely restrictive social states accept these scenes for the same reasons as men do. They also satisfy their deep desire to be protected by strong men without any conditions. They can *accept* Luffy's violence without concern, as he is always under the control of Nami, a mother archetypal image. Thus, the *anime* maintains traditional gender stereotypes. In addition, Luffy fully expresses his feelings of rage, joy and sadness, bringing young people, who can't express their true feeling to authorities, catharsis. It may prevent the explosion of their feelings, which may disturb their social activities. Ironically this keeps Japan at peace.

For Hayashi and Takada, 'Luffy is only a selfish kid'. And they conclude with a worrisome question: 'We have to ask ourselves why such a figure is so popular' (2015, p. 80). If we consider that deeply, perhaps we've been unconsciously waiting for a God Child to make the torn world *ONE PIECE*. The dangers posed by admiring an absolute hero, especially one who can resolve people's frustrations by violence, are legion.

Hayashi and Takada have expressed misgivings about this trend (2015). They focus on how Luffy's fighting is directed at protecting a close circle of friends when they appear defamed or harmed. His dream of finding *ONE PIECE* is deferred (pp. 75–76). The identity of this grail remains undefined. This notion that people will do anything for their friends carries potential dangers, since it prevails in the thoughts or deeds of antisocial groups like terrorists. The rise of demagogic leaders has also given many of us pause. *ONE PIECE* may thus serve as a warning regarding the contemporary pathology of our societies as noted by Jung in Wotan (Jung, 1936/1968, CW 10).

References

Bly, R. (1990/2004). *Iron John.* Da Capo Press.

Hayami, T. (2013). Wan Pisu wa naze San oukubu Urerunoka? [Why have three hundred million copies of *One Piece* been sold?]. *Magunakaruta, 2,* 28–33.

Hayashi, N., & Takada, A. (2015). *Urutoraman kara Wanpisu made Hirotchi no Tatakau Kimochi* [Heros' fighting spirit from *Ultraman* to *One Piece*]. Saizo.

Hirai, K. (2010). *'ONE PIECE' ni manabu Shogoto Jutsu* [Learning Working Style from *One Piece*]. Kabushiki Gaisya data-house.

Hopcke, R.H. (1989). *A guided tour of the 'Collected works of C.G. Jung'.* Shambhala.

Jones, J.M., Dovidio, J.F., & Vietze, D.L. (2014). *The psychology of diversity: Beyond prejudice and racism.* Wiley Blackwell Publishing.

Jung, C.G. (1929/1969). The significance of constitution and heredity in psychology. In H. Read, M. Fordham, G. Adler & W. McGuire (Eds.), *The collected works of C.G. Jung: Vol. 8. The structure and dynamics of the psyche.* (R. F. C. Hull, Trans.). Princeton University Press.

Jung, C.G. (1936/1968). Wotan. In H. Read, M. Fordham, G. Adler & W. McGuire (Eds.), *The collected works of C.G. Jung: Vol. 10. Civilization in transition.* (R. F. C. Hull, Trans.). Routledge & Kegan Paul.

Jung, C.G. (1948/1969). A review of the complex theory. In H. Read, M. Fordham, G. Adler & W. McGuire (Eds.), *The collected works of C.G. Jung: Vol. 8. The structure and dynamics of the psyche.* (R. F. C. Hull, Trans.). Princeton University Press.

Jung, C.G. (1954/1968). Archetypes of the collective unconscious. In H. Read, M. Fordham, G. Adler & W. McGuire (Eds.), *The collected works of C.G. Jung: Vol. 9i. The archetypes and the collective unconscious.* (R. F. C. Hull, Trans.). Princeton University Press.

Loden, M., & Rosener, J.B. (1991). *Workforce America! Managing employee diversity as a vital resource.* Business One Irwin.

Ministry of Health, Labour and Welfare. (2016). www.mhlw.go.jp/file/06-Seisakujouhou.../0000120286.pdf

Macias, P., & Mochiyama, T. (2006). *Otaku in USA: Ai to Gokai no Yunyushi* [Otaku in the USA: A history of love and misunderstanding]. Ootashuppan.

Napier, S.J. (2001/2005). *Anime from Akira to Howl's moving castle: Experiencing contemporary Japanese animation.* Palgrave Macmillan.

Nakamura, I. (2006). Preface. In I. Nakamura & M.M. (Eds.), *Nihon no Poppower Sekai wo Kaeru Contents no Jituzo* [Japanese pop-power, its real contents changing the world] (pp. 15–22). Nihon Keizai Sinbunsha.

Nakamura, K. (2015, 11 July). *Sailor moon:* Feminine images and social status. Presentation at the Fourth Joint Conference of International Association for Jungian Studies, Yale University, New Haven, Connecticut.

Nakamura, K. (2016, 27 June). *Sailor moon:* The moon as healing power for the earth. Presentation at the 2016 JSSS Conference, Earth/Psyche: Foregrounding the Earth's Relations to Psyche, Santa Fe, New Mexico.

Nakamura, K. (2017a). Archetypal images in Japanese anime: 'Space battleship *Yamato* (Star blazers)'. In E. Broderson & M. Glock (Eds.), *Jungian perspectives on rebirth and renewal: Phoenix rising* (pp. 207–218). Routledge.

Nakamura, K. (2017b, 28 June). *ONE PIECE:* The dream of freedom as the 'Other'. Presentation for the 2017 JAJS Conference in South Africa, The Spectre of the 'Other' in Jungian Psychology, Centre for the Book, Cape Town, South Africa.

Oda, E. (2009). *One piece: East blue 1–2–3.* (N. Aneyama, Trans.). VIZ media, LLC.

Oda, E. (2010a). *One piece: East blue 4–5–6.* (N. Aneyama, Trans.). VIZ media, LLC.

Oda, E. (2010b). *One piece: East blue 7–8–9.* (N. Aneyama, Trans.). VIZ media, LLC.

Oda, E. (2010c). *One piece: East blue 10–11–12.* (N. Aneyama, Trans.). VIZ media, LLC.

Samuels, A. (1989/2016). *The plural psyche: Personality, morality and the father.* Routledge.

Samuels, A. (2001). *Politics on the couch: Citizenship and the internal life.* Other Press.

Schodt, F. (1996). *Dreamland Japan: Writings on modern manga.* Stone Bridge Press.

Suzuki, T. (2011). *'Wan Pi-su Sedai no Hanran, 'Gandamu Sedai no Yutsu* [Revolt by the generation of *One piece,* melancholy by the generation of *Mobile suit gundam*]. Asahishinshuppan.

Vries, A.D. (1974/2009). *Elsevier's dictionary of symbols and imagery.* Brill.

Chapter 14

What is it about *The Singing Ringing Tree?*

Amanda Hon

The Singing Ringing Tree (Das singende, klingende Bäumchen [Stefani, 1957]) made a quiet but devastating entrance into the living rooms and psyches of British children when the first of three episodes was broadcast by the BBC during children's peak-time viewing on 19 November 1964. The series was repeated in 1966 and again in the early 1970s as part of the *Tales from Europe* series after it was picked up by the BBC at the 1957 Edinburgh Film Festival (IMDbPro, 2009). In 1990, Rosemary Creeser, director of Westbourne Film Distribution, brought it back into distribution when she realised that there were many adult '*aficionados*' who, like her, remained haunted by the film (1993, p. 118).

There is something about *The Singing Ringing Tree* that gripped – and terrified – many British children – so much so that, as adults, the atmosphere and images remain as present as a powerful childhood dream. The proliferation of internet sites where the film continues to be discussed bears witness to the film's effect (see, for example, IMDb, 2016; Cineoutsider, 2016), as does the attention accorded it by writers such as Rosemary Creeser (1993), Marina Warner (1993, 1995) and Jack Zipes (2000) as well as the numerous references to the film within popular culture.[1]

Shot on 35 mm and in vivid Agfacolor, when my peers and I saw it for the first time in the 1960s it was in black and white, which did not diminish its power. Recorded in German with a male voice-over narration in received pronunciation BBC English, the original language of an *Other* intriguingly faded in and out, recognisable as German but not, this time, barked by soldiers of the already familiar and ubiquitous World War II (WWII) film genre. This was an Other Germany that penetrated young British viewers' minds with the reassuringly paternalistic BBC voice that meant safety but which, at the same time, spoke of ominous deals, enchantment, sensuality, responsibility, cruelty and menace.

One reviewer wrote, 'Imagine a fairy tale conceived by Wagner and directed by Fritz Lang, with nods in the direction of *The Cabinet of Doctor Caligari* [Wiene, 1920] and German Expressionism, and you'd be close' (Thomas, 2016). Elsewhere, it has been described as 'the stuff of nightmares,

DOI: 10.4324/9781003223481-18

like a fairy tale directed by David Lynch' (Smith, 1999). Creeser succinctly captured the eerie beauty of *The Singing Ringing Tree* when she described it as 'Cocteau for kids' (1993, pp. 111–24).

In this chapter, I intend to look not only at the film itself but also at the reception it had and the impact it made on children in 1960s and early 1970s Britain. I consider why it touched so many people of that generation as profoundly as it did. Through the application of the Jungian concepts of *compensation* and *the autonomy of the unconscious*, of *soul/psyche* and of the *Other*, I will consider what gap or gaps the film might have been serving to fill within children's psyches and, perhaps, that of wider society at that time. It is impossible to use a single discipline to explain the mind, and indeed, Jungian psychology makes no claims to providing an overarching dogma, nor to possessing a grand narrative (Rowland, 2005, pp. 7–8). In building on Creeser's psychoanalytical critique of *The Singing Ringing Tree* (1993, pp. 111–24), I will therefore seek to develop a richer analysis, locating the discussion in a wider interdisciplinary context by making use of a sociohistorical lens to focus on changes occurring in arenas such as architecture, technology, prosperity, youth and counterculture, and, more particularly, shifts taking place in women's roles in the 1960s and 1970s. I will also consider the possible agendas of East Germany and of the BBC in showing this film to a British audience at that time.

The story

Inspired by elements taken from several Grimms' fairy tales and the 'Beauty and the Beast' *contes* of 18th-century French women writers (Warner, 1992, p. 32; 1995, p. 297), *The Singing Ringing Tree* tells the story of Princess Thousandbeauty, the motherless only child of an ageing king, who sets her latest princely suitor the task of finding and retrieving the much-whispered-about Singing Ringing Tree. After riding through a mythical landscape, he arrives at a magical kingdom, an otherworldly realm inhabited by strange animals and ruled by a demoniacal dwarf who presents him with the tree on condition that, by sunset, he must succeed in winning the love of the princess. Optimistically, the prince returns to the palace with his prize, but, furious that it will neither sing nor ring for her, the princess refuses him. Subsequently, the dwarf casts a spell, turning the prince into a beast in the form of a bear. As 'Bear', he returns to the palace and snatches the princess from the walled garden where her narcissistic cruelty is revealed when she drains the fountain of its water in order to fill the basin with soil in which to plant the silent tree, leaving the goldfish to die. Kidnapped and ensconced in the dwarf's realm, the princess's unkindness results in her being magically rendered 'ugly', reflecting her inner ugliness. Humbled, she gradually develops empathy, expressed in acts of compassion, for the animals of the Magic Kingdom. Consequently, she slowly regains her former 'beauty', a process that achieves completion when she at last becomes conscious of her love for the bear/prince. At the same time, the spell holding him in beastly form is broken and he manifests once again as the prince. The two finally unite in love, at which the tree sings and rings in approval. The conflict with the dwarf reaches a peak after his attempt to prevent the princess and the bear from uniting fails. Having wrought destruction throughout the Magic Kingdom, leaving one of the animals, a great golden fish, to flounder and, presumably, to die when he empties the lake, the dwarf celebrates his victory by running and laughing maniacally atop a circle of flames that he has conjured up to surround the tree. But his *schadenfreudean* glee is short-lived: discovering himself to be powerless over the princess with her newfound capacity for love, enraged, he vanishes into the earth, as other malevolent fairy tale figures have done before him.

The zeitgeist of the Long Sixties: a child's perspective

'It is always dangerous to speak of one's own times, because what is at stake is too vast to be comprehended' (Jung, 1930/1950, CW 15, para. 154). Perhaps this is even more true when recalling the time of one's childhood. I have some trepidation in writing about the 1960s, not only because it is such a broad subject to which a chapter of this length cannot possibly do justice but also because it is impossible to maintain an objective stance when writing about a time when one lived with the undifferentiated consciousness of a child. However, Andrew Samuels points out that subjectivity has been foregrounded in Jung's approach to psychology, lending some validity to this perspective (1996, p. 19). According to Jung, 'A person sinks into his childhood memories and vanishes from the existing world. He finds himself in deepest darkness, but then has unexpected visions of a world beyond' (1956, CW 5, para. 631). I hope to access some of this darkness, both through introspection and exploring others' narratives, and to use what I find to illustrate my thesis that, for many children of young parents who were energetically swept up in the *zeitgeist* of the Long Sixties[2], the romanticised glory of those years was a different experience altogether, one that triggered an unconscious attempt at 'balancing, adjusting, supplementing' (Samuels et al., 2003, p. 32), a process described by the Jungian concept of *compensation*. I do not deny that this period saw a cultural flowering in which people of integrity with high ideals were engaged and committed to something larger than themselves for the benefit of the greater good, including the Peace Movement, the Women's Liberation Movement, Campaign for Nuclear Disarmament (CND), Gay Liberation, Greenpeace and the Animal Rights Movement, among others. For the first time people realised that they were free and no longer the subjects of a mediaeval system. All these achievements are important and worthy of acknowledgement, as are the innovations that occurred in the arts during these years. But modern Western society is characterised by its plurality, and I will focus here on aspects that have a subjective resonance for me and that, inevitably, cannot reflect the whole story.

Since the Enlightenment, modernity has overvalued psychological consciousness, and the tumultuous developments taking place in the Long Sixties mainstream extended this one-sided emphasis on the outer world, causing *soul*, or *psyche*, that which speaks of 'the non-material aspect of humans – their core, heart, centre' (Samuels, Shorter & Plaut, 2003, p. 140) – to be relatively neglected. *Psyche* is often simplistically translated as 'mind' in academic psychology. While not discounting the importance of rational consciousness as a part of psyche, including the ego and sense of self (Hopcke, 1999, pp. 38–39), Jung considered this view inadequately one-sided because it identifies psyche only with the personal, egoic self. From a Jungian perspective, psyche is 'the totality of nonphysical life, both rational and irrational, both personal and collective, both conscious and unconscious' (Hopcke, 1999, p. 37). Jung's epistemology frequently offers explanations in terms of binary opposition, which, although neat, can fit awkwardly with the plurality of real-life experiences (Samuels, 1993, p. 329). Encompassing the totality of consciousness and unconsciousness, Jung came to use the term 'soul' interchangeably with 'psyche' though, confusingly, sometimes using 'soul' when referring to movement at a depth level and also with 'spirit' (Samuels et al., 2003, p. 140) and with *anima* (Hopcke, 1999, p. 39). Unfortunately, the parameters of this chapter do not allow for an extensive clarification of these terms and usages. However, following Jung's view, 'that the unconscious is primarily, or potentially, creative, functioning in the service of the individual and species' (Samuels et al., 2003, p. 156), I suggest that *The Singing Ringing Tree* carried a *core, heart, centre* quality of soul for many children who saw it, and that they, animated by the experience, were nourished in a way they might otherwise not have been. In turn, they carried this aspect of soul for the wider culture: in later years when adults themselves, drawing on the seeds of increased consciousness activated in them by the film, to participate in and contribute to an expansion of social and collective consciousness as expressed in, for example, the current discourse taking place around the burgeoning forces of our globalised, consumer-driven, nature-destroying society.

By 1961, 75 per cent of families in Britain had a television set; in 1971, 91 per cent (Marwick, 1990, p. 117). With television, the larger world entered the home in a new way, revealing the 'backstage' of adult life (Meyrowitz, cited in Postman, 1994, p. 95). Children could not fail to become aware of the strife, ineptitude and worry that filled the adult world (Postman, 1994, p. 95). What impact might news of specific events have had on children: the abolition of the death penalty and the concurrent debates in 1965, the Aberfan disaster of 1966[3] and the Moors murders of the mid-1960s – the first widely reported case of serial child abduction and murder in British history and the first high-profile case involving a female perpetrator? Between 1955 and 1968, crimes of violence in Britain rose from 5,869 to 21,046 (Marwick, 1990, p. 144). At the same time, 'the guts were torn out of such cities as Newcastle, Glasgow, and Birmingham and replaced with an ugly jungle of urban motorways and high-rise buildings' (p. 119). Television advertising pop-jingles hailed 'the supersonic seventies' over images of brutalist architecture (Banham, 1966), presenting them as 'brave new architectural concepts' and 'concrete symbols of progress' (Marwick, 1990, p. 119).

In 1969, the world saw the first manned moon landing, and in 1971 the decimalisation of currency in the United Kingdom and Ireland. A new irreverence for authority found expression in a satire boom in the early 1960s (Marwick, 1990, p. 121) and in the music and fashion of the growing youth and counterculture, which was embraced by millions, its strength contributing to the lowering of the voting age in 1968 to 18. There were techno-chemical advances in the area of 'suds, shine, and phoney flavours' (p. 111), minutiae of life with which children have a particular intimacy. Even the potato's contact with the earth was rendered tenuous with the launch of instant mash in the 1960s. Changes were occurring all around. Renos Papadopoulos refers to the 'mosaic substratum' that, though generally unconsciously perceived, formed from numerous elements that we take for granted – smells, sounds, architecture, among a multitude of others, provides 'a sense of predictability in the course of our lives', and it is on this that our grounding in reality is built (2002a, p. 17). Papadopoulos's focus is that of refugees who have been uprooted from their homes. I propose that his concept can be borrowed and applied to the context of my focus, too. The ground beneath children's feet in the Long Sixties was trembling and this moved many into an unconscious search for balance. They were too anxious to just join in and do the Watusi.

Simultaneously, Ladybird Books, whose Key Words Reading Scheme was used in many primary schools in the 1960s, portrayed life as simple and good with two-dimensional mothers, fathers and children, all with clearly defined gender roles. The reality was otherwise: between 1961 and 1971 the divorce rate more than doubled from 32,000 to 74,000, creating an accompanying increase in one-parent families (Cunningham, 2006, p. 213). More women than at any time since WWII went out to work in this period (Marwick, 1990, pp. 111–12). Sexual attitudes changed dramatically, due largely to women's new ability to control their fertility with the introduction of the contraceptive pill and improved intrauterine device (p. 113) as well as the influence of the gay liberation movement of the late 1960s and feminism, which, Rozsika Parker asserts, was often misinterpreted as 'the desire to abandon children, home and husband', when in fact it was attempting 'to change the material conditions of motherhood' (1995, p. 54). Feminism was an important influence, even for women who did not consciously align themselves with the movement, as indeed was the counterculture, which similarly had repercussive effects within the mainstream. But what some women – and men – took from these movements was a filtered, misconstrued sense of freedom from responsibility to children and a licence to pursue hedonistic pleasures at the expense of providing continuity and a nourishing, soul-enriching environment in which children could grow up with a sense of security and of their place in the world.

Parker posits, 'Winnicott considered that the capacity to be good enough was often out of an individual mother's hands' (1995, p. 59). Given that many mothers – and fathers, though they have been written about much less – of young children in the Long Sixties had themselves been children during WWII, the majority of their fathers had been absent for a number of years between 1939 and 1945, and their mothers had often undertaken long hours of war work outside the home, some also welcoming freedom from the norms of married life to enjoy social lives ordinarily inaccessible to them outside working hours. This raises a question about the influence of these experiences on the ability of those who were then children to subsequently be *good enough* parents themselves. This becomes particularly poignant when considering that these disruptions to home life were compounded with the terror of bombings – often during the night – and encounters with scenes of massive destruction, perhaps of their own or extended family members' homes, and the loss and maiming of loved ones and peers and, if none of these, empty desks in classrooms after classmates had been killed in raids since the previous day's lessons, and the constant fear of a telegram bearing news of a lost father, brother, uncle ... A rupturing of the mosaic substratum certainly occurred at this time in the urban centres of Britain. Winnicott writes, '... if the facilitating environment is not good enough, then the line of life is broken and the very powerful inherited tendencies [towards integration, growth, development], cannot carry the child on to personal fulfilment' (1990, p. 144). Bruno Bettelheim notes the importance of empathy in good enough parenting, facilitated by a parent's ability to recall their own childhood emotions and experiences (1987, p. 25). I suggest that stress endured in childhoods lived out during WWII created a generation of adults in which many tended to repress the past. Determined to leave the chaos and sense of powerlessness behind and to seek mastery of their own lives, they sought out pleasure in enantiodromic compensation for lack in their early years. This underpinned the spirit of eternal youth that exploded in the 60s and was the shadow aspect of James Hillman's 'one-sided puer' (1983; quoted in Porterfield et al., 2009, p. 31). The Allies had been victorious – what reason was there not to rejoice? As this spirit was prompted by an unconscious, self-regulating, autonomic mechanism, those under its spell were oblivious to its operation and, being unconscious of it, were unable to assert ego control over it (Samuels et al., 2003, p. 53) and so curtail the quality and degree of its manifestation. If defences of the self, become over-determined, a tendency toward omnipotence develops which leads to grandiosity and rigidity; i.e. resulting in a narcissistic personality disorder. On the other hand, autism may result. In either case, the individual is cut off from the satisfactions of relationship because it is *otherness* itself which feels persecutory.

(p. 137)

Consequently, under this widely cast spell of the *puer aeternus,* along with the slums that were cleared from the battered cities, much else of the past was swept away, including extended family networks and many traditions regarded as old and outdated, some of which played an important part in creating a *good enough* environment for children.

Hidden agendas?

Warner argues that 'film is essentially an oral medium and shares many characteristics with storytelling' (1993, p. 24). This view is echoed in Zipes (2000, p. 513). But,

> Storytelling is never neutral, there are always wider considerations of a social and ideological nature, particularly when we are talking about a kind of narrative tradition which has been so enduring in its popularity, has embraced different modes of transformation, and which has been regarded by various critics as both profoundly Utopian and insidiously reactionary in its effects.
>
> (Petrie, 1993, pp. 3–4)

Zipes cites numerous European attempts to politicise the fairy tale by both the left and the right (2000, p. xxix). I can only speculate about the possible agendas of the BBC and the German Democratic Republic (GDR, also known as East Germany) in broadcasting the film to British children. The GDR was not subject to capitalist market pressures to cynically exploit film and myth to generate income, and Deutsche Film AG (DEFA, German Film Corporation), the only official film production organisation in the country, had access to the full resources of the state (Staples, 1993, p. 125). The mid-1950s GDR government urged DEFA to produce fairy tale features 'as an effective means of instilling in children the proper political attitudes, work ethic, and cultural values', and DEFA responded by 'offering the viewer a full palette of red shadings and rose-coloured lenses for the "happy endings"' (Cocalis, 1999). *The Singing Ringing Tree*'s emphasis on the importance of prioritising others' welfare above materialist trappings was arguably socialist: the transformed prince and princess finally leave the tree behind so that it can bring happiness to others who find it. As Creeser writes, 'In many ways the Magic Kingdom in the film conforms to ideas of a Utopian community based upon a symbiotic relationship between the gifts of nature (earth, water, air) and the potential of human cooperation' (1993, p. 118). Some contemporary GDR critics condemned the film as bourgeois, however, claiming that it reflected capitalistic entertainment industry values (DEFA Film Library, 1999; Zipes, 2000, p. 467).

More sinisterly, I see a possibility of anti-Semitism in *The Singing Ringing Tree*, which needs to be examined. The princess, when 'beautiful' is blonde, and

> Blondeness is ... a blazon in code, a piece of a value system that it is urgent to confront and analyse because its implications, in moral and social terms, are so dire and are still so unthinkingly embedded in the most ordinary, popular materials of the imagination. The Nazis' Aryan fantasies were partly rooted in this ancient, enduring colour code which cast gods as golden boys and girls and outsiders as swarthy.
>
> (Warner, 1995, p. 364)

When magically rendered 'ugly', the princess's hair darkens and her nose grows larger. Whether this reflects a lingering anti-Semitism or, possibly, the influence of the Italian fairy story *The Adventures of Pinocchio* (Collodi, 2000) is not clear, but given the context, the former might, arguably, be more likely. Jewish top functionaries and Communists were purged from the upper echelons of the Socialist Unity Party of Germany in the GDR, severely undermining the denazification claims of the republic. Stalin fostered 'anti-cosmopolitanism', associating Jewry with American imperialism and capitalism, though Mike Dennis stresses that 'East German anti-Semitism cannot be equated with the biological racism and mass murder of the Third Reich' (2000, p. 32). Could East Germany have been seeking to plant seeds of both socialism and anti-Semitism in Britain? If so, one can but speculate as to the degree to which the latter was a conscious undertaking.

As for the BBC, Anna Home, former Director, Producer and Executive Producer within BBC Children's Television, states, 'the raison d'être behind showing programmes from eastern Europe was ... that it was thought to be important to introduce British children to other cultures e.g., the *Tales from Europe* series' (personal communication, 19 May 2009). The programmes were meant to be both educational and entertaining and perhaps provide an antidote to the American imports that were starting to dominate British television culture at the time, along with the American music that was captivating the nation's youth. Monica Sims, Head of Children's Programmes (1967–78) at the BBC, states, 'The BBC wanted to prevent children from becoming too insular, or entirely American-dominated' (Smith, 1999). Home has also referred to the ongoing problem of funding children's television: broadcast outside peak-viewing time to much smaller audiences than the evening schedules (Home, 1993, pp. 12–13), and operating within a capitalist system, less money is inevitably allocated to it.

But was there a latent anti-American, socialist presence within the BBC, which, while maintaining a publicly acceptable face in keeping with the BBC's ethos of the time, might have been committed behind the scenes to ensuring that British children received a socialist cultural influence? To some extent, this would fit with the challenging of the status quo that was beginning to gain a voice in Britain at the start of the Long Sixties. Documents declassified by MI5 in 2006 reveal that 'from the late Thirties until the end of the Cold War, MI5 had an officer at the BBC to vet all editorial applicants, stamping the personnel records of anyone suspicious with a distinctively shaped green tag, or "Christmas tree"' (Smith, 2006). Left-leaning 'subversives' were purged from the BBC until the end of the late 1980s. Dr. Peggy Miller, the producer who originally selected *The Singing Ringing Tree* for the BBC (Creeser, 1993, pp. 120–21), is no longer living (Home, personal communication, 19 May 2009), so it has not been possible to ask her for clarification of her political position.

Concluding thoughts

The Singing Ringing Tree stands out in a sea of other programmes in many people's memories from the 1960s and early 1970s. This is due in part to the imaginatively crafted hand-painted sets, the simplicity of the moral message of beauty being more than skin-deep and the importance of kindness, and also to the – then – impressive special effects created by Ernst Kunstmann, one of the most important German film special effects technologists favoured by many acclaimed directors, including Fritz Lang, Friedrich Wilhelm Murnau and Kurt Maetzig, among others (DEFA Film Library, n.d.). The film evokes a magical dream world, remembered more by some as a nightmare, assisted in no small part by the early electronic music of Heinz-Friedel Heddenhausen. A classical musician colleague wrote of the theme tune,

> I was terrified and not from the story. The music totally creeped me out ... scared me, too sinister, pretending to be childlike and, oh so, adult. When I hear that type of music, to me, it's shouting "warning – be careful – things aren't as they appear!"
>
> (Drennan, personal communication, 30 May 2009)

This echoes Max Lüthi's themes of 'appearance versus reality' and that good may be hidden in bad, cited by Creeser (1987, cited in Creeser, 1993, p. 114).

The Singing Ringing Tree prompted reflection. As children, finding ourselves at a cliff-hanging break in the film, it sparked a debate between a friend and me about whether we would prefer to be beautiful and mean or ugly and kind when we grew up. My friend chose the second option with apparent ease, but for me it was a dilemma and the source of some angst: I wanted to be kind *and* beautiful, but unwilling to renounce either of those qualities for my future adult self, it seemed obvious that I was neither. I could almost feel the gravitational pull of a personal inner Magic Kingdom and wasn't sure that I liked it. Papadopoulos points out, 'One of Jung's main principles was that the tension between opposites was the very source of psychic energy itself' (2002b, pp. 170–71). I believe *The Singing Ringing Tree* engaged many children by (re)animating soul/psyche and providing a sense of connection back to myth. It filled a gap in children's quest for meaning at a time when the cultural zeitgeist was dominated by the puer, which has very little interest in looking inwards.

I suggest that, in addition to seeking to compensate for imbalances in their own lives, British children had an unconscious, compensatory collective need to connect with and be horrified by the cultural wounding of their parents' and grandparents' generations to find a way to engage with the enemy Other, including the spectres of Nazism and anti-Semitism as well as with the phenomenon of destruction. Writing about film from the perspective of media theory, Marshall McLuhan states the following:

> When we have achieved a world-wide fragmentation, it is not unnatural to think about a world-wide integration. Such a universality of conscious being for mankind was dreamt of by Dante, who believed that men would remain mere broken fragments until they should be united in an inclusive consciousness.
>
> (2003, p. 149)

The characters in *The Singing Ringing Tree* spoke in the language of our parents' and grandparents' enemies, but softly, and enchantingly, and beneath a voice that reassured us that we were still on home ground. As Papadopoulos writes, 'The problem of otherness is both enormous and complex' (2002b, p. 164). We form our identities in relation to what we are not (p. 166). Citing Winnicott, Farhad Dalal (2003) reiterates that 'I am' is a paranoid statement, as, with the coming into existence of the 'I' that which we are not becomes excluded. He argues that we have all been racialised and cannot help but operate within this framework. Rowland writes from a Jungian perspective: '... the psyche is a dynamic, self-regulating mechanism. By drawing upon its own "other", it aims to heal itself of one-sidedness' (2005, p. 5).

> ... the founding principle of Jung's psychology is to realize that the unconscious is superior to the capacity of the ego to comprehend it. ... It often acts independently of cognitive structures brought to bear by the ego and it is 'collective' because it contains structuring principles inherited collectively by mankind.
>
> (pp. 4–5)

With reference to Terence Dawson's discussion of *Robinson Crusoe* (Defoe, 1994), I further propose that the Magic Kingdom has the qualities of a *temenos*, a sacred precinct, for children. As a place in which the princess rebuilds her identity, it offers reassurance 'that they harbour *within themselves* both the key to their own psychic healing and the "sacred space" necessary to achieve this' (Dawson, 2008, pp. 27–28).

Experiences of 'separation, detachment, and agonizing confrontation through opposition' (Jung, 1940, CW 9i, para. 289) occur ordinarily, to varying degrees, on the journey from childhood to adulthood. They contribute largely to the development of consciousness and insight (para. 289), but what passes into consciousness is determined by an individual's ego strength (Samuels et al., 2003, p. 156).

Bettelheim argues that fairy tales present existential dilemmas in ways that enable children to confront and grasp the underlying essential meanings of these conflicts, providing them with tools with which to work through their own conflicts and experiences (1978, in Petrie, 1993, p. 4). John Izod echoes this in his claim that screened fiction has the potential to help the individual gain greater awareness of his or her emotional being (2000, p. 271).

To conclude, I cite some final words from Jung:

> Every period has its bias, its particular prejudice, and its psychic malaise. An epoch is like an individual; it has its own limitations of conscious outlook, and therefore requires a compensatory adjustment. This is effected by the collective unconscious when a poet or seer lends expression to the unspoken desire of his times and shows the way, by word or deed, to its fulfilment – regardless whether this blind collective need results in good or evil, in the salvation of the epoch or its destruction.
>
> (Jung, 1930/1950, CW 15, para. 153)

The Singing Ringing Tree continues to be screened at independent cinemas around the United Kingdom.

Notes

1   These include a BBC Radio 4 broadcast of a programme about the film and its reception (BBC Radio 4, 2008) and citings in various polls, including a TV special, *The 100 Greatest Kids TV Shows* (BBC News, 2001) and a TV documentary, *The 100 Greatest Scary Moments* (TVTropes.org, 2003). A *Radio Times* readers' poll in 2004 voted 'the twentieth spookiest TV show ever' (Wikipedia, 2009). Other references to the film are found in literature on children's television (Tibballs & Morris, 1991; Home, 1993; Lewis & Stempel, 2001; Lewis, 2002; Sangster & Condon, 2005).

2   The period from the late 1950s to the middle 1970s, so coined by Marwick (2005, p. 780).

3 On 21 October 1966, a colliery spoil tip that had been created above the south Welsh village of Aberfan collapsed catastrophically. It engulfed Pantglas Junior School and a row of houses, killing 116 children and 28 adults. The tragedy had been completely avoidable. The tip was the responsibility of the National Coal Board, and the ensuing inquiry placed the blame for the catastrophe on the NCB and nine named employees. One of the United Kingdom's worst mining disasters, it was the first to be broadcast live into people's homes.

References

Banham, R. (1966). *The new brutalism*. Architectural Press.

BBC News. (2001, 28 August). The 100 greatest TV kids shows. Retrieved March 6, 2016, from http://news.bbc.co.uk/1/hi/entertainment/1513234.stm

BBC Radio 4. (2002, 28 December). *The singing ringing tree*. Retrieved from http://www.bbc.co.uk/radio4/arts/singing_ringing_tree.shtml

Bettelheim, B. (1978). *The uses of enchantment: The meaning and importance of fairy tales*. Peregrine Books.

Bettelheim, B. (1987). *A good enough parent*. Thames & Hudson.

Cineoutsider. (n.d.). Traumatic teutonic TV. Retrieved March 13, 2016, from http://www.cineoutsider.com/reviews/dvd/s/singing_ringing_tree.html

Cocalis, S. (1999). Introduction to *A teaching guide for the DEFA children's film Das Singende, Klingende Bäumchen*: The singing, ringing tree. University of Massachusetts, DEFA Film Library.

Collodi, C. (2000). *The adventures of Pinocchio*. (A. Lawson Lucas, Trans.). Oxford Paperbacks.

Creeser, R. (1993). Cocteau for kids: rediscovering *the singing, ringing tree*. In D. Petrie, (Ed.), *Cinema and the realms of enchantment: Lectures, seminars and essays by Marina Warner and others* (pp. 111–124). British Film Institute.

Cunningham, H. (2006). *The invention of childhood*. BBC Books.

Dalal, F. (2003, 1 February). IGA seminar 'Race, colour and the process of racialisation' [Personal notes].

Dawson, T. (2008). The discovery of the personal unconscious: Robinson Crusoe and modern identity. In S. Rowland (Ed.), *Psyche and the arts: Jungian approaches to music, architecture, literature, painting and film* (pp. 25–34). Routledge.

DEFA Film Library. (1999). A teaching guide for the DEFA children's film *Das Singende, Klingende Bäumchen: The singing, ringing tree*. University of Massachusetts.

DEFA Film Library. (n.d.). Ernst Kunstmann. Retrieved July 3, 2016, from https://ecommerce.umass.edu/defa/people/938

Defoe, D. (1994). *Robinson Crusoe* (2nd Ed.). (M. Shinagel, Ed.). W.W. Norton & Company.

Dennis, M. (2000). *The rise and fall of the German Democratic Republic, 1945–1990*. Longman.

Hillman, J. (1983). *Inter views: Conversations between James Hillman and Laura Pozzo on therapy, biography, love, soul, dreams, work, imagination and the state of the culture*. Harper & Row.

Home, A. (1993). *Into the box of delights: A history of children's television*. BBC Books.

Hopcke, R.H. (1999). *A guided tour of the* Collected works of C.G. Jung. Shambhala.

IMDb. (2016). User comments. Retrieved March 6, 2016, from http://www.imdb.com/title/tt0052199/usercomments

IMDbPro (2009). Fun facts. Retrieved from May 3, 2009, from http://pro.imdb.com/title/tt0052199/funfacts

Izod, J. (2000). Active imagination and the analysis of film. *Journal of Analytical Psychology, 45,* 267–85.

Jung, C.G. (1930/1950). Psychology and literature. In H. Read, M. Fordham, G. Adler & W. McGuire (Eds.), *The collected works of C.G. Jung: Vol. 15. The Spirit in man, art, and literature.* (R. F. C. Hull, Trans.). Routledge & Kegan Paul.

Jung, C.G. (1940). The psychology of the child archetype. In H. Read, M. Fordham, G. Adler & W. McGuire (Eds.), *The collected works of C.G. Jung: Vol. 9i. The archetypes and the collective unconscious.* (R. F. C. Hull, Trans.). Routledge & Kegan Paul.

Jung, C. G. (1956). The sacrifice. In H. Read, M. Fordham, G. Adler & W. McGuire (Eds.), *The collected works of C.G. Jung: Vol. 5. Symbols of transformation.* (R. F. C. Hull, Trans.). Routledge & Kegan Paul.

Lewis, R. (2002). *Encyclopaedia of cult children's TV.* Allison & Busby.

Lewis J., & Stempel, P. (2001). *The ultimate TV guide.* Orion Publishing Group.

Lüthi, M. (1987). *The fairy tale as art form and portrait of man.* Indiana University Press.

Marwick, A. (1990). *British society since 1945.* Penguin Books.

Marwick, A. (2005). The cultural revolution of the long sixties: Voices of reaction, protest, and permeation. *International History Review, 27*(4), 780–806.

McLuhan, M. (2003). *Understanding media: The extensions of man. Critical edition.* (W. Terrence Gordon, Ed.). Gingko Press.

Papadopoulos, R. (2002a). *Therapeutic care for refugees: No place like home.* Karnac.

Papadopoulos, R. (2002b). The other other: When the exotic other subjugates the familiar other. *Journal of Analytical Psychology, 47*(2), 163–88.

Parker, R. (1995). *Torn in two: The experience of maternal ambivalence.* Virago.

Petrie, D. (Ed.). (1993). *Cinema and the realms of enchantment: Lectures, seminars and essays by Marina Warner and others.* British Film Institute.

Porterfield, S., Polette, K., & French Baumlin, T. (Eds.) (2009). *Perpetual adolescence: Jungian analyses of American media, literature, and pop culture.* State University of New York Press.

Postman, N. (1994). *The disappearance of childhood.* Vintage Books.

Rowland, S. (2005). *Jung as a writer.* Routledge.

Rowland, S. (Ed.). (2008). *Psyche and the arts: Jungian approaches to music, architecture, literature, painting and film.* Routledge.

Rowland, S. (2009). Puer and hellmouth: *Buffy the vampire slayer* and American myth. In S. Porterfield, K. Polette, and F. Baumlin, T. (Eds.), *Perpetual adolescence: Jungian analyses of American media, literature, and pop culture* (pp. 31–46). State University of New York Press.

Samuels, A. (1993). *The political psyche.* Routledge.

Samuels, A. (1996). The future of Jungian studies: A personal agenda. In M. Stanton & D. Reason (Eds.), *Teaching transference: on the foundation of psychoanalytic studies* (pp. 15–26). Rebus.

Samuels, A., Shorter, B., & Plaut, F. (2003). *A critical dictionary of Jungian analysis.* Brunner-Routledge.

Sangster, J., & Condon, P. (2005). *TV heaven*. Collins.

The Singing Ringing Tree (n.d.). Wikipedia. Retrieved February 1, 2009, from http://en.wikipedia.org/wiki/The_Singing_Ringing_Tree

Smith, A. (1999, 24 May). Fast forward to fear. *The Scotsman*.

Smith, D. (2006). BBC banned communists in purge. *The Guardian*. Retrieved May 22, 2009, from https://www.theguardian.com/media/2006/mar/05/broadcasting.bbc

Staples, T. (1993). Doing them good. In D. Petrie (Ed.), *Cinema and the realms of enchantment: Lectures, seminars and essays by Marina Warner and others* (pp. 125–39). British Film Institute.

Stefani, F. (Director). (1957). *Das singende, klingende Bäumchen*. DEFA.

Thomas, R. (2016). Reviews of *The singing ringing tree*. Amazon. Retrieved March 13, 2016, from http://www.amazon.com/Singing-Ringing-Tree-Christel%20Bodenstein/dp/B00004YS9R/ref=sr_1_1?ie=UTF8&s=dvd&qid=1242474717&sr=8-1

Tibballs, G., & Morris, J. (1991). *The golden age of children's television*. Titan Books Ltd.

TVtropes.org (2003). The 100 greatest scary moments. Retrieved March 6, 2016, from http://tvtropes.org/pmwiki/pmwiki.php/Series/The100GreatestScaryMoments

Warner, M. (1992). The uses of enchantment. In D. Petrie (Ed.), *Cinema and the realms of enchantment: Lectures, seminars and essays by Marina Warner and others* (pp. 13–35). British Film Institute.

Warner, M. (1995). *From the beast to the blonde*. London, England: Vintage.

Wiene, R., (Director). (1920). *The cabinet of Dr. Caligari*. Decla-Bioscop.

Winnicott, D.W. (1990). *Home is where we start from*. Penguin Books.

Zipes, J., (Ed.). (2000). *The Oxford companion to fairy tales*. Oxford University Press.

Index

Note: *Italic* page numbers refer to figures and page numbers followed by "n" denote endnotes.

For Product Safety Concerns and Information please contact our EU
representative GPSR@taylorandfrancis.com
Taylor & Francis Verlag GmbH, Kaufingerstraße 24, 80331 München, Germany

www.ingramcontent.com/pod-product-compliance
Lightning Source LLC
Chambersburg PA
CBHW050641280326
41932CB00015B/2743